From the Well of Life, Nobody Can Drink Alone

From the Well of Life, Nobody Can Drink Alone

Fundamental Theology and Youth Ministry in Conversation

FRANTIŠEK ŠTĚCH

Foreword by Bert Roebben

WIPF & STOCK · Eugene, Oregon

FROM THE WELL OF LIFE, NOBODY CAN DRINK ALONE
Fundamental Theology and Youth Ministry in Conversation

Copyright © 2026 František Štěch. All rights reserved. Except for brief quotations in critical publications or reviews, no part of this book may be reproduced in any manner without prior written permission from the publisher. Write: Permissions, Wipf and Stock Publishers, 199 W. 8th Ave., Suite 3, Eugene, OR 97401.

Wipf & Stock
An Imprint of Wipf and Stock Publishers
199 W. 8th Ave., Suite 3
Eugene, OR 97401

www.wipfandstock.com

PAPERBACK ISBN: 979-8-3852-6069-0
HARDCOVER ISBN: 979-8-3852-6070-6
EBOOK ISBN: 979-8-3852-6071-3

VERSION NUMBER 01/09/26

Contents

Foreword by Bert Roebben | vii
Preface: A Biographical Key | ix
Acknowledgements | xxi
List of Abbreviations | xxii

(Patchwork) Introduction | 1
1   What Is Theology? | 20
2   The Story of Fundamental Theology | 51
3   The Story of Youth Ministry and Emerging Youth Theology | 124
4   "Who Do You Say I Am?": The Way of Theologian | 184
Conclusion: Doing Theology Together | 227

Bibliography | 233
Name Index | 245

Foreword

NOBODY CAN DRINK ALONE from the well of life. What we deeply share as human beings is life, both as a gift and challenge, from the cradle to the grave. For many fellow human beings, however, life has lost its gift character and has become much more than just a challenge. It has become a life-and-death struggle amidst war, hunger, and violence. Young people in particular are facing hard times. For many, the promising horizon of life seems to be closed and the road from cradle to grave shorter than ever. Moreover, their life's resources on the road are lacking because no one shows them, or worse, because they are simply no longer available. There is a drought, both physically and mentally. As a world community, we have a huge moral responsibility in changing this situation. No time to waste.

The invitation of this book is a theological re-sourcement, close to the wells of everyday life, in the here and now, where we find ourselves as fellow human beings, alive and kicking, stilling our existential thirst together. Again, no time to waste. František Štěch is challenging us to reconsider Christian theology as a source of life from which we drink together. Academic as well as lay theologians, young people as well as adults, bishops as well as the people of God, all of them crossing boundaries of culture, background and authority—all of them should be doing theology together, should be drinking from the same fountain of life.

The author is a bridge-builder. Over the course of many years I've followed his work and engagement in theology. For the International Association for the Study of Youth Ministry, he brought scholars together for their conference in the Czech Republic, in the heart of Europe. He mutually opened the discourses of liberal theology in the West and the East. For many projects he became a sparring partner of colleagues in other fields. He coordinates exciting new developments in the Theology and Contemporary Culture research group at the Protestant Theological Faculty of the Charles University in Prague. His recent work on theology and artificial intelligence is groundbreaking.

In this book, he testifies to his personal academic journey as a bridge-builder, specifically between his work and study in youth ministry and systematic theology. This is more than a cool interdisciplinary meeting between two academic fields. František Štěch is committed to truly working *intradisciplinarily*. He carries two souls in his body, two passions that he organically connects. In this book he shows the reader not only how the encounter of disciplines advances academic theology as a whole but also how "doing theology together" in an autobiographical modus can be experienced as a life-giving enterprise. This becomes real in the way he takes the theological journeys of young people seriously and reinforces their voice in eloquent ways: "It is like the systole and diastole of the cardiac rhythm; a vital theological circulatory system. A theology of youth welcomes young new partners into the beating hearts of the Christian life."

Standing on the shoulders of his three teachers in systematic theology (Vladimír Boublík, Karel Skalický, and Avery Dulles), learning from their "faith seeking understanding," and adapting the methodology of youth theology from the German religious pedagogy to reinforce both faith and understanding *(fides et ratio)*, František Štěch provides a helpful theological lens to explore, to explain and to experience the "landscapes of salvation" in today's culture. This personal theological endeavor is at the same time vulnerable and powerful. It is put to the test of the reader, but it is also critical about those places where the Christian tradition has evaporated, or its mission has been misused. In the words of Marian Füssel, reflecting on the idea of "landscape" in the work of Michel de Certeau, one could argue that František Štěch's work addresses both "the dead places and the lived spaces" of the Christian tradition in today's world. In that respect, his work is not only a plea for re-sourcing the life of faith but also a reliable guide to find these sources at work for a world, thirsting for peace and justice. Thus, there is no time to waste in reading and studying this book.

Bert Roebben
University of Bonn

Preface
A Biographical Key

IT ALL STARTED DURING the year 1986, in Communist Czechoslovakia, when I joined the group of young people preparing for their first holy communion in the Roman Catholic Church because I was baptized as a child, and my parents (my mother more than my father), as well as my grandparents (my grandmother more than both of my grandfathers), were Catholic churchgoers. I was told that I was to be initiated into the mystery of the Eucharist. I did not know what that meant; all I knew for sure was the fact that I would be allowed to go to the altar together with adults and take a wafer. I thought that was "cool," and I went for it. It was two or three years prior to the well-known "Velvet Revolution"—the relatively peaceful political coup that put the former Czechoslovakia on the road to democracy. But nobody knew it was going to happen that soon in autumn 1986, when I started to prepare for first communion, together with six or seven other children.

The first meeting was unforgettable. The priest came on his motorcycle, dressed in a leather jacket, and I remember his smell mixed with oil, petrol, and leather. Immediately I thought of him as a hero. He by no means reminded me of other priests I knew. They were mostly old and somehow inaccessible for me as a boy—they were "strange." When we entered the room, we set around the table and introduced ourselves. At the end of that initial activity, he gave us sturdy paper, crayons and colored pencils, and said, "Kids, if anyone whom you do not know is entering this room today or during any other of our sessions, start drawing and tell them that we are an art class. Or if someone on the street or in school asks you, tell them the same. You must tell them this, because we are here undercover." After that, I devoured everything he said—catechism seemed to me a kind of secret teaching (*mysterium arcanum*) we were initiated in. It was not for everyone and moreover, it was adventurous—like an esoteric school of subversive thought.

When the preparation was done, I received my first communion in spring 1987, and when I look at the pictures taken during the celebration in my local town cathedral, I can spot people in the background in leather coats observing what was happening and, especially, who was present at the event. Those men were plainclothes secret police. I did not care about them at that time because I had just made another step in my career of being nominally Catholic, and I was happy with it. I made my family happy. That kind of social Catholicism, however, started to collapse together with collapse of the Communist regime in my country. In the early 1990s I entered the religious education classes as early as possible. It turned out to be a disaster. My earlier picture of faith as an esoteric school of subversive thought melted in the pot of sweet, pious porridge for goody-goodies who are just asked to go to the church and behave well. Christianity lost its sense for me during that time. I hated to go to my religious classes, and a few times I made RE teacher cry in the classroom, for she thought I did not love our Lord Jesus Christ enough because I constantly misbehaved and made fun of the holy things. Despite that, I prepared for confirmation, but it was because my grandparents promised to buy me a guitar as a gift for confirmation, not because of religious reasons. My peers received traditional gifts like earrings or necklaces for girls and watches for boys, but I pursued my grandparents to buy me a guitar. So I received my guitar, and I was divorced from my faith—at least from its ecclesial expression.

At that time, I experienced more sacredness during my hiking trips with my friends, camping in deep woods along the frontiers between Czech Republic, Austria, and Germany, where we explored a no man's land into which these woods turned after the Communist border guards left them. We enjoyed enormous freedom wandering through places where almost no one had been allowed to go for four decades. Each weekend was an opportunity for the next adventure, and naturally there was no time for going to church on Sundays. What for, after all? It was boring, and the mystery, trembling and fascinating, was present not in the church within the pious community of my local Roman Catholic parish but out there in the wild landscape and with my adventurous friends. People in my parish seemed to me to be a bit strange, and I never precisely knew why. When I think about it now, with more than thirty years of distance, I think it was not because the community was bad or people were strange; it was rather because the mainstream-style Catholicism in the 1990s Czech Republic was not able to meet the expectations of the raging teenager during the early days of freedom, where everything seemed to be possible after the former Eastern bloc finally dissolved. If anything from the Bible was my creed during those days, it was the Pauline call from 1 Thess 5:21: "Test everything; hold fast to what is good." And I did, even though I sometimes held fast to what I thought was good for me and not to that what was good for real. But who had not been there at least once?

When my first opportunity to travel to Italy came in 1997, I immediately said yes. I convinced my grandfather to support this high school study trip financially, which was not very difficult since he was a great supporter of anything that was connected to my studies. His passion was history, and I always wanted to become a historian. And so, we were a group of seventeen and eighteen-year-old young people heading to Italy—Florence, Rome, Napoli, Pompeii, San Marino, Assisi, and many other places.

Immediately as we entered the first church in Italy (Cattedrale di Santa Maria del Fiore, Florence), my fellow travelers noticed that I made a sign of the cross. That created a strange situation for me. My peers started to ask me questions related to religion, faith, Christianity, saints, etc. They wanted to hear stories behind the signs that we saw in sacred sites we visited. They demanded answers to their questions and with conviction or perhaps only with hope that I was the one who could (or even should) provide the answers, they continued approaching me. On the one hand I was happy to be in the center of attention, but I was not always able to satisfy their curiosity and respond to the criticisms or accusations they voiced about Christianity and Catholicism. I felt sometimes like Peter when he was asked, "You are not also one of his disciples, are you?" (John 18:17, 25–26) and sometimes like the one who was advised by Peter to be ready to make defense to anyone who demands an account of hope (Cf. 1 Pet 3:15). But what hope? I racked my brain over that question. Did I still have some hope like that? To be honest, I still felt hope for good things to come inside of my young soul, but the source of that hope was not clear to me. I had a feeling that I once had access to its source, but in those days, all Christian religious symbolism seemed to me to be empty shells and made no sense to me. Only much later I realized I was already doing fundamental theology and youth ministry at once at that time, during that trip to Italy. I ministered to my peers just by talking with them about faith I was not sure about, and even without realizing it, I also started to construe my own fundamental theology. I thought a lot about my own Christianity, and my secular peers made me do it. I never left the faith for real; I just stopped going to church, and in the discussions (and confrontations) I had in Italy, the Christianity buried deep inside of my young soul started to come back to the surface.

On the last day of our tour through Italy we arrived in the beautiful town of Assisi. If you ever visit, you cannot miss its fabulous basilica from the thirteenth century, known for the crypt where St. Francis of Assisi is supposed to be buried. St. Francis was my confirmation patron, but being there I felt nothing special. I wandered around the upper and the lower church together with the whole group, and at the end, when we had some time left before the scheduled departure of our bus, I went to explore the site for myself, since I was tired of people after ten days of being together. I just gave my friends the last of my money to buy wine for the farewell evening and disappeared into the shade of the sacral complex. After a while I discovered that we had not visited the crypt, and I decided to rectify that for myself. It was almost time for the bus to leave when I entered the crypt. When I opened the door with a characteristic creak, the bell rang and Mass started. It was not crowded. A few elderly, probably Italian women, a priest, a ministrant, and myself. And that was the moment when nothing and everything happened at the same time. I had no vision, no revelation, nothing like that, but suddenly it became clear to me that I am Christian, and I want to be available to whatever God may wish. I remember I just started to pray in silence by the words of Jeremiah—maybe slightly different but certainly similar in terms of meaning: ". . . here I am, in your hands. Do with me as seems good and right to you" (Jer 26:14).

It was a rather quick, intensive inner experience or resonance with the divine in my life, which I named for myself in Christian terms, and I set off in direction of searching for my own Christian identity. I soon left the Mass in the crypt, maybe even before the preaching. I did not understand any of the Italian anyway. And I went to the bus, headed home, and we high school students started to enjoy our farewell wine, some of us freshly adult and some of us (including myself) pretending to be already adult—which was possible only when the teacher closed both eyes and pretended he did not see, feel, or hear anything. Starting from that day, I never doubted my Christianity in general. Of course, I continued my fights with God and the church, but in principle I've always known I was Christian since then.

Time went on. In 1999 I finished my high school education and applied for university. I always wanted to study history, but because of a confluence of different reasons, both internal and external (my own stupidity, youthful pride, high numbers of applicants, etc.), I was not accepted to any of the history study programs for which I applied. I was lucky enough that my mother—together with my local priest, who was cool and inspired me to become active in the church again—convinced me to apply for a leisure time pedagogy and religious education study program through the local faculty of theology. It was the only place I got accepted. I was not against studying leisure time pedagogy because I wanted to become a teacher of history anyway, and I was a committed leader of the Woodcraft youth group at that time. But I had difficulty with the religious education part of that program. Influenced by my own experience, I thought that any religious education is (more or less) indoctrination and brainwashing. Well, at the end I went for it. My decision was partly motivated also by the fact that I wanted to avoid military service, which was still compulsory for young men of my age at the end of 1990s. However, my father was very disappointed by the fact that I was unsuccessful with my admission exams to study history. He told me that I am an idiot, and I'd better go buy myself sandals and a candle and start learning how to pray. I did not care much about that. I just left home and went hiking and camping with my friends. It was summer, and my first university semester still seemed far away.

But the first year at the faculty surpassed all my expectations. All my former prejudices vanished because I encountered an open environment full of seekers rather than fanatic Christians. I fell in love with my studies, even with its religious education component. Already in my second year at the university, I started working as religious educator, and I did this as one of my many part-time jobs for nearly a decade. I also became active in Christian youth ministry, which I never thought I would be able to do. However, there was a plan for me different than becoming a professional RE teacher, woodcraft leader, or youth minister. I never finished my pedagogical training. After five semesters (right at the midpoint of studying to be a professional educator), I switched my program of study to theology on the advice of our main theology professor, Karel Skalický. He recognized a talent for theology in me. Soon after becoming a student of theology, I left to study intercultural theology for a year in Nijmegen in the Netherlands through the Erasmus exchange program. That confirmed my new direction. I wanted to become theologian.

Despite this, I was always interested in the development of new technologies. I hold my A-level certificate in computer science and was always interested in motorcycle sports and their industry. I grew up in an environment of a local vintage motorcycle club of which my father has been a member since the late 1960s. Maybe because I was connected to that environment from childhood, I worked for four years as a part-time lathe operator in a small family factory, producing heavy machinery for the manufacture of pencils. For quite some time, I worked also as a test driver for the sales department of the Peugeot company in the Czech Republic, and I should not forget my great experience of working six years for a cleaning company. I spent a lot of time cleaning on construction sites. I have met hundreds of workers, engineers, and technically oriented people, and I must admit, they taught me a lot. They were my "professors" as much as those who taught me theology.

By the time I graduated from the faculty of theology in June 2005, I had been already accepted into the doctoral study program in systematic theology at the same institution. At the same time, I received a scholarship for the winter semester at the Free University in Amsterdam. New horizons opened ahead, especially when my PhD supervisor asked me to assume part of his teaching responsibilities lecturing on fundamental theology and the introduction to theology, starting in the autumn of 2006. I was just a freshman within theology when I was plunged into the depths and fathoms of academia. It was either sink or swim. But it was, nonetheless, exciting.

Soon after I started to work for the university, I realized that the academic environment was a bit sterile for my tastes. I wanted to maintain contact with the world of high school and with those who are outside academic circles and debates. Therefore, I continued to work with both religious and secular youth groups. I remained active in the local Catholic Church, and I also continued to serve as the Woodcraft youth group leader. My group was interested in the culture, craft, and lifestyle of the native and indigenous peoples of North America. This, of course, involved an interest in religion. I remember numerous discussions about similarities and differences between Christianity and native religions of the North American Indians. It was a proper fundamental theological task to discuss with young people matters like the Christianization of native American tribes. It required a lot of reading from histories of different Christian churches and local religious movements. But that was not the end. I had to enter the field of cultural anthropology, ethnography, religious studies, and ecumenical theology. I found particularly useful works from intercultural hermeneutics and postcolonial studies.

In short, working with youth is not all fun and games. It requires a lot of study and research too. It requires one to be well informed and yet sensitive and attentive to the opinions, arguments, needs and contexts of young people. Especially in the environment of "secular" youth ministry, I realized a presence of (even though mostly implicit) religious questions (e.g., life, death, sin, forgiveness, meaning of life, different moral issues, ecology, power, etc.) among the youth, and when they discovered that I am a practicing Christian, I had the chance to express my Christian attitudes and standpoints. It was a great opportunity to give witness to my religious path, as well as to learn from young people about their ideas, convictions, and standpoints. It was a fruitful dialogue, and they often came to consult with me on any kind of "spiritual" matter. Some continue to do so even though they have now their own careers and families. I've come to realize that I still am doing the same thing I've been doing since that high school trip to Italy back in 1997. No matter if I do youth ministry, religious education, or if I lecture on theology or write theological texts, it is one and the same vocation. I live my Christian life, and thus I also do theology. It cannot be otherwise because once I set off in the direction of Jesus Christ on the path of faith seeking understanding (plausibility in action), everything that I do has at least a theological undertone and is part of my theology, which is being constantly tested in dialogue, exchange, and interaction (both positive and conflictual) with others.

In January 2009 I defended my doctoral dissertation and became full time lecturer of fundamental and systematic theology, so I had to stop being (hyper)active in youth ministry and youth work. There was simply not a time for that anymore, and I decided to leave it to younger folk, since I was just about to get married. Meanwhile I started to teach part-time civics at one of the local high schools, which I did for four years. That was another great experience: working with young people in an ordinary school environment. I did this job to get some extra income for our family budget since my wife and I had moved to the old stone house we bought in one of the villages close to the borders with Austria. Of course, it needed some work. And it still does. When I work on our house, it always appears to me as another valence of doing theology. I realized that even manual household labor can be experienced as theology: perhaps, the theology of house maintenance or housekeeping (after all, the prefix of "ecu-menical" derives from the Greek term for "house": *oikos*). My perspective on theology as a profession and discipline started to change. I became more attentive to what people think "theology" is (or might be).

For the first time I asked myself: *What is theology?* What do you do? What is the purpose of what you do? And is it somehow useful? And for whom? At about this time, the first lines of this text were written, and its first thoughts started to mature. I kept asking myself these and similar questions from that time on, and as far as I can see, I will continue to do so for the rest of my life. When I think about it, this text can be read also as a personal confession of the white, male, European, Roman Catholic, lay theologian reaching his midlife crisis and searching for possible ways forward.

I've been walking through the woods around the house where I began living with my wife, dog, and cat. During my work on this text, our pets died and three kids were born. Hours, days, and years passed until one day I came back home and knew that an initial foggy vision was finally coming into sharper contours and focus. I commenced writing the prospectus for this text. I thought it would be quick and easy to turn my ideas into written lines, paragraphs, and chapters. But that was not the case. I went out again, this time to my professors, to my fellow theological friends, as well as to my friends who do not have anything to do with theology. I talked with them all, shared what I intended to write, and received many comments and recommendations, as well as helpful criticisms.

I kept studying fundamental, systematic, and practical theology, I kept reading books about religious education and theological interpretations of Christian youth ministry, and I started to perceive a certain pattern which seemed to me present in nearly all of them. Consequently, I became convinced that all divisions and differentiations in theology are just technical and that theology must be perceived holistically as a particular and distinct modus of human life and that academic theology is just one piece of the rich mosaic of theology. I started sorting out my memories, trying to remember experiences from the past near and far, reflecting on them, interpreting them, and imagining all possible consequences of different theological considerations. I realized that working with young people and being a fundamental theologian by profession both marked my life story and, as such, became indispensable parts of my personal *auto/Theo-biography*—the story of my life which intertwines with the story of the Christian God from the beginning.[1] I realized that practicing (fundamental) theology is what I have been always doing and that the time has come to pause and reflect about it.

But there was no time for pausing within the vibrant atmosphere of full-time academic job with many extra involvements here and there. The stop came unexpectedly in 2016, when the new faculty leadership decided to cancel my position. Suddenly, I became jobless. Losing your job changes a lot, especially when your firstborn child is two months old and you are the main provider for the family. When I look at it from a distance now, I have to say it was the best thing that could have happened to me. I was forced to pause. During that pause I had a chance to "recharge my theological engine," as one of my favorite Asian theologians, Choan-Seng Song, might say. In other words, my system rebooted, and I realized that I was already burned out and that if I want to continue doing theology in the future, I had to rethink my own discipline (fundamental theology) in terms of its identity (What is it?), narrativity (How is it narrated?), and mission (How it can contribute towards development of the humanity and wellbeing of our society? Is it somehow useful at times, though many people regard it as useless?). I also realized that I must do the same with my own life.

Luckily enough I was not a jobless father for long. With help of friends, I soon became researcher of Charles University in Prague, the capital of Czech Republic, and I gained more freedom that I could have ever imagined. I was blessed once again in my life with being able to continue doing theology as my profession. I found the time spent doing research—reading and writing—as a very opportune time (*kairos*) for myself. Everything around me was suddenly quiet and slowed down. I enjoyed a year of doing nothing but reading and writing. But after that I started to miss my teaching because I found out that it is one of my major inspirational sources, and without being able to teach or work with young people, there is an abyss in my life. It is good when something becomes clear to you, if only

1. The term "auto/Theo-biography" is not new. It was introduced by the English practical theologian Pete Ward to describe "reflexivity," which he adopts from the area of cultural studies as his own theological method, emphasizing the importance of personal story and cultural context to a theologian for the whole process of writing and doing theology. Our personal stories cannot be detached from our theologies. It is also necessary to note that Ward writes "auto/theobiography" (Ward, *Participation and Mediation*), but I decided to write this term in a bit different way to emphasize three elements present: the self, the story of one's own life, and God, who is present in lives of those who have relationship with him. Thus, I write "auto/Theo-biography."

for a moment. In that kind of moment, I reloaded the work on this text and finished its first version in 2018. Meanwhile, I started to teach again. Due to other moments of academic turbulence, I went through at the end of 2018 and beginning of 2019, I set off from the environment of the (Roman) Catholic Theological Faculty into the stormy sea of other existential uncertainties, only to land in the safe harbor of the Protestant Theological Faculty of Charles University. Working as Roman Catholic in Protestant environment brings another valuable element into my life, and that's a spirit of ecumenism. For seven years now (in 2025), I've been well balanced between teaching and research, remaining in academia but having time to scout other terrains too. I was finally able to find a fragile balance between work and family and fully enjoy the blessing of living in nature and working in the capital city. Recently, everything has seemed calm—at least until the next storm comes. And I know that it is already there, still behind the horizon but surely coming some time in future.

And this is why I decided to present you with a brief story of the life I've lived so far, because all that happened to me and what I have been through I regard as the deepest sources of my theology, a theology which originates from within a chaotic dynamic of everyday life. I believe that my theology (including my academic texts) is not detached from what I live. My theology cannot be anything other than interwoven with the complex story of my life, with my personal auto/Theo-biography—the story where God has its indispensable place. In this sense I am perhaps the "*Anthropos theologicos*—human being before God and fellow human beings."[2] Therefore, I am bringing all my relationships and all that I do before God's face, and precisely in this way, all elements of my life are parts and parcels of my theology—my auto/Theo-biography. Theology is my life, and my life is theology. It could not be otherwise.

At this place I would like to express my thanks and enormous gratitude to my wife, Marie Štěchová Žáková, who patiently tolerated her grumpy husband, busy with writing his "important" text. She always encouraged me to continue writing when I was discouraged and stood at my side when I was down and desperate. I wish to thank my parents for their continuous support and for giving me a wood-carved statue of St. Francis in a time when I thought I was not going to finish this text at all. It meant (and means) a lot to me. I must give thanks also to my grandparents (who passed away before I finished this text), to my brother

---

2. Roebben, *Theology Made in Dignity*, 59.

and sister, and to the whole extended family for their support and help whenever it was needed. I am especially grateful to my wife's parents for helping us during messy but beautiful times, such as when my wife and I became parents. A special word of gratitude must be addressed to Professor Karel Skalický, who continues to be my generous supporter, source of inspiration, and spiritual advisor. We spent hours and days talking about my growing text for several years, and I am grateful for every minute we have been thinking and doing theology together. Further, I am indebted also to my friend Professor Bert Roebben, for his friendship and support. With him I learned what it means to do theology together. I wish to give thanks to Ludmila Muchová, who was my former teacher of religious education and who linked me to the International Association for the Study of Youth Ministry (further abbreviated as IASYM).[3] Ludmila became my colleague and friend, and she believed in my theological capacities even in times when I did not believe in them myself. She was also one of my main sources of inspiration for writing this work. There are a few other friends who deserve my gratitude for being both spiritually and physically available for me whenever needed. Among them special thanks belong to Standa Wawreyn, Roman Míčka, Pavel Pokorný, David Vágner, and Tomáš Veber. The last tragically died before this text was finished. Another big thanks goes to Virgil W. Brower, who patiently proofread the first version of this text in 2019.

I cannot name here everyone who contributed in one way or another towards the blossoming of this book because it would be simply impossible. They were numerous. But I carry them all in my heart, and I am grateful that (regardless of if they are religious or not) I am allowed to do theology together with them. Finally, I would like to dedicate this work to my children—Žofie, Josef, and Irma—in the hope that one day they may come to understand their place in their father's life story, a story into which they entered without ever being asked.

Olešnice, Czech Republic,
29. September 2025

---

3. To learn more about IASYM, see www.iasym.org.

Acknowledgements

I RECALL MANY BLESSED times when I was able to make progress on writing my book. Among them I would like to mention the one specific, intensive time. In November 2017 I was able to concentrate on writing first parts of this book during my 30-day visiting professorship at the Technical University Dortmund supported by its generous Gambrinus fellowship.

This work has been supported by Charles University Research Centre program No. UNCE/24/SSH/019.

The title (and subtitle) of this book is taken from my earlier article: František Štěch, "From the Well of Life Nobody Can Drink Alone: Fundamental Theology and Youth Ministry in Conversation," *Theology and Philosophy of Education*, 1:1 (2022) 24–31.

All quotations from sources in Czech language and languages other than English are translated by author, unless otherwise noted.

All Scripture quotations are taken from the *Holy Bible. New Revised Standard Version (NRSV)*, Bible Society Resources Ltd. 2008, unless otherwise noted.

All documents of the Second Vatican Council quotations in this text are taken from *The Documents of the II. Vatican Council*. http://www.vatican.va/archive/hist_councils/ii_vatican_council/

List of Abbreviations

AA	Apostolicam Actuositatem (Decree of the 2nd Vatican Council on the Apostolate of the Laity)
CCC	Catechism of the Catholic Church
DCE	Deus Caritas Est (Encyclical letter of the pope Benedict XVI—25th December 2005)
DV	Dei Verbum (Dogmatic Constitution of the 2nd Vatican Council on Divine Revelation)
FR	Fides et Ratio (Encyclical letter of the pope John Paul II—14th September 1998)
GE	Gravissimum Educationis (Declaration of the 2nd Vatican Council on Christian Education)
GS	Gaudium et Spes (Pastoral Constitution of the 2nd Vatican Council on the Church in the Modern World)
IASYM	International Association for the Study of Youth Ministry
ITC	International Theological Commission of the Roman Catholic Church
LG	Lumen Gentium (Dogmatic Constitution of the 2nd Vatican Council on the Church)
RCIA	The Rite of Christian Initiation of Adults
TT	Theology Today: Perspectives, Principles and Criteria (document of the ITC from 2011)
UR	Unitatis Redintegratio (Decree of the 2nd Vatican Council on Ecumenism)

(Patchwork) Introduction

THE IDEA TO RETHINK fundamental theology in relation to youth ministry and youth theology had started to occupy my mind already almost two decades ago, as I struggled to define my professional identity. Consequently, I also asked questions about the identity of the academic discipline where I find myself at home. I am a fundamental theologian of Roman Catholic background, born and settled in the Czech Republic, the post-communist, central European country often presented in various sociological studies as one of the most secularized countries in the world.[1] Contrary to that, many contemporary thinkers (e.g., Halík, Noble) are convinced that the process of secularization already passed its peak in the Czech Republic a while ago, and nowadays various kinds of recent religiosity (highly privatized, individualized, de-traditionalized, often syncretic and hybridized) enjoy full swing. In the words of Ivana Noble, "Despite the fact that the Czech Republic (like Estonia or Bulgaria) statistically displays the smallest presence of traditional religions, as well as mistrust of institutions (including religious ones) and a tendency to privatized worldviews (including religious ones), there is a big shift away from atheism and towards new forms of religiosity."[2]

It seems that it is no longer possible to talk about religion, or more specifically about Christianity, living an exclusively secular, cultural environment contextualized in the Czech Republic. Czech society is not secular anymore. It is not a society where God is absent. It is a society where God seems to be absent but is being rediscovered and witnessed once again, although in ways that are often surprising and different than

1. Vido et al., "Czech Republic," 201–31.
2. Noble, *Tracking God*, xiv. See also: Noble, *Theological Interpretation*, 2–9.

were usual in the past. Perhaps it would be possible to say that new forms of religious practices or new religiosities are emerging "after religion," religion understood (e.g., in terms of Emile Durkheim) as a unified system of beliefs and practices.[3] Plurality and relativity entered the realm of Durkheimian "religion" and set in motion the transformation process of "religion" but also of "the religious."

Since the start of my university teaching career (early autumn 2006), I wrestled with a few (fundamental) questions: 1. What is theology? 2. How can theology be communicated to those who do not have a religious background? 3. What is fundamental and substantial to theology? And consequently: What is fundamental theology? These questions emerged from the situation I experienced firsthand, and which is common to many of the contemporary theological institutions in Europe. They do not have students in their theological study programs; thus, they must attract them with something else. Either they succeed, or they most likely will be closed or absorbed by other faculties or different institutions. Thus, they are extremely creative in developing non-theological study programs, and they try to smuggle at least a bit of theology into them. However, theology is present in these curricula only as an additive to other sciences like pedagogy, social sciences, philosophy, religious studies, etc. As a result, students often do not understand why they must study theology during their studies of e.g., leisure time pedagogy, or they do not see the point in it at all. To be clear, there is no problem in having different disciplines present in one coherent study program, but my usual experience was not one of consonant interdisciplinarity but of rather dissonant hybridity instead. However, I am convinced that it is simply a matter of carefully designing the program of study. It does not have to represent only danger or a threat to theological faculties. It might be understood rather as an immense opportunity to reach out beyond the borders of the classical study of theology as well. Theology finds here the new audience among young adults who encounter it, while being themselves untouched by any former ecclesial education and without any church affiliation. In my case, most of my students were agnostic or religiously indifferent, claiming vaguely that there is, maybe, something out there. Despite their (oft-claimed) religious "unmusicalness,"[4] they were still showing signs of spirituality and some sort of individualized

---

3. Durkheim, *Elementary Forms of Religious Life*, 44.
4. Vahland, *Max Webers entzauberte Welt*, 48.

and privatized spiritual life. For them I had to forfeit the possibility of teaching fundamental theology as a purely academic discipline, and I had to become instead a witness about perspectives on life of which they had never heard, opening not only my mind but also my heart to them. It was hard gaining their attention and showing them that theology is not a set of boring, outdated dogmas or boldly claimed propositional truths but rather attest to theology as an everyday practice of venturing, of true relationships, a struggle for meaning in life. On the one hand, it was often uncomfortable for me (especially in terms of time investment), but on the other hand, it was extremely challenging as well. I realized that I am not educating future priests (even though a few of my former students became ordained) but an extremely diverse group of young people ranging from Catholic "fundamentalists" and convinced agnostics to spiritually exalted "New Age" kind of believers in something or all kinds of things. Most of them, naturally, except those committed to Christianity (who were the minority), had (sometimes very strong) prejudices against Christian religion and the church (in my context predominantly Roman Catholic), yet most of them were open to conversation about religion, spirituality, beliefs, etc. While introducing religiously indifferent or unmusical young adults to the fundaments of theology, I had to rethink for myself one of the crucial questions for each believer (theologians included): What is theology? What do I do when I claim I do theology?

Contrary to these types of students, there were a few others who studied theology. With them I tried to do fundamental theology in a traditional way. I started with history of the discipline, the origin of the term "explanation," talked about the transition from apologetics to fundamental theology, and continued with topics like revelation, the concept of the divine, the relationship between faith and reason, resurrection, etc. This naturally involves a lot of theoretical (speculative) thinking. But many of these students soon told me that it is too much, that they do not need speculations about nature of theology and its fundaments. They thought that only the church and expert theologians should care about such things. They wanted to gain a "how-to" knowledge for praxis. All their questions could perhaps be subsumed under the following one: What is the practical use of fundamental theology? Encountering this reality, I always tried to explain and emphasize the practical use of theology in general and fundamental theology in particular. For that purpose, I searched for contemporary theories among the latest trends in theology (like post-critical, postmodern, public, or intercultural theology) to catch up with the "spirit of the time." However, such effort did not attune well with some of my fellow colleagues (especially those in favor of scholastic and neo-scholastic theology) and their ideas about what theology is and how it should be done. Other colleagues often regarded theology as an exotic fruit to decorate the traditional tables of their respectful disciplines, but "let's not have it too much." Yes, there were many dark nights during my teaching career, but I also had an experience that sometimes an initial cacophony of different sounds and voices from my diverse portfolio of students started to sound well together during our discussions and seminars. It was sometimes quite an effort to mediate between different "instruments" but "at the end we had a wonderful jam session," as one of my students once expressed his reflection on our discussion, which supplemented my lectures. "Yet we still have been doing good theology," I replied. Only couple of years later I came across the book by an American woman, a processual and Lutheran theologian, Ann Pederson, entitled *God, Creation, and All That Jazz*. Pederson emphasizes creativity and improvisation in process of doing theology to that extent that she does it as jazz jam session.[5]

Following this personal discovery, I realized that my first "perpetual" question (What is theology?) suggests that theology today is all about jamming with others and trying constantly to find a way how to attune together different perspectives, opinions, traditions, and faith backgrounds. It is sometimes extremely difficult, but it is worthwhile. One just needs to be modest and should not try to be a conductor or musical director of the group but rather an initiator, a mediator, or an inspirator, playing its part but giving space to others that they may also play their parts.

In relation to what has just been said, my second "perpetual" question constantly returned to me in all my attempts to communicate theology to my students, colleagues, friends, and to those I encountered outside academia. How to communicate theology to those who ask: "What do you do?" "What is your job?" "Theology?" "What is it?" "Is it somehow useful?" "What is your contribution to the wellbeing of society?" It is always a difficult task to justify what you do, especially when you do something like theology in a context where people hardly see any use of it. And even if they see it, all of them have different backgrounds, pre-understandings and ideas about what theology is and what use for it could be. Some of them are academics, some of them students, some

5. Pederson, *God, Creation, and All That Jazz*, 16.

of them are workers, technicians, divorced—or even angry with religion for whatever reason, indifferent to religion, or the contrary: zealous for religion or spirituality of various forms. Communicating theology to those who ask theological questions but do not know about it is always particularly challenging for me. Therefore, my theological journey so far is marked by constant effort to discover better answers for all those who ask.[6] "Always be ready to make your defense to anyone who demands from you an account of the hope that is in you; yet do it with gentleness and reverence." (1 Pet 3:15–16).

This passage from the first letter of Peter is sometimes called the Great Charter of fundamental theology,[7] the theological discipline in which I've found myself at home during the academic career I've led so far. That brings up my third crucial question: What are the fundamentals of theology if we consider it as an ever-changing process of theologizing—believing in mystery revealed, reflecting upon our faith and mystery revealed, and re-interpreting our former ideas and standpoints amid diverse communities in which we are engaged and live? Theology is a process. It is faith seeking understanding and love, generating hope in a shared realm of public life, where all people are involved in one way or another. But what is fundamental to this process? How to understand theology in a substantial way? That returns us back to question 1 (What is theology?) again. Through the development of this text, I will move within this circle of principal questions. I want to show that it is not a vicious circle but a spiral instead—a spiral moving forward in cycles, developing not only our understanding to faith, hope, and love but also their practice. The spiral of history evolving towards an eschatological future—the time already present, yet to come. Even though my perpetual questions are not explicitly mentioned in the following text, they are ever present between the lines.

---

6. Such effort is related to searching answers for many "how-to" questions like: How to teach and develop theology useful for praxis and yet remain properly theoretical matching all criteria of the proper academic discipline? Is theology something useful today? Or shall we study it only as a relic from the past, or as an interesting intellectual exercise having nothing to say to people today? How can I make my own discipline not only applicable but also attractive? Does it have anything to say also to broader society and not only to believers? Is there anything useful in doing theology for people who think they do not need it at all? How can I get into conversation with people who do not have religious experience(s) and thus are not able to recognize a divine presence in their lives? How can I present the relevance of theological investigation to a particular believing community as well as to non-believers? Is my theology understandable and existentially relevant, and if it is not, how could it become like that?

7. Kropač, *Religionspädagogik*, 352.

Being interested in the fundamental principles of Christian theology, I always perceived an importance in being in touch with young people, with those who represent the future steps of entire humanity. How are they going to shape faith, religious, or church traditions in the coming decades? What faith will they hand over to their own youth? While people live the summers, autumns, and winters of their humanity, young people represent its spring. Each generation of young people is a return of humankind's spring. But as each returning spring is different from the previous one, each generation of young people differs from the last. Of course, the same is true about other the seasons of human life. But as farmers sometimes say: spring always shapes the whole year.

In the "swan song" of my own spring of my life, I met the IASYM and joined its members for a couple of conferences, where I received the clear impulse to relate my own research and teaching to the field of practical theology and reflection on the practice of youth ministry. Convinced that each systematic and fundamental theology, too, must be deeply embedded in pastoral ministry, the question of the relation between theoretical (systematic and fundamental) and practical (pastoral) theology came under scrutiny. They both have their own methods, topics, and research areas. Their relations may be (and are) discussed, but they hardly meet, at least within academia. A different story appears when we talk about theology in non-academic terms. The theological and the practical meet in "everyday theology."[8] Differences anchored in scientific developments, methodology, and rationale within fundamental, systematic, and practical theology do not matter much in everyday life. People just live their ordinary, daily lives from a religious perspective. They recognize God as being present and working in the world and in their lives. They believe in God, or at least they try. They live their faith. They fight for it, and they accept it as a divine gift of grace. People affiliate with the church, or they directly express their belonging to the concrete church community. They are from this world, breathing the same air with everyone else around. Yet they expect the kingdom to come, which is far from being here (John 18:36). And, of course, they reflect upon their life experience at different levels, everyone according to their own gifts and dispositions.

* * *

---

8. Vanhoozer et al., *Everyday Theology*. More labels for the concept of "everyday theology" could be found, for instance, in Borgman, *Foundations*, 77.

Reflecting on fundamental theology and youth theology together may seem to some like mixing apples with oranges. But such a connection arose out of my experiences with young people asking fundamental questions about their life and faith, seeking understanding of themselves and the world around them. Many times I was surprised by their pithy theological insights without any previous theological studies. At the same time, I witnessed disagreements among theologians of diverse disciplines, especially between practical and systematic theologians. I met several biblical scholars looking down on other theologians, incognizant of contextual interpretations of what is said in the Bible. Is one allowed to do theology with only a poor knowledge of biblical Hebrew, Greek, and Latin, and with no knowledge of Aramaic or Coptic? This was a question I confronted quite often during the start of my theological career. I always concluded that yes, one is at least allowed to endeavor to do so. But I always felt a bit stupid and guilty, that I was not gifted enough to learn these languages well. But there is no perfect and all-knowing theologian, and in the words of the womanist poet Audre Lorde, if "we wait in silence for the luxury of fearlessness, the weight of that silence will choke us."[9] More importantly, I am convinced that in addition to the significant theological disciplines, we also need good fundamental theology to remind us that theology is not fragmented in separate fields or systematic tractates. Theology is one common discourse for all believers. Its task is to unite different points of view, separated discourses, and divided perspectives into a unity in diversity. Such interpretation of theology also has great potential for ecumenical dialogue, since it does not presume fundamental oppositions between different Christian denominations but rather celebrates their mutual differences as possible sources for mutual enrichment rather than just conflict. This holistic concept of theology could also enable Christians today to be better equipped for dealing with multiple kinds of diversities with which the contemporary world is marked (religion, gender, power, etc.), in terms of dialogue. This way of seeking theology as one discourse despite a vast plurality of voices is fundamental to any kind of further theological enterprise. However, it is a matter of choice (fundamental option), while maintaining a quest for reasonable, understandable, and existentially relevant theoretical frameworks for Christian faith. As such, it is not merely a matter of speculative, academic reasoning but also a matter of lived experience asking for reflection and interpretation.

9. Lorde, *Sister Outsider*, 44.

Apart from practicing inner interdisciplinarity within theology, theologians must seriously consider contemporary cognitive pluralism present in the "shared realm of public discourse,"[10] as Wenzel van Huyssteen would put it. If it wants to take part in the public discussion, theology must be able to enter the arena of interdisciplinarity beyond its own boundaries. That means "to accept the unavailability of consensus, and to work at creating a communal framework of wide reflecting equilibrium of thought and action."[11] In other words, to stop the attitude of "if we think like them, they will think like us."[12] This is certainly not a way forward. Instead, we need to let the space open to the genuine otherness of the other, which is what Emanuel Levinas meant by "exteriority"—to respect the otherness of the other, who has the right to his/her own territory.[13] Together with van Huyssteen, I am convinced that true interdisciplinarity in theology only becomes possible "when our conversations proceed, not in terms of imposed 'universal' rules, nor in terms of purely ad hoc rules, but when we identify this (post-foundationalist) space where both strong Christian convictions as well as the public voice of theology are fused in public conversation."[14]

However, I am also aware that interdisciplinarity might by criticized today as becoming a programmatic necessity in contemporary theology. As Aaron Ghioni writes, for instance, "I would soon find that this was a motto in today's university culture, in which interdisciplinarity is put forward as prerequisite for employment and an expectation of approved syllabi."[15] Of course, interdisciplinarity is not the only self-salvific way for today's science, including theology, but on the other hand we need a certain openness to keep our theology up to date, understandable, and (existentially) relevant to contemporaries. However, Ghiloni is far from ideologizing interdisciplinarity. He opts for a balanced and nuanced interdisciplinary theology. He sees it as a mission. "A mission mindset understands the necessity of communicating between cultures, thus balancing interdisciplinarity's competing demands for clarity and nuance. Indeed, early missiologists such as Saint Luke and Eusebius might be seen as proto-interdisciplinary theologians, inasmuch as they develop

---

10. Van Huyssteen, *Shaping of Rationality*, 279.
11. Van Huyssteen, *Shaping of Rationality*, 279–80.
12. Van Huyssteen, *Shaping of Rationality*, 280.
13. Halík, *Night of the Confessor*, 87.
14. Van Huyssteen, *Shaping of Rationality*, 280.
15. Ghiloni, "On Writing Interdisciplinary Theology," 13–14.

narratives which deliberately draw on 'non-religious' sources in addition to sacred writings."[16]

As such, a kind of proto-interdisciplinarity would be at least as old as the gospel itself. For the sake of a balanced interdisciplinarity with a certain missionary drive, the (perhaps unlikely) interconnections between fundamental theology and youth theology seem not only interesting but even necessary. However, both disciplines come from different theological backgrounds. While fundamental theology is often seen as prolegomena to systematic theology,[17] or at least as overlapping with systematic theology,[18] youth theology originated in the realm of youth ministry and religious pedagogy—disciplines traditionally linked to the dominion of practical theology. Therefore, it dwells in an area very close to various empirical sciences and to cultural change. Youth theology is a discipline very hospitable to new ways of thinking, and the same is true of fundamental theology, because it is a discipline "not only evidently dependent and living on the edge of empirical sciences and theology but . . . also enormously sensitive to changes of cultural environment and new ways of thinking."[19]

Therefore, I am convinced that right in this area, a platform for mutual encounter opens. Practical and fundamental theologians alike shall come out of the "totem" of their own profession and take courage to meet and embrace each other. It is a matter of decision to behave according to the principle of "totemic exogamy,"[20] to practice interdisciplinarity in science, because "whoever wants to be 'fertile' and wants to 'deliver' must leave the shelter of one's own 'disciplinary totem' and search somewhere else. Just as totemic exogamy obliges tribe members, interdisciplinarity . . . is gradually becoming urgent."[21]

* * *

This text will deal with youth ministry and youth theology, as well as with different practical theology topics, but it shall be an exercise in fundamental theology, attempting to establish a new link between practical

16. Ghiloni, "On Writing Interdisciplinary Theology," 25.
17. Geiser, *Community of the Weak*, 438–39.
18. O'Collins, *Rethinking*, 12.
19. Říha, "Fundamentální teologie," 146.
20. Frazer, *Totemism and Exogamy*. Principle of totemic exogamy according to Frazer obliges tribe members to find their partner in the different tribe or totemic clan.
21. Skalický, *V zápase s posvátnem*, 12.

and theoretical ways of understanding and practicing theology. Is fundamental theology just theoretical or rational reflection on Christian faith? Or could it be also practical, as Johann Baptist Metz suggests in *Practical Fundamental Theology*?[22] What is going to happen when young people or youth ministers start a theological conversation with fundamental theologians? What will happen when people with no knowledge of academic theology challenge theologians with disturbing questions? Having been often involved in debates with young people, I've observed a certain reluctance to talk to me when they were told I was a theologian. Having participated in meetings of the faculty staff preparing events for young people to promote our theological programs, I often witnessed an effort to make it a very low threshold, as if we go out to hunt for stupid people whom we will eventually educate. All in all, I think there used to be very little space for encounter between young people and professional theologians. It appears to me to be very similar to situation of Saint Paul speaking about the resurrection of the dead in Athens and proclaiming the "unknown God" (Acts 17). I always had the impression that when theologians speak to young people, they preach of a God who is unknown to the youth.[23] This works both ways. I often heard young people say similar things as that which the Athenians did in response to Saint Paul: "We will hear you again about this" (Acts 17:32). Of course, not all these meetings in which I participated (either as theologian, religious educator, youth minister, or when a young person myself) ended like that. But it is my experience that theologians and young people often miss each other. How could we make this situation better? A few events where I witnessed mutual understanding and genuine learning from each other (even an experienced professor of theology may learn something from meeting with young people) motivated me to meditate more about this and ponder not only the possibilities but also the difficulties of such encounters.

In general, I believe an authentic sharing and mutual learning occurs when stories of particular people are narrated and heard. Everyone deserves to tell one's own story and deserves to be heard. Hearing stories is sometimes difficult, especially in times when listening is becoming more problematic. But telling stories may be equally hard, if not even harder, when it comes to sharing life stories, personal struggles for identity, or deep experiences of meaning or relevance. And I think religious

22. Metz, *Faith in History and Society*.
23. Even though, many Pauline scholars (e.g., Jakob Taubes) celebrate the apostle specifically as a "lay" theologian, rather than a professional or systematic one.

experience is certainly one of that kind. Therefore, I decided to write in a personal, autobiographical[24] way, because I fully agree with Asian-American theologian David Ng's conviction that

> a person of faith is inclined to review one's life in terms of faith, interpreting and extrapolating the events of life through the eyes of faith. One's life story becomes a life-story, a way of relating events to providence. "Life" is connected into a reasonable (and sometimes paradoxical) series somehow taking on a story structure informed by faith. The stories of faith in the Bible serve as models for a Christian person of faith. One's life is seen as a story that is a part of larger story. The story is social, and it includes other persons and groups of one's life.[25]

I also believe that personal stories of Christians include God as well, because in terms of Christianity, God is present (and active) in the history of the world as well as in the lives of individuals and communities. God is present in our contexts and places where we live. From a Christian perspective, all that is happening in this world happens between humans and the divine. The world, and its appearance, mirrors a mutual human-divine relating to each other. Understanding this relationship is essential for our dwelling in the world. People have developed tools to reflect upon their lived relationship with the supernatural. Such a tool is called theology in Christianity. Understanding theology and consequently also living in a theological way (living faith, hope, and love) is necessary for each person who calls him/herself a Christian. Theology as such is a principal reflection. To deepen our understanding, it has developed a well-worked system of concrete reflections. Certainly, one of the essential theological disciplines is fundamental theology, which provides reasonable grounds for interpreting one's own faith and Christian identity and narrates the story of theology as a discipline.

For myself, who grew up during the close of the twentieth century in the former Eastern bloc, saying goodbye to the old communist regime and welcoming a new era of being free "Middle Europe," a theologian was a synonym for the old wise (clergy)man (not woman) who "knows it all." But even at the beginning of my theological studies, I had a feeling that

---

24. I accept the following etymological definition of autobiography: "Autos, bios, and graphein together suggest that a work becomes autobiographical whenever it contains a text written by life of that life itself." Štofaník, "Popularization and Autobiography," 73.

25. Ng, "Path of Concentric Circles," 81–82.

there must be a different way. Later, when I advanced in age, I worked with young people myself (as youth minister and as theologian too) and recalled my earlier feelings. I sensed that they were not just objects to inform about theology, educate in certain religious traditions, or teach catechism to. On the contrary, I experienced that they could challenge my theological interpretations and convictions because they have their own. Soon enough, I realized that I had to first learn from them, if I was ever to be able to teach them. Theology is not only about education, studying, and reasoning. It is also about sharing stories, speaking, and listening. It is about "convivence"—living together.[26] Theology means telling stories, in which God and I (We) play a central role. Through narrating their stories, Christians bring the gospel message (about faith, hope, and love) to human society. There is an evangelical aspect deeply embedded in each theology. Generally, I understand evangelization as a way of practicing theology—narrating the story of Christianity and its theology (faith, hope, and love seeking understanding). It is an ongoing process of discerning God's presence in the world through the human experience of God's revelation and stealth in history (*Deus revelatus* and *Deus absconditus*). Such experience is not reserved for professional theologians or clergymen. It is not reserved for adult Christians either. All Christians and non-Christians too, all people of faith, seek the roots of their faith. They also strive to communicate them to others in an authentic way. Fundamental theology facilitates the broad dialogue of the whole of theology within the complex structures of the world, reminding believers that their faith and mission are exercised within the whole breadth of human society. Each Christian, no matter if young or old, needs to see that his/her being is essentially Christian (human in Christ) and fundamentally theological (in relationship with God). Christians shall mutually empower each other to make the key story of the Bible the key story of one's own life; in other words, to live-tell one's own life-story in the perspective of eternal salvation. In the words of Bert Roebben, "Every generation will need to tell the story again and think about how it illuminates 'the signs of the times.' The old lesson of Anselmus of Canterbury—*fides quaerens intellectum* (faith seeking understanding)—needs to be actualized in every new generation. Young people deserve therefore good ministers who encourage them to see, to reflect and to act with the

---

26. "Convivence" (Ger. Konvivenz) is the term adopted from Latin American liberation theology by Theo Sundermeier. It means "living with attention to one another." Sundermeier, *Den Fremden verstehen*, 189–90.

eyes of faith—especially in times in which many people decide to close their eyes to the Mystery of Life."[27]

Church ministers, clergy, theologians, and adults in general need young people as companions in their exercise of faith (seeking understanding). Young people can encourage them to see, to reflect, and to act with their eyes of faith always wide open. They can enable them to see their own faith always anew. They can teach them that there is still more to come, that there is still something we can expect. They can remind them that all people remain "young" in the sight of the eternal One.

* * *

Several years ago (in 2005), when I started to pursue my dissertation on aspects of fundamental theology in the writings of the late Cardinal Avery Dulles, SJ, I began reflecting upon his life. I entered his theology through reading his autobiography.[28] I learned that each story has its face, and each idea has an author.[29] The author, his/her face, and life story are always important for deeper understanding of his/her concepts and ideas. Later in 2008, I was blessed with the opportunity to meet Cardinal Dulles personally. Even though he was at the end of his amazing life, he opened his personal archive to me. He graciously gave me audience for a few months on a regular basis. He read my texts and commented on them. All this made a great impression on me. At that time, I was a very young "theology student from nowhere," and he was "the cardinal from New York" and surely one of the leading Catholic theologians of his time a few months prior to his death and suffering while battling with serious health problems. Yet despite these differences, we met, we talked and discussed, and I always felt welcomed. I was always encouraged. He never made me feel like my questions were stupid. He patiently explained himself as he replied to my questions. Above all, he taught me a lesson of intergenerational respect and collaboration. On February 14, 2008, I received a letter from Cardinal Dulles in which he summarized the essentials of his own theological method, which we had discussed before. Among other things, he wrote, "Before I am a theologian, I am a Christian and a Catholic. Theology is an exercise of faith; it presupposes faith.

---

27. Roebben, *Seeking Sense*, 226.
28. Dulles, *Testimonial to Grace*.
29. Štěch, *Tu se jim otevřely oči*, 21.

As a reflective believer, I ask questions about the content, grounds and implications of my faith."[30]

A personal story always matters for any kind of theological work done. Theological work does not mean merely writing articles or books alone. It also means living our lives in a theological way. My encounter with Cardinal Dulles (both in writings and in person) was enabled by my teacher, the excellent theologian Karel Skalický. His adventurous life story will be further addressed through the course of this work as well. He was the one who discovered me as "theologian" and initiated me into academic theology. He was and still is (even in his advanced age) my respected guide on my own theological journey. Meeting professor Skalický and Cardinal Dulles, I learned about the importance of biography and autobiography for academic theology. A life story is part of one's own life. It is tightly bound to it, and it springs out of its richness. Following their example, my attempt will be to write this text in an *understandable* and *existentially relevant way*. These are the two principles Štefan Štofaník, a young theologian of Slovenian origin who tragically died in 2014, identified—in his last published essay—with the complementary, related factors needed for theology to make sense and become accessible.[31] Understandable and existentially relevant theology is not only a question of "what theologians are doing and why"[32] but also of how they write theology. It is a matter of style. Štofaník proposes autobiography as a narrative style of writing contemporary theological works and states (quoting Giuseppe Mazzota) that autobiography makes a scholar's scientific praxis and achievement intelligible.[33] It is because my story is not just mine. Each story also includes social dimensions. For Christians (and theologians too), it is related to their faith and to God. Thus, those who consider themselves believers narrate their autobiographies as auto/

---

30. Štěch, *Tu se jim otevřely oči*, 14.

31. Štofaník, "Popularization and Autobiography," 68.

32. Hellwig, "Foundations for Theology," 1. When we do something, it is always important to know why we do it. Just think of Aldous Huxley and his vision in *Brave New World*, where, as a member of a certain class, you are not supposed to know why you do things; you simply must do them. "You're so conditioned that you can't help doing what you ought to do. And what you ought to do is on the whole so pleasant." Huxley, *Brave New World*, 182. Therefore, as those who do theology, we shall not only focus on knowing what we do (systematic theology) or how we do it (practical theology), but we must also consider why we do it. Otherwise, we may end up doing what we ought to do, and then it is just up to someone else to convince us that it is so pleasant.

33. Štofaník, "Popularization and Autobiography," 72.

Theo-biographies—stories of their lives where God is not absent but rather very present in each moment and act.

Each Christian theology is (or shall be) an echo of the interpersonal encounter between a human person and the personal (Triune) God, between the story of self and story of God, where the "self" is never solely alone but realized always in community with other human "selves." It was Edward Schillebeeckx who, in the third volume of his trilogy about Jesus of Nazareth (*Church: The Human Story of God*), clearly expressed the communal character of theology. He suggests that people are words with which God tells his story (as evoked in the original Dutch title of his book, *Mensen als verhaal van God*). Schillebeeckx declares a negative ecclesiology approach and focuses on the lives of "men and women and their bond with God, as God has become visible above all in Jesus of Nazareth, confessed as the Christ by Christian churches."[34]

If God tells his story and all human beings are words of this narrative, can our theology be something else then storytelling?[35] Through telling my stories, indicating some key experiences in my (Christian) life, reflecting on them theologically, and relating them to particular theological influences, I will try to locate myself in a particular (theological) tradition, context, and culture. I will attempt to connect my life story/stories with concrete theological questions, and I will also take up the challenge of presenting fundamental theology anew, maybe in a more imaginative, creative, inspiring, accessible, understandable, and existentially relevant way. In that effort my encounters with young people, youth theology, and youth ministry play an essential role.

Employing personal stories as theological resources presupposes a decision to put experience first and reflect on the traces of God in personal lives.[36] Narrating, reflecting, and sharing experiences will become important for shaping the future of Christianity and its theology since it surely departs from the shape it took throughout modernity and has become "postmodern." Today, discussions about the postmodern condition of Christianity goes on. But some theologians already attempt to foresee the "tomorrow" of Christianity. For instance, Tomáš Halík is "convinced that the Christianity of tomorrow will neither be 'ideology' nor religion in terms of 'the system of beliefs and rituals' (according to the definition of Durkheim), but it should and could be a school of faith, hope,

---

34. Schillebeeckx, *Church*, xiii.
35. Song, "Five Stages," 3.
36. Geiser, *Community of the Weak*, 253.

and love; a school on the basis of medieval universities' ideal, a common life of prayer and study, where truth was searched in free discussion and only that was handed over to the others, what was previously meditated through."[37]

If this vision shall come to pass, the Christianity of tomorrow will need a different mode of theology, reflecting more on personal stories; enabling free discussion across nations, cultures, and generations; and becoming a school of faith, hope, and love rather than only a rational reflection of them. It seems that the future of Christianity must become a responsible religiosity, individually shaped yet realized in communities (schools of faith) carrying on traditions of recognizing, interpreting, and understanding revelation, faith, and the community anew. In theology, an authority of experience (as well as its reflecting and sharing) is slowly taking over the juridical authority of hierarchical church, which lost its power in society and support in mainstream culture during the process of secularization. Some theologians call it "the end of Christendom"[38] and see the future of Christianity in a return to "core stories of Christian identity."[39] "Ultimately, Christendom collapsed in the face of the overwhelming power of secular nationalism. Later, Christian scholars struggled to live in the new age of 'post-Christendom,' when one could no longer assume any connection between religion and political order. By the start of the twenty-first century, however, the whole concept of the nation-state was itself under challenge."[40]

The world changes fast, bringing opportunities but also threats.[41] On the one hand, we may benefit from rapid technological developments and information exchange, but on the other hand, we experience growing individualization, crises of identity, and the gradual fragmentation of society.[42] Such a context gives a lot of space for individualistic syncretism as well as for fundamentalism. In the past, society found in religion and theological reflection a profound source of reference and support, but after the secular "disenchantment of the world," these often proved to be irrelevant, outdated, or inadequate to the task.[43] The "fluidity" of the

37. Halík, *Chci, abys byl*, 10–11.
38. Hall, *End of Christendom*.
39. Dean, *OMG*, 37.
40. Jenkins, *Next Christendom*, 10–11.
41. Beck, *Risk Society*.
42. Lyotard, *Postmodern Condition*; Boeve, *Theology at the Crossroads*.
43. Gauchet, *Disenchantment of the World*.

world[44] is surely a valid metaphor of contemporary times, derived from its quickly changing forms, as well as from the relativity resulting from individualization and privatization. The ability to anchor identity from the spiritual core of our personality has at least the same importance as flexibility and an ability to adapt in ever-changing conditions. A cursory look at contemporary European societies would very likely indicate that while some people experience new and exciting opportunities, many others experience disorientation, brokenness, and loss. At the same time religious faith and theology continue to experience a decline at the level of society. This means that the resources that people accessed in the past in times of crisis are often no longer available to them. This causes a certain fragility within society, creating a challenge to theology as well as to other disciplines like philosophy, psychology, sociology, and pedagogy. They, too, struggle to maintain their function to provide answers to questions about human destiny and the meaning of life.

In this context, both unsettling and full of potential, the Christian theological tradition may carry a new meaning and a new promise for our culture and society. This involves a search for an interpretation of contemporary religious experience enabling Christianity to renew its potential to inspire contemporary culture(s), where theological thinking has become, to some extent, somewhat obscure. Such a situation asks for a renewal of types of reflection. Perceiving these developments well, some (mostly practical) theologians today emphasize "doing theology" instead of only thinking it.[45] Such a theological renewal requires a search for new methods, new ways, and new styles of formulating and communicating theology. As one of the apostles of such a change wrote, "New themes, new debates, new references, and new walking partners in the social sciences, cultural studies, ethnography, and art and music theory have contributed to a different feel and style (of theology) that may not be so familiar in traditional academic circles. And yet it all finds its common center in theology as autobiography."[46]

Why not add youth ministry and youth theology to the list of Geiser's proposed dialogue partners for (fundamental) theology? The theology of the future must become our own story once again—stories of our lives. Therefore, an interdisciplinary encounter with fundamental and youth

---

44. Bauman, *Liquid Modernity*.
45. Bevans, *Introduction to Theology*, 1.
46. Geiser, *Community of the Weak*, 253.

theology may bring interesting benefits for the constant reshaping and development of Christian theology as such. Fundamental theology deals with the grounding principles of Christian faith and studies them in relation to contemporary cultural and societal shifts as newly emerging contexts. Youth theology emerged as a reflexive tool of youth ministry, which is an area where the practical life of the church is emerging and the future of Christianity is reshaping the church.

* * *

I hope this introductory patchwork of thoughts can serve as a brief degustation of the different notions and perhaps also new links I am going to explore and discuss in more depth throughout the next four chapters, which are structurally organized in the following order. Chapter 1 asks a very fundamental question which everyone who does theology in one way or another must answer many times: What is theology? It often seems that everyone knows what it is. But when we look closer, we find out that there is actually very little agreement on what it is and how it should be done. I am convinced of the necessity to clarify what I understand (at least when writing this text) by theology, in general, before I proceed to chapter 2.

There I set myself the task of reiterating the story of fundamental theology as particular theological discipline in which I found myself professionally at home. However, you should not expect an authoritative, comprehensive summary of the nature, method, content, and style of fundamental theology. Instead, I opted for an improvisational and biographical narration starting with my interpretation of the history and origins of the discipline. I continue by paying homage to three of my great theological sources (Vladimír Boublík, Karel Skalický, and Avery Dulles). I will try to show the ways they influenced and shaped my own theology in general and my understanding of fundamental theology in particular. The last part of chapter 2 attempts to find a bridge to cross from fundamental theology to the realm of youth ministry and youth theology. As a newcomer, I decided to adopt a curious tourist perspective when attempting to narrate the story of youth ministry and emerging youth theology.

For that reason, chapter 3 will be a report about my exploration in the unknown terrain (*terra incognita*) where the theological voices of young people might be heard, where the future of theology and the church may be prepared and shaped. Landscapes of youth ministry and youth theology are quite far removed from my own professional domain. Yet my own experience of working with young people gave me hope that I could find there a profound source of inspiration and perhaps also new companions for doing theology with. Are there possibilities for mutual encounters? Is it possible at all for fundamental theology and youth ministry or youth theology to do theology together? And if so, what could be their common themes? From where they can start doing theology together?

An attempt to answer these last two questions will be made in chapter 4. It seems to me that in principle, there are three areas of common interest about which both disciplines are concerned: (1) Christian religious identity in relation to human identity in general; (2) the investigation of how to pursue a truly Christian life, i.e., how to do theology; and (3) the question of meaning in both Christian and human terms. I strongly believe that an enhancement and renewal of both disciplines concerned in this work may come from their mutual encounter and attempt to start doing theology together, a theology which would not be entrenched within theological faculties and academic conferences yet would still flourish from human experience and from life itself.

1

What Is Theology?

"Theology is taught and written, danced and sung, sculpted and painted, even dreamed and cried."[1]

WHAT IS THEOLOGY? WHAT do I do when I *do theology*? These are questions that theologians, as well as all believing Christians across denominations, must ask during their lives. However, that is often not the case. More likely, people usually have a vague notion of what theology is, and academic theologians generally assume that everyone is clear about it. Nonetheless, experience has taught me that these assumptions often vary a lot. Therefore, it seems that different misunderstandings in particular theological debates, ecumenical as well as intra-denominational, may stem from insufficient reflection on what theology is in essence and what its meanings are. To avoid such difficulties, we must repeatedly attempt to answer the fundamental theological question: What is theology? And how does it connect to the everyday life of Christian believers? Thanks to this kind of questioning, we can see that theology is a question; it can "bring itself before itself" as a question, and therefore it can reach a kind of self-transcendence. It is like what Karl Rahner suggested as the essence of human subjectivity. According to Karl Rahner, human beings question

1. Sedmak, *Doing Local Theology*, 11.

themselves analytically and open themselves to the unlimited horizons of such questioning. Thus they have a certain capacity to transcend themselves in a basic way.[2] The same is true about theology if we consider it as part of human subjectivity and activity. Theology as human activity transcends itself because it persistently asks about its own meanings and origins. But is theology only a human activity? Is it only part of our subjectivity? Can we consider human beings as the only source of theology?

When it comes to its many shades, theology is very much fragmented. But it remains a common heritage, an everyday task, and a common future of all Christians too. Theology teaches us to live in relationship with the eternal One. Each theology is an auto/Theo-biography[3] of its own kind. It is a story of a particular human being, living his/her life in a concrete sociohistorical context of the world. It is a story of life, which is not Godless but full of God instead. It is life, where God has its own indispensable place as person (tri-person) and partner, as the One (and three) who is not only present but the One (and three) who also acts as the One (and three) who is the very source of theology. Through him, with him, and in him we live, and thus we can do theology similar to the way God does it. Speaking words about himself and acting according to his own will, God certainly does Theo-logy. Consequently, it might be said that auto/Theo-biography is a story of God as well as a story of a particular human being. Therefore, I hold the view that this concept has considerable potential for the development of ecumenical (as well as interreligious) discussion about the nature of theology.

Theology is generally defined as human faith asking and seeking answers to its own questions. In the words of Saint Anselm, theology is faith seeking understanding (*fides quaerens intellectum*).[4] But this famous Anselmian definition of theology most probably comes from Saint Augustine's: "Do not seek to understand in order to believe but believe that you may understand." A similar description one also finds in the Septuagint by the prophet Isaiah: "Unless you believe, you shall not understand" (Isa 7:9).[5] Even though Augustine and Anselm had different visions of theology,[6] it is obvious that there is a long-standing

2. Rahner, *Základy křesťanské víry*, 61.
3. Ward, *Participation and Mediation*, 2–4.
4. Grenz et al., *Pocket Dictionary*, 52.
5. Becker, *Fundamental Theology*, 70.
6. While Anselm "thought human reason itself to be fully capable of discovering on its own the rational coherence of the truth of the faith, apart from any appeal to divine

tradition of interpreting theology as the possible meeting point of faith with reason in a particular context. Theology is always contextual and universal at the same time. It starts from a concrete situation and experience of and in this world. But simultaneously, it attempts to be universal because it attempts to "name" the One who is universal. Theology thinks about and longs to know God—its universal foundation. Consequently, theology can be understood not only from this "below" perspective but also from the "above" perspective, where God is theology itself. As we shall see later in this text, this is because theology essentially dwells between humanity and the divine. Theology is universality seeking particularity (God searching for human beings) on the one hand and particularity seeking universality (people searching for God) on the other. It is the universalization of particularity and the particularization of universality that is at the center of Christian theology. The theory of globalization, as it is described by Roland Robertson, not only knows such two-facedness,[7] but long before, the Gospel of John spoke about it in its prologue (John 1:1–4). This text reveals Jesus Christ as the Word incarnated, as God, who became man, as absolute power becoming a powerless[8] child, as absolute power hanging powerlessly on the cross, and as absolute power rising from dead as the Lord of history.

---

revelation or the Scriptures . . . [Augustine] stressed the mutual interaction of faith and understanding in the interpretation of the Scriptures for the sake of true knowledge of God." Becker, *Fundamental Theology*, 71.

7. Robertson, *Globalization*, 102.

8. From my point of view, this theological notion is extraordinarily valuable for public debates on power. For those who might be interested, I recommend reading Václav Havel's essay "Power of the Powerless" (Havel, "Power of the Powerless") through theological optics and then trying to apply one's own conclusions to problems we face in public debates today. I am sure it will be a salutary experience and an exercise in public theology. A theologian who may have been inspired by Havel's outstanding essay was Clemens Sedmak. He writes, "We do theology not because of hope in a magically liberated, sorrow-free happy life. We do theology because we hope that wounds may be the source of strength. . . . We do theology because of wounded people who have touched us. Jesus surrendered his power and became vulnerable, defenseless, and wounded . . . We do theology because people suffer. Doing theology is a way to attend to the wounds of our time. There are the wounds of ignorance and stupidity, the wounds of broken promises and unrealized dreams, the wounds of innocent suffering and of guilt, the wounds of open questions and burning concerns. We all do theology as wounded healers, as people in need of healing and comfort, and as people who can share the life-giving strength of our wounds. . . . We could not do theology without this trust in the power of our wounds and the wounds of our fellow creatures. This is the power of the poor in history, the power of the children, the power of the powerless." Sedmak, *Doing Local Theology*, 9–10.

Ecce homo! Behold! Human being (particularization of universality)! Behold! Lord (universalization of particularity)!

Such cohesion of universality and particularity in theology, and theology as such, must be studied before we approach fundamental theology and youth theology in the later stages of this text. It is the task of this chapter to introduce a fundamental perspective, to unveil what theology was, is, and may be. I would like to remind readers about the importance of the principal question asked in the title of this chapter: to describe the different shades of the term "theology," and finally, I want to point out the substantially ecumenical character of theology. To meet such resolutions, it will be helpful to think gradually about the possibilities and limits of defining theology, about in which sense theology is a science, and eventually about theology as holistic activity which is not only accessible but also characteristic to both expert theologians and all believing Christians as well.

1.1 DEFINING THEOLOGY

Everyone who asks about meaning of the word "theology" usually receives a typical dictionary answer: theology as a term signifies a "science (doctrine) of God" or "speaking (study) of God" and comes from the Greek words "theos" (God) and "logos" (word), or "logia" (sayings). This etymological exposition could be found almost in all introductions to theology.[9] It is also common to understand theology as specifically a Christian "thing." However, the origin of the word is not Christian. The term "theology" had been used already by Plato and Aristotle in their efforts to conceptualize and describe any kind of thinking or speaking about gods.[10] One of the great theologians of antiquity, for instance, was Marcus Terentius Varro, who was called "the most learned and the brightest of all Romans"[11] by Augustine, who discusses Varro in *City of God*. With a bit of clarification, we possibly also can talk about Jewish and Islamic theology, as suggested by one of the prolific proponents of dialog among the monotheisms of the Abrahamic tradition, David Burrell.[12]

---

9. McGrath, *Christian Theology*, 102; Plantinga et al., *Introduction to Christian Theology*, 5; Mueller, *Theological Foundations*, 28; Schüssler Fiorenza and Galvin, *Systematic Theology*, 3.

10. Noble, *Tracking God*, 3.

11. Jüptner, *Civilní náboženství*, 11.

12. Burrell, *Towards a Jewish-Christian-Muslim Theology*.

With time, theology became almost exclusively the domain of Christianity and anchored firmly in its structures. This specifically occurs in medieval times.[13] In his treatise on the nature and origin of theology, Francis Schüssler Fiorenza specifies that theology got its contemporary meaning in the thirteenth century.[14] Up until that time, the word "theology" was only scarcely present in patristic literature to contrast Christian *theology* and pagan *mythology*.[15] The concept of theology is completely missing in Biblical Greek.[16] However, a purely linguistic exposition of theology is rather fragmentary and encourages deeper research. It is not surprising that throughout history, there were numerous and sometimes very diverse definitions of "theology" given. Therefore, an attempt by the Czech theologian Karel Skalický to offer a kind of typology is very much welcome.[17] Skalický does not consider one, all-embracing definition of theology but presents together three complementary definitions in his account: Theocentric, Anthropocentric, and Theo-Anthropic.[18] He noticed that each definition of theology assumes one of the mentioned perspectives. Each one is relevant in a certain sense. But to decide which one is the most accurate or the most comprehensive would be misleading. Skalický's typology thus sets off in direction of a dynamic understanding of theology, which can be defined as:

1. Science/knowledge about God (Theocentric definition).

2. Science/knowledge about faith (Anthropocentric definition)

3. Science/knowledge about revelation of God to humankind (Theo-Anthropic definition)

The first definition introduces theology as an attempt to find out whatever we can know and discover about God. Sometimes it even understands God as an object of our intellectual curiosity. No wonder. After all, God is a mystery that fascinates trembling human beings, attracting attention and stimulating the search for knowledge since time

---

13. McGrath, *Christian Theology*, 102.

14. At the same time, he maintains (quoting Joseph Ratzinger) that today we use the word "theology" to label human knowledge of God. Schüssler Fiorenza and Galvin, *Systematic Theology*, 4.

15. McGrath, *Christian Theology*, 103.

16. Plantinga et al., *Introduction to Christian Theology*, 5; Noble, *Tracking God*, 4.

17. Skalický, "Současná křesťanská teologie," 33–42.

18. Skalický, "Současná křesťanská teologie," 33.

immemorial. The second definition changes this perspective. A focal point of its interest is not God anymore but human faith instead. What can we know about the One who infinitely transcends us, who is ever greater (*semper maior*) and thus unknowable in the final analysis? If there is anything to be investigated, if we can think about something, it is faith as an anthropological phenomenon. Skalický's third perspective interconnects the two preceding ones and presents them as complementary. Both grasp an important aspect of the relationship between the personal God and the human person. Theology is a free act of God, who, in his revelation, shares himself with human beings. But it is also a free act of the human person, who answers or responds to such revelation by his/her faith.[19] An act, if it should be genuinely free, must be an act of the free will. It can be said that theology, in the third perspective of Skalický, discerns God, who in his power and through his will, reveals himself as Love and thus invites humans into relationship with himself. People can reply to this confession of (L)love by their own love, or more precisely, by directing their own power with the help of will towards God, who is Love.[20] Theology as it is defined in the Theo-Anthropic way is reflection of the God-humanity relationship.

According to Skalický it is possible to escape the shallow water of theology considered as a *genitive objective* (science/knowledge about something) and dive into the greater depths of the term. The real meaning of the term "theology" remains shrouded in mystery because of its (mysterious) substance. Getting deeper, we may find out that theology is not only a knowledge/science about something, but it is also (and maybe mainly) a knowledge/science of something. "Such a genitive is no longer a genitive objective (about something) but a genitive subjective (of something), in a sense that God, faith, and revelation are not anymore just objects of science but are also its subjects."[21]

In the light of such a "linguistic" modification, we may see a glimpse of the other meanings of theology, which can be defined in the *genitive subjective* as:

---

19. Revelation as a mutual encounter of God and human beings based on reciprocal free activity (revelation—accepting/recognizing revelation) is presented for instance in the Documents of the Second Vatican council, especially in the *Dogmatic Constitution on Divine Revelation "Dei Verbum"* (DV), and more specifically, in DV 2 and 6.
20. Štěch, "Love as the Core of Theology," 179–89.
21. Skalický, "Současná křesťanská teologie," 33.

1. Science/knowledge of God (Theocentric definition)
2. Science/knowledge of faith (Anthropocentric definition)
3. Science/knowledge of God's revelation to humankind (Theo-Anthropic definition)

In the logic of the first definition we may speak of God, who has knowledge about himself through his own Word (*Theou Logos*), which he produces (in himself), thinks, and pronounces. God pronounces himself. He says his own name aloud; he reveals himself as the One who freely determines not only his own being but also everything else, because everything receives existence from his power, will, and love. From a Christian perspective, the first and the most substantial Word of God is Jesus Christ. God, the Son, the preexistent Logos of the prologue to Saint John's Gospel: the Word of God through which God pronounces the truth about himself, through which God pronounces himself, shows who he is, reveals himself to himself and to the whole of creation. Through Jesus Christ, with him, and in him, God not only has self-knowledge but also self-consciousness and opens towards partnership with humankind. If a particular person answers positively to such a call, his/her life becomes "theology" too, and the Word of God may be perceived in the human word about God. Already at this place we can see that "shallow" meanings of theology are substantially related to "deep" ones. And even from shallow water we may catch sight of the depths. It is also necessary to note that the whole of creation exists in a theological way because it is called into existence by God's word, which is an act (act of creation) at the same time. In broad sense, all that exists can be considered "theology," since everything that is celebrates God the Creator in its own way. Such deep intuition is expressed in some of the psalms (Pss 69:35; 148:7; 150:6), or the song of three young men in the fiery furnace from the third chapter of the apocrypha book of the prophet Daniel. In modern times the theological existence of the universe is further perceived, for instance, by Pierre Teilhard de Chardin.

Usage of the *genitive objective* in the case of the second definition exposes the reality that even knowledge coming from the transcendental component of human faith may be called theology. Consequently, the Christian faith may be understood not only as "a decision, standpoint, or human activity but also as a supernatural gift of God. The reflected interaction between human and divine can occur at the level of faith, which is possible on the basis of mutual love, and may even lead to eschatological unity."[22]

From this perspective, faith is emphasized as subject, which mysteriously strives for self-understanding. The faith itself is a true *fides quaerens intellectum*, but at the same time it wants to be voluntarily accepted with gratitude. Finally, Skalický's third definition of genitive subjective suggests that divine revelation works inside the human soul as an invitation to understand, follow, and engage in the relationship with the Revealer. Revelation is the Revealer, alone, incarnated, tortured to death, and resurrected Jesus Christ. In him, love is revealed—the love of God as well as the love of human beings.[23]

Christian theology can be defined in many ways. However, God, human beings, and their relationship will ever remain its fundamental coordinates. Theology is happening between humanity and the divine. God shows himself in human lives as revealing God (*Deus revelatus*) but also as God in hiding (*Deus absconditus*). He empowers people to recognize him and to know him,[24] but at the same time, he remains mysterious and hidden, and people experience powerlessness in all their efforts to know him. Could this God be an object of our scientific interest and inquiry? Could theology be a science?

1.2 IS THEOLOGY A SCIENCE?

If we shall be able to answer this question, we must extend the intertwined pair, God—humanity, with a third quantity, and this is the world. No relationship is played out in absolute vacuum. It needs always its proper context, where it can be perceived, developed, and understood. Of course, the quality of relationship is not easily measurable by an external

---

22. Štěch, "Love as the Core of Theology," 183.
23. Zvěřina, *Teologie agapé I.*, 79.
24. An interesting Trinitarian reference is provided by Czech theologian Ctirad V. Pospíšil: "Our integral knowledge (thus not only intellectual) of the Triune One does not happen outside of us. Based on how the Triune One manifests himself in the history of salvation and in our lives, we find that he places human beings in the center of his interest, which shall be mirrored by human beings, who should place the Triune One in the center of their interests. As such, 'God's anthropocentrism' and the 'disciples' Theo-centrism' do not exclude each other, but they even inevitably complement each other. These are two faces of the same (one) love having traits of the Man from Nazareth, the incarnated Son of God, truly the One from the Trinity and truly a human being as we are." Pospíšil, *Hermeneutika mystéria*, 22.

observer. However, it is possible to estimate the quality of a particular relationship from the way those involved in it treat each other and their surroundings. Each relationship manifests itself in its environment. The garden of those who love each other blossoms and is beautiful because they work together in it. The garden of those who quarrel is overgrown with weeds and the fruit of trees that nobody harvests. Relationships and their quality are expressed in their tangible contexts. The context of theology, understood as a multifaceted relationship of free persons (God-human beings), is the "garden" of the world and its history. Therefore, theology can be a science about the meeting of God with human beings inside the world. Theology can also be an academic discipline about the referentiality between God-human-world. However, it must accept that the finest shades of these relationships will always remain hidden to any of its inquiries, because they are not, and even cannot, be captured in purely rational discourse. On the one hand, theology has its object (or better a "chief interest")[25] and is grounded in human, rational thinking. But on the other, this does not exhaust all its possibilities, because it is also a relationship of free persons. It lives inside the most intimate recesses of the heart as faith, hope, and love.

Some think that theology is science when it "clearly marks its foundations and proves itself to be a controllable, and thus, in principle, a disputable way of thought."[26] Such conviction was established in history mainly thanks to the fact that theology had to defend its own scientific character against the positivism of natural sciences and the enlightened critique, i.e., that it uses matters of faith for their scientific reflections. During the twentieth century, theology continued to prove its own scientific character and (it is necessary to note) with admirable success. For instance, two influential Czech Protestant authors (Gallus and Macek) thinks that theology is undoubtedly a science. "Foundations of theology may be hard to understand by others, but its deductions and argumentation are scientific in modern sense of the word."[27] And Gallus adds that

---

25. It is very problematic to talk about an object of theology. Particularly because God is a person and not a thing. When Christians confess their faith in God, they do not confess faith in something but rather faith in someone. Therefore, I accept theses that, in the case of academic theology, suggest that it is better to talk about its "chief interest" than about its "object" (Pospíšil, *Hermeneutika mystéria*, 20). Ivana Noble even writes, "God resists being treated as an object." Noble, *Tracking God*, 2.

26. Machula, "Teologie jako věda," 47.

27. Macek, "Teologie mezi vědami," 201.

theology is "subordinated to all rules of logic and scientific discourse."[28] It seems that today, everybody believes that theology is a science. True atheists may be possible exceptions. To be honest, I have not met many genuine, real atheists during my life so far. But I have met at least one: former Protestant pastor, philosopher and scholar of religion Otakar A. Funda. He does not consider theology a science and understands it rather as a distinct kind of poetry[29] where imagination has priority over knowledge. Such critique is sound, and it raises an important question: Isn't it possible that theology has become perhaps too much of a science?

An attempt to prove theology as a science face-to-face with other formal, natural, and interpretative sciences,[30] as well as the emphasis on its academic character, led theology into the trap of its own scientism. Theology became an esoteric issue of academics, and it is often written by scientists for scientists only.[31] Also, we must admit that many believing Christians (not to mention non-Christians) consider academic theology unintelligible, inaccessible, boring, and frequently obscure. Despite this, some theological books enjoy a certain popularity among readers. But academia often refuses them as "non-scientific." Some Christians even think that we do not need any academic theology. Why is that? Is it due to a kind of misunderstanding or reluctance to read difficult texts? Is it because people in general do not read today? Maybe the mistake is not at the side of an "audience."

Maybe there is a mistake at the side of an academic theology. Maybe it is a time to reconsider the way theology expresses itself. Maybe there is no need for academic theology anymore in the ways it is written and published today. Maybe theology does not only refer to the university research and writing theological publications. Maybe theology must once again emphasize that it is not only a presentation of its own content (i.e., the content of faith) but a process and activity instead.[32] Maybe we must ask again: What is theology? How should it be done?

---

28. Gallus, "Orientující teologie," 80.

29. Funda, "Je teologie vědou?," 105–35.

30. Theology most likely ranks among the interpretative (or cultural) sciences. These sciences always assume some starting point. Thus, theology is a science in an interpretative or cultural sense. It is a science explaining the world from a Christian perspective. Pospíšil, *Hermeneutika mystéria*, 138–44.

31. Whapham, "Foreword," 8.

32. Bevans, *Introduction to Theology*, 1.

In connection with such questions, some authors are aware of the importance or necessity of extracting or salvaging theology from the exclusive group of experts and return and deliver it back to all Christians amid Christian communities. At the same time, they do not question the importance of scientific discourse. This is well perceived by Ivana Noble when she writes, "Theology is not a science in terms of the natural sciences. This does not mean, however, that it is not a science."[33] According to her, the scientific character of theology resides in its adequateness to its "subject" and its addressees (audience). Skalický's perspective is like Noble's. However, he does not speak about adequacy but about "delimitation of acceptable boundaries" for theology, although he most probably thinks like Noble.[34] Following their thoughts, I would describe the scientific character of theology as an effort to search for the right relations (acceptable and adequate) between God, humanity, and the world.

In addition to classical academic theology, many authors have started to develop concepts of non-academic theology, including lay theology,[35] lived theology,[36] everyday theology,[37] or ordinary theology.[38] All approaches mentioned consider theology as an inseparable part of daily life and suggest that theology should leave its rigid effort to be scientific and return to the human experience of subjective encounters with God, other people, and the world back into the center of its core reflections. Theology should be interested in both what these experiences are and how people share them. The academic way of doing theology always springs from "popular" theology practiced by ordinary believers and is developed alongside. "Theology begins when a person wants to understand his/her life-journey and realizes that, for it to be complete, it has to include a spiritual dimension and, moreover, that this spiritual dimension is a source of life for all other dimensions of our existence."[39] In relation to this, Hans-Peter Geiser points out one very important fact: "There is no engraved rule that academic writing has to be only one way. There is no general law that says that theology can only come in one shape."[40]

33. Noble, *Tracking God*, 16.
34. Skalický, "Současná křesťanská teologie," 41.
35. Hoebel, *Laity and Participation*.
36. Doehring, *Practice of Pastoral Care*.
37. Vanhoozer et al., *Everyday Theology*.
38. Astley, *Ordinary Theology*.
39. Noble, *Tracking God*, 235.
40. Geiser, *Community of the Weak*, 438.

All in all, ordinary and academic theology can intertwine, inspire, enrich, and co-determine each other. Theology may become a way of live, encompassing rational and spiritual dimensions, theoretical reflections as well as practical activities. Theology is more than just science or knowledge. If theology would be just knowledge without love, or just science without its practical overlaps or motivation to everyday conversion, then it would be only dead orthodoxy. If theology shall be alive, then it must always unite orthodoxy with orthopraxis[41] and one's spiritual journey with rational (even scientific) reflections. "There is a difference between devout reflection and theology, that theology is both a spiritual journey and a science with all the requirements that makes on it. Theological reflection needs to be, or at least needs to struggle to be, historically accurate, terminologically correct, systematically unconfused, and clear in its interpretation."[42]

It is important for the integrity and future of theology that its scientific character be maintained. But if it must stay actual, if it must touch human hearts, if it must be *beautiful, compelling,* and *engaging,*[43] as well as *understandable* and *existentially relevant,*[44] then it must not be merely, only, or exclusively a science. Its engaging beauty must always infuse its scientific rigor and vice versa. Theology should overcome its one-sided emphasis on its own academic character and enter a close contact with the world. Theology as an interpretative science can be understandable only within the world. Only within the world is theology able to reflect a web of stories, meetings, and relations of people towards their God and vice versa. A product of reason, or science if you want, can be only a hypothesis of God. The idea of God can originate only at the level of lived faith. "If we search for the meaning of human dwelling in the world, and thus also the meaning of this world, it is necessary to leave the hypothesis of God and find courage to enter into relationship with him."[45] This leads me to the conviction that attentiveness to experience and its sharing, sense for relationship, reflexive method, and rational reasoning should merge in contemporary theology once again. Theology should return to itself, to its own foundations, to the richness of its own meanings. Maybe we can call this kind of change (analogous to what has been called the "theological turn in French philosophy") a "theological turn in theology."

41. Noble, *Tracking God*, 5.
42. Noble, *Tracking God*, 235.
43. Roach and Dominguez, *Expressing Theology*, 19–22.
44. Štofaník, "Popularization and Autobiography," 68.
45. Štěch, "Fundamentální teologie a křesťanská identita," 30.

Theology is not only a matter of tractates of systematic theology presented in heavy manuals. We cannot simply divide theology into theoretical and practical. These are just some of the possible ways of theology, and their divisions are just technical. A theological turn in theology must try to remove these traditional ways of structuring theology and attempt to offer a holistic theology. All the bits and pieces of theological reflection upon lived realities could be interwoven into one colorful tapestry of a *Vita Theologica*—a lived theology. Even academics must practice theology and not only write about it.[46] To live theologically (or to practice theology) means to see our lives in the light of the Scripture (read, heard, and interpreted); creative acceptance of the church tradition in constant tension between individual and communal experiences of revelation.[47] To live theologically means to narrate our lives as auto/Theo-biography.

Auto/Theo-biography as a personal and communal narrative about the human relationship with God implies the practice of theology. Practicing theology is an exercise of the relationship in which human stories and God's story meet in a common narrative expressed both in words and deeds. Ward presents his concept of auto/Theo-biography as a method for exercising practical theology which "shows, how practical theology can be embodied theology."[48] But I think this concept has much more of potential for the whole theology, both as method and as its specific kind or modus. In the following section I will attempt to argue that the term auto/Theo-biography refers to the narrative nature of theology and enable Christians to discern the fundamental condition of their identity. Therefore, it may serve as an appropriate prolegomenon to my further exposition of the story of fundamental theology.

1.3 THEOLOGY AS AUTO/THEO-BIOGRAPHY

"Theology clearly relates to rational discourse, but it is much more than that."[49]

So far, we've considered that giving a comprehensive definition of theology is impossible without an inevitable simplification of some kind. At

---

46. Roach and Dominguez, *Expressing Theology*, 17.
47. Štěch, "Písmo a Tradice," 159–63.
48. Ward, *Participation and Mediation*, 18.
49. Ward, *Participation and Mediation*, 20.

the same time, we cannot claim that theology either is or is not a science (in the strict sense of the word). Most probably the best definition of theology would be the lived relationality including the self, other selves, God, and the world (the extended Theo-anthropic perspective). One of the many ways we could exercise theology is a reflexive narration of the human life story, which is lived, reflected upon, and told in relationships with God, fellow people, and the world. How do I see God? And how does God possibly see me? How do I see myself, others, and the world? And vice versa, how do others and the world see me? How does God see the world and human beings? For the Christian believer these questions are interrelated and inseparable at the same time. This chapter suggests that they might be answered when we focus on the contemporary theological concept of auto/Theo-biography as (1) theological method (for academic theology), and (2) a way of doing theology today (for those who live theological lives). While zooming in on this way of doing theology, we must also investigate developments in *narrative theology*, since it helps usher (auto)biography into theological debates.

Biography and autobiography have a long tradition in theology as literary genres, at least since the time of the famous Saint Augustine's *Confessions*. But only as late as the second half of the twentieth century has the broad stream of a so-called "narrative theology" opened the road for personal stories to become part of the human theological enterprise once again. In general, narrative theology deftly argues that stories of the individual matter for theology and that language functions as a medium for theology being articulated as a narrative of lived experience. Contrary to that, some still raise objections that academic theology should be seen as a coherent and comprehensive analysis of ideas about God and that narrative could at best serve only as source of such ideas.

Because of these contrapositions, we may see that every narration of an individual life and theological experience is in certain tension with the theological norms of the believing community developed in a long discernment process of shaping doctrines. They are organized into a system describing how the living community of faith understands (or shall understand) God. Contrary to that, (auto)biography tells a story, the story of a particular life which contains certain religious ideas and is also interpreted through them. Theology as narrating life-stories is often not organized into the gradually developed argument of an established theological methodology (even though sometimes that could also be the case) but rather revealed through describing experience instead. It is more accidental than systematic. Yet it is still theology because it thinks (about) God and witnesses to his works in human lives.

1.3.1 Story of Narrative Theology

"God is not a concept; God is story. God is not an idea; God is presence. God is not hypotheses; God is experience.... What is the best way to gain access to this God? Surely not by means of concepts, ideas, hypotheses, or principles, but by means of the life we live, the experiences we go through, in a word, by means of the stories we weave, the stories we tell and share."[50]

Even though narrative is a dominating literary form in the Bible, the academic theology of the Enlightenment generally downplayed the importance of biblical stories as narratives and largely "aimed to extract propositional truths"[51] from them. But already during the first half of the twentieth century, some theologians started to perceive the importance of life-stories and narrativity for the renewal of theology. This tendency can be traced back to Richard Niebuhr's introduction of the category of story into the discussion about the meaning of revelation.[52] From the 1960s on, narrativity and storytelling appeared more frequently in the agenda of theologians across Christian denominations. Especially groundbreaking was *The Eclipse of Biblical Narrative*, the book published by Hans Frei in 1974. Frei pointed out that scholars in the modern era withdrew the meaning from the text and placed it somewhere behind or outside of the text. He mentions Schleiermacher as an example. According to Frei, this kind of an "unduly" abstraction led to hermeneutics suggesting that the Bible communicates only a general truth about God and human beings. Contrary to this, Frei proposed reuniting meaning with narrative again while asserting that "the meaning emerges from the story form, rather than being merely illustrated by it."[53]

Although there is a common consensus about the importance of story or stories for theology, there is still little agreement on what the

---

50. Song, *In the Beginning Were Stories*, 7.
51. McGrath, *Christian Theology*, 129.
52. Niebuhr, *Meaning of Revelation*.
53. Frei, *Eclipse of Biblical Narrative*, 280.

term "narrativity" precisely means.[54] And the same is true about narrative theology as such. It is widely agreed that it is an important theological movement, but it is somewhat vacuous and not a very well-defined trend.[55] However, according to Stroup, narrative theology can be divided into three main categories on the basis of its focus within a narrative.[56] Some theologians (1) were interested in narrativity as an introduction to the study of religion in general,[57] and Christianity/Christian theology in particular (e.g., Frei, Navone). Others (2) understood narrativity as life-stories of persons related to human experiences (e.g., McClendon Jr., Hauerwas). And yet others (3), dissatisfied with previous approaches to narrative, proposed biblical stories as providing specific examples of narrative and dealt with questions of how these narratives function in Christian communities, regarding them as authoritative and speaking to their contexts (e.g., Cullman, McFague). Another typology was offered by Gary L. Comstock, who was dissatisfied with Stroup's categories and divided narrative theologians into two camps to describe the tensions between (1) pure narrative theologians and (2) impure narrative theologians.[58] Comstock describes his categories this way: while the first ones (e.g., Frei, Hauerwas, Lindbeck, Kelsey)

> believe narrative is an autonomous literary form particularly suited to the work of theology [and] oppose the excessive use of discursive prose and abstract reason, insisting that Christian faith is best understood by grasping the grammatical rules and concepts of its texts and practices, [others (e.g., Ricoeur, Tracy, Hartt)] deny narrative a unique theological status. Believing that Christian sacred narratives are irreducibly infected with historical, philosophical, and psychological concerns, they seek

---

54. Stroup, *Promise of Narrative Theology*, 71.

55. McGrath, *Christian Theology*, 129.

56. Stroup, *Promise of Narrative Theology*, 71–84. However, Stroup introduced these categories already in the first edition of his book in 1981.

57. The narrative nature of religion is also well perceived in the field of religious studies. For instance, *Oxford Handbook of the Study of Religion* includes a full chapter on the narrative mode of the study of religion (Jensen, "Narrative," 290–303). "In this insightful chapter, Jensen not only discusses the value of narratology and narrative semiotics for the study of religious texts but also points out that religious identities and religious worlds are constructed and constituted through narrative. Davidsen, "Fiction and Religion," 497.

58. Comstock, "Two Types of Narrative Theology," 687–717.

to apply the methods of those disciplines to their interpretation. For them, narrative is neither pure nor autonomous.[59]

Despite these distinctions, I think that one of the basic theological problems with narrative is whether it is a prolegomenon to theology or whether it can function as a fundamental part of theology (doctrinal or systematic) itself. One of the proponents of the later division is evidently George W. Stroup, who claims: "The real significance of narrative for doctrinal theology is not that it provides a novel or heuristically useful introduction to discussions about the meaning of Christian faith. Narrative is an important theological category because it is essential for understanding human identity and what happens to the identity of persons in that process Christians describe by means of the doctrine of revelation."[60]

While most of the early authors saw narrative from the first perspective (as prolegomena to theology), more recent understandings of narrative in theology incline to the second (part of theology). When, for instance, Alexander Lucie-Smith summarizes contemporary narrative theology, he writes, "The human story is the meeting place between men and women and divine revelation, and not something that can be considered the opposite pole to revelation."[61]

Today, narrative theology covers quite a broad spectrum (perhaps apostate to its origins) and establishes itself as a legitimate way of academic theological performance. In terms of its method, narrative theology starts not with exploring abstract principles (deductive method) but rather with a particular story (inductive method) where theology is present in both explicit and implicit ways. Narrative theology certainly has made important contributions toward seeing particular life-stories (biographies) of human beings as theology.

> By recognizing that Christian beliefs are not so many propositions to be catalogued or juggled like truth-functions in a computer but are living convictions which gave shape to actual lives and actual communities, we open ourselves to the possibility that the only relevant critical examination of Christian beliefs may be one that begins by attending to lived lives. Theology must be at least biography. If by attending to those lives, we find ways of reforming our own theologies, making them truer, more faithful to our ancient vision, more adequate to the age now

---

59. Comstock, "Two Types of Narrative Theology," 688.
60. Stroup, *Promise of Narrative Theology*, 88–89.
61. Lucie-Smith, *Narrative Theology*, 3.

being born, then we will be justified in that arduous inquiry. Biography at its best will be theology."[62]

However, theology is not only a series of human life-stories, where human experiences of God's revelation, faith, and the world are shared. Through narrating our biographies in a theological way, we actually "situate our stories within a larger narrative of our faith."[63] Theology equally involves the story of God (Life itself and the Giver of life), the stories of human being(s), and the story of the world (where life is being lived). Consequently, we may perceive human lives as living stories. John Shea, a Roman Catholic thinker inspired by the work of Elie Wiesel, wrote, "We tell our stories to live . . . [and] we are stories God tells. Our very lives are the words that come from his mouth."[64] This is in accord with the already-cited famous claim of Edward Schillebeeckx: "People are the words with which God tells his story."[65] It is precisely because of this that I hold that Christians can neither exclude God nor the world from their stories. Christian life is not just the human story. It is the story of God and the world as well. Therefore, a strict theological focus on biography or autobiography seems to me either too *anthropocentric* (too focused on our human way of seeing and interpreting things) or as too *Theocentric* (narrated as if a person can adopt a stance of seeing things from God's perspective). However, as we have seen, personal story still matters for theology. In order to avoid a clash with either the Scylla of *narrative anthropocentrism* or the Charybdis of *narrative theocentrism*, I suggest presenting theology as the lived and narrated auto/Theo-biography where the personal story of human being is appropriately attuned with the story of God and the story of the world within the communal (cultural and contextual) narrative of Christian faith. Therefore, it is well balanced between *biography as theology* and *theology as autobiography*. While the first concept may fall into the trap of false objectivity or one-sided hagiography, the second concept is always at the risk of self-deception. Auto/Theo-biography, from my point of view, has the potential to avoid both extremes because it chooses a *perichoretic perspective* of being neither strictly *anthropocentric* nor strictly *theocentric* but rather attempts both fully at the same time. Aligning human story with the story of God

---

62. McClendon, *Biography as Theology*, 22.
63. Fischer, *Inner Rainbow*, 1.
64. Shea, *Stories of God*, 8.
65. Schillebeeckx, *Church*, xiii.

through an act of faith rooted in recognition that our story is part of the God's story does not mean we are giving up our personal biography but quite the opposite. In relation to the story of God, a human biography becomes more authentic and enhanced in its humanity. We may sum up by saying that auto/Theo-biography dwells within a *Theo-anthropic* perspective, which does not refer merely to the space in between but rather to the fullness of the space in between the human and divine, which is filled by the perichoretic dwelling of human stories and the story of God.

1.3.2 Auto/Theo-biography as Reflexivity and a Theological Way of Life

From my point of view, auto/Theo-biography benefits the most from giving equal space to all agents of theology—the (1) self, community, (2) God, and the (3) world as contexts for all three narratives—human stories (personal as well as communal), the story of God, and stories of the world—intertwined in a perichoretic way. Auto/Theo-biography also offers and opens possibilities for interlinking academic and everyday theology. It emphasizes personal story, which is always connected to other personal, communal, institutional, disciplinal, and even implicit[66] auto/Theo-biographies. It was suggested earlier that auto/Theo-biography could be seen as (1) a theological method and (2) a theological way of life. As regards the first, auto/Theo-biography, as suggested by Pete Ward, uses the method of "reflexivity" adopted from cultural studies. The application of this method in academic (written) theology emphasizes that "commitments of the writer are a part of the academic process."[67] Reflexivity helps theology to situate its theories into concrete contexts and offers a clearer perspective of the blurred and liquidized postmodern world. Reflexivity, writes Ward, "is an intentional and disciplined form of reflection on how the personal, social and cultural context of the researcher not only affects what is researched . . . but also the way that that

---

66. Holding that the universe is created by God (maybe not in particularities but certainly in principle), I am convinced that all that exists (creation) narrates through its being a certain kind of auto/Theo-biography as witnessed, for instance, in Ps 19: "The heavens are telling the glory of God; and the firmament proclaims his handiwork. Day to day pours forth speech, and night to night declares knowledge. There is no speech, nor are there words; their voice is not heard; yet their voice goes out through all the earth, and their words to the end of the world."

67. Ward, *Participation and Mediation*, 4.

research is conducted. . . . At its most basic, reflexivity relates to a process of disclosure and dialogue that is intended to make evident the situated and interested nature of academic work."[68]

According to Heather Walton, Ward's method "entails making plain the processes of theological formation that have generated particular research agendas within the researcher."[69] In fact, by employing a method of reflexivity, Ward launched a new theological method itself, a method of auto/Theo-biography which "suggests that theological reflection and cultural expression coexist in biography and practice."[70] And Sedmak thinks that "doing theology takes place within the framework of a particular culture. This has an impact on the language we speak, the categories we use, the experience we rely on, the problems we deal with, the assumptions we make."[71]

Following Ward and Sedmak, we may conclude that theology as human practice is a culturally embedded phenomenon. But at the same time, it goes beyond culture because it opens for the ever-greater mystery of God. If theology is to be honest in holding constant God's supremacy over his creation, it must admit its own fallibility. Theology done from within a human culture is always potentially wrong. In simple words, God is always different from what or who we think he is. But at the same time, we are constantly invited to think about him and even to have relationship with him. People remain embodied in the physical world and the world of culture. But at the same time, through experiences of revelation and faith, they can perceive transcendence. Auto/Theo-biography may be considered a relevant theological method because it is formed during life in the process of doing and thinking theology. It is being developed in reflexive moments, when theologians stop working and mulling over the secrets of life in the world and instead reflect on their relationship with the transcendent God and their fellow human beings. Past and future meet in the presence of a reflexive moment. I particularly like the expression of the Reformed Chinese theologian Choan-Seng Song, who writes on this matter, "Theological method is something of an after-thought. It is a pause you take after you have done the work, an exercise you do to recharge your theological engine, an effort you make to chart again your theological course. Method will not come at the beginning of your doing

68. Ward, *Participation and Mediation*, 3.
69. Walton, *Writing Methods*, 97.
70. Ward, *Participation and Mediation*, 18.
71. Sedmak, *Doing Local Theology*, 80.

theology. You do not define and restrict—is not to define to restrict?—what you have to do even before you get started."[72]

However, auto/Theo biography should not be reduced only to a particular theological method. It is not a narration which would set up its path and destination in advance. Rather, it unwinds itself as it is told. It is a theological method. But it is also, and maybe predominantly, a theological way of life (*vita theologica*).[73] To put it in a more radical way: theology is not only a study or critical reflection of the sources of Christian faith, but it is also walking in the countryside, washing dishes, helping the neighbor, taking the children to school, praying, chopping wood for winter, rejoicing in the coming spring, caressing a partner, having dinner with friends, attending church service or a mass, riding a motorbike, going to a concert, cleaning the toilet, or taking out the garbage. In all these (and much more), the human life-story is related to (hi)story (his-story) of salvation and discovers its firm roots within the "spectrum of life" (divine-human-world) or the "divine milieu," as Pierre Teilhard de Chardin puts it.[74] Auto/Theo-biography is a meditation of these roots. It is thinking and pondering about life which is common to God and human beings. Saint Paul says, "And it is no longer I who live, but it is Christ who lives in me" (Gal 2:20). Such unity is not identical with simple unification, when the greater subject somehow absorbs the smaller or weaker.[75] The unity Saint Paul speaks about consists in the inseparability between (and discernibility of) God, human, and the world.

The revealing God (who is an active, free tri-personality) is perceived by human faith and is searched for and praised individually (as well as in communities) formed to better understand the Trinitarian mystery too far and too big to be grasped by any single individual. Personal life stories comprising Christian religious experience participate in the narrative of God perceived in revelation. This participation is further "mediated in the expression of the Christian community"[76] and makes theology a communication above all. Theology as a multidimensional process of communication is

---

72. Song, "Five Stages," 2.

73. Lacoste, *From Theology*, 85.

74. Teilhard de Chardin, *Divine Milieu*, 114. For Teilhard de Chardin, God even reveals himself as a universal milieu.

75. Skalický, "Současná křesťanská teologie," 41.

76. Ward, *Participation and Mediation*, 106.

both lived in as a culture and at the same time it is indwelt by God. In communication theology is animated within the community. Animation relates to a quickening that gives life to the theological as it is communicated. Communities and individuals animate theology through expression and identification, and, as such, animation is a way of life. At the same time, animation relates to the way that theology is made alive (as reflection) through the freedom of the Spirit of God. So, theology is animated as it is moved or circulated within the Christian community, and as it is animated it becomes theology, that is, a participation in transforming glory.[77]

Theology circulates as blood in the veins of the church, the mystical body of Christ, who is the incarnated and resurrected Theo-Logy, the Word of God (*Logos tou Theou*). This Christological (and Christocentric) character of Christian theology originates as auto/Theo-biography in an intimate conversation with God present in the uttermost depths of the human heart and soul. Yet it also goes public when an overwhelming religious experience (of God's presence) is shared with others. In short, theology as auto/Theo-biography equally values common as well as individual (human and religious) experience, spiritual praxis, and intellectual efforts. It brings together faith, reason, and imagination. As such, it may be perceived as an effort to understand "our part in the divine narrative."[78]

It was suggested, together with Dominguez, Roach, and Štofaník, that theology should be beautiful, compelling, engaged, understandable, and existentially relevant. But above all theology should be truthful. The truthfulness of theology resides in its authenticity, and therefore it is necessary that our lives become theology and theology becomes our lives (orthodoxy meets orthopraxis). Theology calls us to search for truth, even in the contemporary context of post-truth societies. It calls us to be truthful because the first theologian is God, who pronounces (reveals) the truth about himself, the world, and human beings. Through his only Son, who is "the way, the truth, and the life" (John 14:6), God invites us to participate in this Truth. Therefore, we may conclude that theology is the calling of God ("Human!") and human beings ("God!") which carries through the world. These two are searching for each other. They walk to each other. They will perhaps, eventually, fall into each other's arms, when God and human will no longer be separated, but rather God and

---

77. Ward, *Participation and Mediation*, 106–7.
78. Borgman, *Foundations*, 10.

human will become one (John 17:20–24) in a tight embrace: God and human finally discernible in the freedom of personal being but inseparable in a decision of the free will and adherence of love. This is what Jesus Christ, the only Son of God, who rests in his arms (John 1:18), teaches, points out, and represents by his very being. He is the incarnated and resurrected Word of God. He is the incarnated and resurrected *Theo-Logy*.

1.4 FAITH, HOPE, AND LOVE SEEKING UNDERSTANDING

"Although the word 'faith' appears more frequently in the New Testament than the word 'love,' faith in this context does not mean 'belief that God exists' but 'belief in God's love.' What makes a Christian is not the belief that 'God exists' but the belief that God is love."[79]

If we decide to believe in the Christian God, we start to narrate our auto/Theo-biography, and thus we practice (think and do) theology. At the same time, we open ourselves to hear the story of God. Moreover, we become aware that we are words of God's narrative. We do theology together with an eternal teacher, prophet, and the king. We do theology with Jesus Christ. But at the same time, through him and in him, we become theology ourselves. This suggests that we are what we do (and vice versa). As creatures living the freedom of human beings, we practice and we are *theology*. In terms of theology understood as *genitive objective*, we practice theology, and we seek understanding of who God is, which is also who we are and what our experience of faith, hope, and love is and means, etc. But in terms of theology perceived as *genitive subjective*, we are theology because we enter the relationship with the eternal theologian, and we seek (desire) eternal fulfilment of and with this relationship. As creatures in creation, we are already part of God but not yet fully. It is because the full partnership with God requires discernment and free acceptance of the divine gift of faith, hope, and love from one side, and God's final word of salvation in the *eschaton*, which will bring about (and transform) our faith, hope, and love into their desired fullness from the other. Therefore, we may technically distinguish between *practicing theology* as *seeking understanding* and *being theology* as *seeking/desiring fulfilment*. However, they always remain inseparable because

---

79. Halík, *Chci, abys byl*, 40.

each hint of faith, spark of hope, and trace of love desires their fullness and seeks understanding. Considering such argument, we may express conviction that human beings already exist in a theological way but not yet in fullness.

Claiming theology as a form of practice or using terms like "practicing" or "doing" theology may seem problematic, and therefore it requires broader explication. In the remaining part of this chapter, I want to argue that it is worthwhile to think of theology not only as faith (*fides*) seeking understanding, as Saint Anselm proposed but also as hope (*spes*) and love (*caritas*) seeking understanding (*quaerens intellectum*). This conviction was quite recently expressed by the International Theological Commission (ITC) of the Catholic Church in the document "Theology Today: Perspectives, Principles, and Criteria" (TT): "Because of the close bond between faith, hope and love . . ., it can be affirmed that theology is also *spes quaerens intellectum* (cf. 1 Pet 3:15) and *caritas quaerens intellectum*. The latter aspect receives particular emphasis in the Christian East: as it explicates the mystery of Christ who is the revelation of God's love (cf. John 3:16), theology is God's love put into words" (TT 19n27).

Despite this pronouncement, the whole document rather sticks to the traditional exposition of theology as faith seeking understanding and does not specifically relate to the other two. The primary function is assigned to (living) faith, which, in perspective of the TT, subsumes hope and love. "Living faith can be understood as embracing both hope and love" (TT 11). What then is the merit of treating theology not only as faith but also as hope and love seeking understanding?

As far as I can see, there is a danger that hope and love may become empty words if we simply subsume them under the rubric of faith. Even though we may understand (as TT does) living faith as (lived) hope and love, there is still a certain risk of thinking faith only in propositional terms, like a preset system of truth claims/doctrines we shall believe because they were proven truths and attested by generations affirming them before us. In other words, there is a danger that an act of faith (*fides qua creditur*) may be reduced to a mere affirmation of its content—doctrine (*fides quae creditur*). I am not suggesting that the concept of faith seeking understanding is wrong but merely supplementing it with the other two (i.e., hope and love) might contribute towards a more colorful unfolding of the meaning and character of theology as such, which must be relational (or perichoretic). That means that there must be always an openness to more to come, and this openness is hope. Theology also means reflection on the hope that our imperfect, uncertain, and also sometimes distorted faith will be transformed through the encounter with Jesus Christ into a faith enabling us to be true witnesses to God. "Hope gives us an orientation towards God and anchors our desire to live by faith."[80] Furthermore, Ivana Noble reminds us of that faith, hope, and love were always considered key experiences or building stones of Christian existence.[81] They were called cardinal (and theological) virtues. They are interrelated. But the greatest of them—the umbrella for the other two—is love.

> Love never ends. But as for prophecies, they will come to an end; as for tongues, they will cease; as for knowledge, it will come to an end. For we know only in part, and we prophesy only in part; but when the complete comes, the partial will come to an end. When I was a child, I spoke like a child, I thought like a child, I reasoned like a child; when I became an adult, I put an end to childish ways. For now, we see in a mirror, dimly, but then we will see face to face. Now I know only in part; then I will know fully, even as I have been fully known. And now faith, hope, and love abide, these three; and the greatest of these is love. (1 Cor 13:8–13)

Theology is a way of expressing a level of understanding our faith. It is a way to show how we discern and live our hope. But above all, it is a way to express our practice of love. Theology reflects on our deeds of love and searches to understand where our love may grow stronger. Love cannot be demanded, nor it can be imposed or possessed. Love can only be hoped for and practiced. I can love and hope that I will be loved or that I will be given love. Love is a gift that only a free person can give. Love is realized by and grows from faith and hope.

Even though faith and hope must remain indispensable part of each theological reflection, I am giving priority to the notion of love, as has been prioritized before at length by canonical thinkers such as Kierkegaard (*Works of Love*) and Marion (*The Erotic Phenomenon*; *Prolegomena to Charity*). It is because the true core of theology is L(l)ove—revealed and accepted, believed in, hoped for, and practiced (seeking understanding as

---

80. Noble, *Tracking God*, 10.

81. There were numerous authors occupied with the faith, hope, and love triad. Gerald O'Collins may serve as an example. He considers faith, hope, and love as representing three different styles of doing theology. But he puts them into a slightly different order (faith, love, hope). For O'Collins, faith seeks a knowledge and understanding that it will never be exhaustive, love seeks social justice that can never completely come in this world, and hope seeks to anticipate liturgically the final vision of God. O'Collins, *Rethinking*, 326.

well as its fullness). Revelation as an invitation into a relationship with God is certainly a transformative life experience. It ontologically transforms the lives of those who encounter God's revelation.[82] It gives to its recipients a new life and a new perspective of the whole universe. Theologians today widely accept that creation is the very first act of revelation. In creation, "God showed his love, wisdom, and power. He inserted the deepest mystery and the highest aim into the whole of creation—focus on the Creator. Through his word of creation, he established the truth and meaning (logos) of creation; by his love and holiness—if it is possible to say—he inserted the undeletable desire for unity into creation, the inclination towards fullness."[83]

Such original, general revelation develops further in history, where we may observe various peculiar events recognized as extraordinary revelation by believers. The sequence of these extraordinary revelations might be called a history of salvation. Various authors have attempted to sketch their structure. One of these was Oscar Cullman. For him, God's revelation has a fundamentally soteriological character. God reveals things to human beings because he wants them to recognize the truth about their lives' meanings, which is salvation (becoming "theology" in fullness). In other words, God wants to share his love with humanity and calls us to love as well. Such love, or the Creator's logos—the incarnated, resurrected, and eschatological Christ—is the scheme and principle of salvation history.[84]

Christian theology holds that at the beginning, everything was created out of the love of God, and through this love (Christ, the logos), the Creator's revelation of God's loving nature opens its salvific-historical dynamic. But an original love relationship between God and humankind is perverted by the pride of original sin. In the Christian tradition, the symbol of eating fruit from the tree of the knowledge of good and evil in the garden of Eden symbolizes this original sin (Gen 2:9). That fruit is commonly associated with an apple. This may be due to resemblance of the Latin words for "apple tree" (*mālus*) and "evil" (*malus*). But as Jan Samohýl, for instance, points out,[85] in the Jewish rabbinic tradition this mythical tree of the knowledge of good and evil is sometimes interpreted as the *etrog* tree (*hadar*). Etrog is a kind of citrus fruit (*Citrus medica*)

---

82. Skalický, "Geneze koncilního dokumentu," 23.
83. Zvěřina, *Teologie agapé I.*, 77–78.
84. Cullmann, *Christ and Time*, 179.
85. Samohýl, *Židovské inspirace*, 104.

which in Hebrew is called "*peri ez hadar*" (or else "*pri etz hadar*"),[86] literally "fruit of the beautiful tree." This fruit has a shape of the human heart, and because of that shape it symbolizes the heart during the Jewish feast *Sukkot*, in its ritual bouquet called "lulav."[87] Such interpretation comes most probably from rabbinic commentaries to Midrash Vayikrah Rabba 30:14.[88] Lulav consists of palm leaf, willow branch, myrtle, and etrog fruit. In this context, the story of Genesis gains a new dimension. First people were seduced by the wily serpent not to eat just any apple or fruit but their own heart. And if we eat our own heart, aren't we losing our ability to love? I understand this interpretation of the biblical narrative as very actual for today's society characterized often as "consumption society." A consumer wants to enjoy primarily. It seems that in such enjoyment the contemporary "homo con-sumens" (human consumer) finds "consummatio" (completion) of his/her life.[89]

Humankind's embarrassing and fatal stagnation of love is surmounted by God's promise, which is later repeated many times in the history of Israel and specified by concrete deeds and covenants.[90] Israel's history, as found in the Hebrew Bible, is the story of the assurance of God's love for his people. The only thing God wants from his people in return is their love. But what they can give when they have a gaping wound in place of their heart? What can they give when they replace their eaten heart by heart of stone? Is it possible to love with a heart of stone? Human love always requires God's intervention and help. "I will give you a new heart and put a new spirit in you; I will remove from you your heart of stone and give you a heart of flesh" (Ezek 36:26) calls God through the mouth of the prophet Ezekiel.

The Christian understanding of the fulfilment of all Old Testament promises culminates in the event(s) of the death and resurrection of Jesus Christ. Through the risen Christ, all of creation again meets its balance and reconciliation with God, the Creator. It is Jesus who connects God's

---

86. This transcription is used for instance in Feldman, "Sukkot."

87. This interpretation is mentioned also in Brofsky, *Hilkhot Mo'adim*, 299; the same interpretation we may find also in Scheinerman, "*Sukkot*," para. 8: "Another famous interpretation of the four species likens each to a body part: the Etrog is the human heart; the palm fronds are the spine; the myrtle is the eyes; the willow is the mouth. Just as one waves all four species before God on Sukkot, so too one uses all the parts of one's body to worship and serve God: heart, spine, eyes, and mouth."

88. Berman, "Sukkot," para. 8.

89. Štěch, "Od věrohodnosti," 96.

90. Zvěřina, *Teologie agapé I.*, 78.

requirement of love with a love commandment to the whole of humanity (cf. DCE 1). Human love is no longer a requirement or a commandment but a free human decision to respond to the invitation to participate in life of the very source of love, mediated through revelation. Therefore, we can see that God's revelation is fundamental to Christian theology, and above all, it is a salvific revelation of love, culminating in the paschal event of Jesus Christ. "For God so loved the world that he gave his only Son, so that everyone who believes in him may not perish but may have eternal life" (John 3:16). The one who stays in Christ also stays in the Triune One, who is eternal love and thus stays in love. The commonly used phrase "God is love" shows here a totally different dimension of its essential importance.

Since the risen Christ is a first taste of the second creation, his presence starts to work as a ferment in the history of the first creation. Christ begins to recast step-by-step the first creation into the second (new) one from within, which we may identify with the so-called kingdom of God. This kingdom is already present (cf. Luke 17:21) but also yet to come (cf. Luke 10:9; Mark 1:15; John 18:36). It is not yet present in its fullness. Saint Paul puts it like this: "So if anyone is in Christ, there is a new creation: everything old has passed away; see, everything has become new!" (2 Cor 5:17). The one who is in Christ already has a share in the second creation. While Adam ate from the tree of knowledge, the new creation will eat from the tree of life. While the logic of the first creation implies practicing or doing theology, the logic of the new (second) creation suggests theology as a new mode of existence (being theology), or more precisely, a continuous rebirth of the human practice of theology into the fullness of being theology; being united with the Word of God when time will reach its crowning in the eschaton. "God is love, and those who abide in love abide in God, and God abides in them" (1 John 4:16b). The late Pope Benedict XVI calls such loving co-action between God and human beings "an expression of the essence of the biblical faith: that man can indeed enter into union with God—his primordial aspiration. But this union is no mere fusion, a sinking in the nameless ocean of the Divine; it is a unity which creates love, a unity in which both God and man remain themselves and yet become fully one" (DCE 10).

In conclusion, in this text, I would like to propose theology as *spiritualizing rationality* and *rationalizing spirituality*, encompassing both theoretical reflection and practical action. As such, the practice of theology is a spiritual rationality, as it was understood by Cappadocian fathers or Saint Anselm.[91] Theology is a critical reflection nourishing the experience of faith, maintaining and generating hope, and practicing love. That invites us not only to pray and act or pray and work (*ora et labora*), as an ancient Christian monastic principle suggests, but also to think. Practicing faith, hope, and love imply thinking about and reflecting on our practice (faith, hope, and love seeking understanding). Practicing theology as an activity is heading towards the fullness of "being theology." From the perspective of theology suggested as auto/Theo-biography, people are words of God (Theou-logos) and thus they already are theology. But at the same time, since they are not yet fully united with Jesus Christ—the Word of God—they are not yet theology in a full way. Practicing (or doing) theology helps us to keep the right direction of our faith, hope, and love aimed at the goal of being united with Jesus Christ. Through him, with him, and in him we can become discernible but inseparable parts of the eternal dwelling of Love within the Holy Trinity. In this respect, we may call theology a science of Love—*Scientia caritatis*.

> Scientia caritatis—It is not enough to know that love is a beautiful thing, to sing love's praises, or to sweetly pronounce her name. Nobody denies that, after all. But to know where I can make a good impression by my love, where I can employ her; to search for opportunities where I can offer my love to the other—to everyone without exception; to love—not by words but in deeds; to love—not only to wait, but to search for the opportunity to show love.[92]

While science grounds our knowledge based on our reason, love points us towards the higher ground of knowledge based in contemplation and meditation, as well as in prayer and the spiritual experience of meeting with the divine. "Scientia deals with temporal things. It helps us to understand the world and to find the right direction for our acting in the world. Scientia grants us knowledge on the basis of observation, in which our rational faculties are used."[93]

But rational faculties and the abilities of reason cannot wholly grasp the notion of God, who is always greater and wholly different than anything we can even think of. The scientific nature of theology is therefore twofold. On the one hand, it can reflect on the mystery of God and create

---

91. Ward, *Participation and Mediation*, 24, 100.
92. Boublík, *Duchovní deník*, 125.
93. Noble, *Tracking God*, 17–18.

concepts for our understanding, but on the other, it remains in silent prayer, overwhelmed and stroked by the experience of love. Theology can provide a true scientific reflection within its field. Yet it always remains partially apophatic. Theology is both: a spiritual journey and a science. Ivana Noble further provides us with an exact expression of this simultaneity when she says that as a spiritual journey, theology is rooted "in a pre-reflective religious immediacy, in the spiritual, liturgical, and social practice of believers,"[94] and as a science, theology is practiced as (and participates in) "an on-going struggle for clarity, historical, and conceptual accuracy, interpretative and systematic coherence."[95]

Thus, theology may be seen as a complex way of living, including rational and spiritual dimensions, theoretical reflections, as well as practical actions. This could perhaps be called the "theological turn" within theology—an attempt to heal the artificial division (characteristic to modern thought) between the theoretical and the practical, between thinking and acting, and thus reconnecting theology again with real life, in which thought and deed work together. From my perspective, a theological turn in theology suggests an *unsystematic theology* which is based not on doctrinal presuppositions but instead on personal experiences and sharing them within a believing community (the church) and broad society (the public sphere). There is not much of a system in such an unsystematic theology, but there is a meaning.

This brings us back to fundamental theology as a theological discipline opening our minds to higher levels of intellectual reflections of our theological living. Fundamental theology connects contexts where we love, hope, and live our faith with the whole story of Christianity (including Scripture, tradition(s), doctrine, and practices). Fundamental theology may serve as a portal through which we can move back and forth between the worlds of academic and practiced (lived) theology. To keep the door open, fundamental theology offers a service by constantly posing the question "What is theology?" No answers are exhaustive. Each understanding of theology is rather provisional, but theology remains a way of thinking, acting, and being. Thus, it encompasses rational reflection, practical action, as well as silent contemplation. The Australian fundamental theologian Gerald O'Collins puts it succinctly: "We need theologies that know how to sit studying the past, that know how to walk

---

94. Noble, *Tracking God*, 43.
95. Noble, *Tracking God*, 43.

the streets with the poor, and that know how to kneel in adoration of the Savior who has come."[96]

They all need to become one if we are striving for an understandable and existentially relevant theology. As an example of a concrete step in the process of this slow convergence (of different styles and ways theology is done), I would like to propose the meeting of fundamental theology with the environment of youth ministry and youth theology. The first one is certainly closer to the world of academic theology, and the second is a reflection upon a particular age-related group practicing theological life. Let us now hear the story of fundamental theology first, and then the story of youth ministry closely related to youth theology, that we may further elaborate on the possible grounds for their eventual encounter—where they can meet and listen to each other's stories. I believe such an encounter has a strong potential to be fruitful not only for both environments mentioned but also, and maybe more importantly, for the whole of theology at least in two ways: (1) it can contribute towards seeing theology as both a spiritual journey and a scientific discipline, and (2) it has the potential to strengthen theology in terms of its relevance for contemporary society and make it again a voice that matters.

---

96. O'Collins, *Rethinking*, 331.

2

The Story of Fundamental Theology

IN THE INTRODUCTION OF his monumental book entitled *Fundamental Theology*, one of the most significant fundamental theologians of the twentieth century, Heinrich Fries, wrote, "It is no longer enough merely to proclaim or solemnly assert the Christian faith. One has to lay out its grounds in the face of the overwhelming power of the contemporary experience of world and existence and of the challenges which accompany this experience. It is a massive task, but also a great opportunity."[1]

Fundamental theology is a specific, relatively young[2] theological discipline responding to challenges of contemporary contexts, relating them to scriptural as well as doctrinal texts. It attempts to use all possible opportunities to fulfil the task of giving an account of the hope Christians have to anyone who demands it (cf. 1 Pet 3:15–16). It provides Christian theology with reflections on its own foundations. Fundamental theology operates on the frontier, studying the core principles of Christianity and investigating possibilities of engagement and dialogue with everyone and everything outside Christianity (see 1 Thess 5:21). It further strives for partners among theological disciplines as well as other sciences. It plays a mediating role between church and society. Fundamental theology is "an integral part of the critical and methodical reflection on Christian faith. Beginning from within the Christian tradition, it seeks to spell out

1. Fries, *Fundamental Theology*, 5.
2. Driscoll, *Theology*, 99–100.

what is implied by the stance of faith. Fundamental theology, however, is predogmatic because . . . it does not rest on a finished theory regarding revelation and its mediation through tradition and ecclesiastical pronouncements."[3]

Thus, it is central for fundamental theology to show that there is such a reality as revelation. It helps enable theologians (as well as ordinary believers) to discern revelation as an event in human history. It wants to point out its basic content and seeks appropriate interpretations. But at the same time, it reminds people that their understanding of revelation is still in some respect provisional. As Gerald O'Collins puts it, "Insofar as they deal with the mystery of God, theologians cannot be too 'knowing' but must remain provisional, modest, and apophatic in what they say and claim."[4] Based on this kind of thinking, fundamental theology wants to trace reasonable foundations of the Christian faith and yet still bows to the great mystery of Christianity, which resides in the death and resurrection of Jesus Christ. Fundamental theology is always radically open to more to come (soteriological openness). It is a story to be continued. It is the story of God, who is the ever-greater mystery (*Deus semper maior*). It is the story of human persons and their relating to God (faith); it is the story of the community of faith (the church). It is also the story of God who seeks his people (revelation), offering them an eternal future in everlasting communion with him (salvation). Thus, fundamental theology maintains the common quest for an ever-open search for Truth and becomes a shared *diaconia* (service) to the ever-greater Truth that can be touched and felt. But ultimately it always remains ungraspable for people of this world.

Fundamental theology was developed in the church as a tool to balance extreme epistemological polarizations between fundamentalism and foundationalism. These positions were found in the church, as well as in the whole of society, a long time ago. But each era deals with them in its own way. A continual rebirth of classical apologetics into fundamental theology at the turn of nineteenth and twentieth century was characterized by attempts to balance both these tendencies. On the one side, there is fundamentalism, asserting that the recognition of first principles (and their meanings) is determined by conviction (faith). Foundationalism, on the other side, wants to discover recognition of first principles

---

3. Dulles, *Models of Revelation*, 15; Similar expression could be found in Joest, *Fundamentální teologie*, 11–12.

4. O'Collins, *Rethinking*, 336–37.

based on certain given epistemological facts that are found through a continuous structuralizing of knowledge.[5] In other words, while fundamentalism knows because things are this way, foundationalism comes to its knowledge through so-called "regressive argumentation," asking for the first causes of all things. Such a philosophical method has been well known since the time of the Aristotle and became particularly influential in Christian theology with Thomas Aquinas. From a theological perspective, fundamentalism usually takes the form of irrationalism or fideism, while foundationalist positions often present themselves as a kind of theological rationalism. Therefore, against *fundamentalism*, fundamental theology traditionally plays up an exercise of reason that reflects upon the foundations of the church and its doctrine. Against the positivistic rationalism of an extreme *foundationalism*, fundamental theology emphasizes faith as not being a result of affirming doctrinal presuppositions but rather a consequence of an effort of the whole personality based on experience to a great extent.[6]

Today, we see displays of fundamentalism and foundationalism not only within the church or Christianity but in the whole of society. This is not only the case in Europe. With its long experience of balancing various extremes, fundamental theology can help to find a *via media* not only within the church but also in broader society overall. Let us seek genuine foundations of the Christian faith to avoid the ideologies of fundamentalism and foundationalism. Let us now feel invited to unveil roads and paths of fundamental theology. Their stories could be heard while walking them either alone in silence or in conversation with others who share the road with us. Let us first hear the story of fundamental theology's origin and development. Let us hear the stories and songs of experienced walkers, before we start to tell and sing our own songs.

---

5. Hábl, "Problem."

6. This was already perceived by John Henry Newman: "I do but say that it is antecedent probability that gives meaning to those arguments from facts which are commonly called the Evidences of Revelation; that, whereas mere probability proves nothing, mere facts persuade no one; that probability is to fact, as the soul to the body; that mere presumptions may have no force, but that mere facts have no warmth. Mutilated and defective evidence suffices for persuasion where the heart is alive; but dead evidences, however perfect, can but create a dead faith." Newman, *Fifteen Sermons*, 200.

2.1 FROM APOLOGETICS TO FUNDAMENTAL THEOLOGY

In its own way, fundamental theology has existed ever since Christians began seeking explanations for their experiences of faith, hope, and love. In the previous chapter, we met with theology. Now it is time to deepen our encounter. What are the fundamental principles of the Christian story? And how were they presented in the long history of Christianity? Why is there a theological discipline dealing with them? How did it develop? A brief sketch of the history of fundamental theology may help us to answer these questions.[7]

During the first centuries of Christianity, the new religion was often confronted with opposition and misunderstanding from different sides of that epoch's society. The justification and defense of the fundamental issues of Christianity were mostly needed to confront (or defend against) those outside the Christian community. Thus, the ancient Greek term *apologia* (verbal defense) was used as a headline for the early church's writings defending its young beliefs against various adversaries. Some of the early church authors are referred to as apologists, e.g., Justin Martyr, Origen, Tertullian, etc. However, at the end of the period of early Christian apologetics, we encounter more introspective or even existential (Augustine) ways of dealing with the foundational questions of Christianity.[8] Monika Hellwig, in her excellent historical sketch of theological foundations, praises Saint Augustine as the "greatest fundamental theologian of Christian antiquity"[9] because he was not only taking a defensive stance but employing a genuine (personal) witness as a positive way of presenting Christian faith. According to Hellwig, Augustine "considers the grounds a human person can have for recognizing the call of the transcendent God and for making the response of faith within a particular religious tradition and community."[10] Augustine bears witness to hope. In weak and strong moments of faith; it is the hope that our lives do not end in our physical termination but may be ontologically transformed by the enormous love we can touch upon by our faith. It is a witness about the adventures of brave people who decided to enter a relationship with God.

---

7. There are of course more comprehensive texts then this one, written by Catholic as well as Protestant theologians, which I would recommend consulting for those who have a deeper interest in this notion (e.g., Metz, *Development*; Dulles, *History*; O'Collins, *Rethinking*, chapter 1; Becker, *Fundamental Theology*).

8. Hellwig, "Foundations for Theology," 3.

9. Hellwig, "Foundations for Theology," 2.

10. Hellwig, "Foundations for Theology," 3.

"Augustine's existential approach to theology shows the connections of faith, knowledge, and action. It reflects the experience of his conversion and a gradual interpretation of the experience, something that Augustine perceived as his life duty. This developing and changing interpretation of faith lies at the roots of what Augustine sees as adequacy for the subject of theology, even if he uses a different terminology."[11]

During medieval times, the mere defensive approach of Christian antiquity dealing with fundamental notions of the faith, changed into the one searching for legitimacy for the Christian tradition. Continuity, connectedness to sources of tradition, and its authenticity—guaranteed by true authority—were main topics for medieval apologetics. The focus turned from outside to inside. Medieval authors enjoyed the privilege of living in the security of "Christendom," where Christian faith was generally accepted and practiced. Scholastic thinking, characteristic of this period (from eleventh to thirteenth century), is fascinated with rationality within the faith and wants to come closer to God through the powers of reason. If I believe, my faith is searching understanding (*fides quaerens intellectum*), says Anselm of Canterbury, and returns the question of God's existence into the main scope of scholastic theologians.[12] Slightly more than a dozen decades later than Anselm, Thomas Aquinas, the "Doctor Angelicus," had to deal not only with question of God's existence but also with the justification of theology as such. Theology is a discipline that involves critical reason as well as faith. Based on this conviction and Aristotle's conception of science as searching for causes of the effects, he presents theology as the "sacred" science "about the primary principles and causes they presuppose, and about the ultimate fulfilment of all things."[13] These primary principles may be found in God's revelation. Therefore, Aquinas defined theology as a science of faith involving critical reason. His theology fundamentally divided "natural reason and supernatural faith in such a way that each of them has its place and competence."[14] From the perspective of Aquinas, faith and reason are distinct yet closely related.

---

11. Noble, *Tracking God*, 17.

12. Anselm is most probably building upon Augustine's expression "Do not seek to understand in order to believe but believe that you may understand." Becker, *Fundamental Theology*, 70.

13. Becker, *Fundamental Theology*, 20.

14. Becker, *Fundamental Theology*, 22.

The criticism that nominalists (e.g., Roscellinus), or better "moderate nominalists" (often called "conceptualists," e.g., William Ockham or Peter Abelard), had of realism (the scholastic theological methods and conclusions held by Thomas Aquinas or Duns Scotus) was, at the end of the Middle Ages, a prelude to the spring of the Renaissance. With its entrance into history, we observe the return of an anthropological focus and growing interest in non-Christian religions (also partially because of overseas discoveries). Both societal changes resulted in a considerable shaking of "Christendom," tightly bound within the Roman Catholic Church. Is this church the only possible and true mediator of Christian revelation? What has priority: Scripture or grace? What makes church authority (doctrine, hierarchy, and teaching) legitimate? These and similar questions about true faith and the church were raised by the reformation, starting already in the late fourteenth and early fifteenth century with authors like John Wycliffe and Jan Hus. Early theologians of the reformation focused more on practical theological issues and ecclesiology. But as the reformation further developed into the sixteenth century, a new approach to foundational issues of Christian theology became urgently needed in the Catholic as well as the Protestant Churches.

> At this stage of Western history, it was not a question of justifying the theological project of Christians against unbelievers, as it once had been and would be again. Nor was it then a question of defending the validity of theology against the claims of philosophy to be all-sufficient, as it had been in thirteenth century and would be again in modern times.... The primary concern of this phase of Western Christian theology was to justify a particular way of appealing to revelation to establish the data with which theological construction would be concerned.[15]

While Protestants constructed their theology on the primacy of Scripture, Roman Catholics insisted on the continual ecclesial tradition proving its continual truthfulness in all eras. Fundamental theological questions asked again for their answers in a new historical context and appeared once more at the center of theological debates. Unfortunately, these debates were soon ideologized and politicized. Consequently, they moved from universities' auditoriums to European battlefields, where they caused deep wounds on the souls of European nations. Arguably,

---

15. Hellwig, "Foundations for Theology," 5.

only the ecumenical movement in the twentieth century has started the process of healing.

The breakdown of medieval "Christendom" and the process of religious (maybe better, denominational) fragmentation according to the principle "*Cuius regio, eius religio!*" slowly led to the disrepute of Christianity in the European milieu together with the arrival of modernity, a period also known as "the Enlightenment" or "the Age of Reason." It came to full blossom during eighteenth and nineteenth century, and new fundamental questions regarding Christian faith came to the fore. The most popular issues were the autonomy of reason, the concept of revelation, secularization, and also—for the first time in history—atheism. The term "revelation" became an especially crucial problem. "In the late nineteenth and twentieth centuries, the theology of revelation, no longer viewed as a department of mystical psychology or as an apologetical prolegomenon to theology, took shape as a comprehensive systematic treatise emerged, foundational for the whole of dogmatics."[16]

While modern rationalists displayed tendencies to reject faith and placed human reason in the spotlight, their opponents often took the opposite standpoint and emphasized faith over reason. Adherents of fideism (e.g., Schleiermacher) stated that revelation, as well as all other truths of faith, cannot (and should not) be justified rationally but by faith alone. On the contrary, rationalists (e.g., Fichte) ruminated about revelation and other truths of faith exclusively within the limits of reason, often thinking that what is not possible to explicate by reason does not exist. In other words, revelation is either possible to verify by reason, and therefore it is not necessary to believe it, or it is not, and so it does not exist.[17]

Sometimes I encounter allegations that fundamental theology is only typical for Roman Catholic theology, but this is certainly not true. Fundamental theology was not a brand-new discovery of Roman Catholic scholars of the late nineteenth century. They were rather "influenced by widespread concerns of Protestant theologians,"[18] who coined the term even earlier. However, fundamental theology in a Catholic context developed through modernity as a theological discipline distinct from former classical apologetics,[19] which used the method of three *demonstrationes*"

16. Dulles, *Models of Revelation*, 21.
17. Štěch, *Tu se jim otevřely oči*, 82.
18. O'Collins, *Rethinking*, 2.
19. "Classical apologetics" is a term used for modern theological genre of logical

(demonstrations, evidence) to defend the truthfulness of Christianity. First, *demonstratio religiosa* defended the existence of God and the importance of historical revelation against the idea of "natural religion" held in the Enlightenment. Secondly, *demonstratio Christiana* had the task to show that God revealed himself legitimately and fully in Jesus Christ, against the claims of non-Christian religions. The third argument concluded that revelation is fully and most devoutly kept in the Roman Catholic Church. *Demonstratio Catholica* was a reaction to the Reformation and ecclesial truth claims of various Protestant churches. Classical apologetics generally showed strong marks of evidentialism, claiming that it is possible to prove the truthfulness of Christianity through miracles.[20] But in modernity, people were already able to produce sort of "miracles" themselves. Just think about the enormous velocity of technical revolution during the "century of steam." In such a context, even to see a miracle, for real, does not necessarily mean to believe it (not to mention encountering the proclamation of miracles by the church and their authorities). It is no wonder that this narrow-minded argumentation, oriented merely as systematic defense of the Roman Catholic faith (and the solemnly asserted truth of Christian revelation attested by authority of the teaching office [*magisterium*]) failed, and a change of focus, once again, came into the agenda.[21]

I would like to mention here just one of the many people who caused this refocusing of apologetics and inspired its later rebirth into fundamental theology. His name is Maurice Blondel (1861–1949), a French philosopher who attempted to revitalize apologetics. Blondel rebuked traditional apologetics for approaching only reason alone and for always remaining too abstract. Contrary to this, from his perspective, faith calls for the involvement of the whole personality. Blondel was convinced that

---

argumentation serving to discern, justify, and understand fundaments of Christian faith. It was developed on tradition of the literary genre of the apologetics known in the church since the time of early church fathers. However, the term "apologetics" was used even earlier by Plato, for instance in the title of his defense of Socrates (*Apologia tou Socratou*).

20. This kind of evidentialist apologetics was criticized already by John Henry Newman. I tried to summarize Newman's arguments against evidentialism in my article for the journal *Communio* (see Štěch, "John Henry Newman," 114–15). Later, thinkers like Alfred Loisy, Maurice Blondel, George Tyrell, and many others criticized the method of classical apologetics from different angles. "They gave rise to a number of new beginnings from old sources, and these new beginnings continue in our own times to refocus the whole matter of foundational theology." Hellwig, "Foundations for Theology," 8.

21. Hellwig, "Foundations for Theology," 8.

"a speculative proof of God's existence does not touch the heart nor fascinate the will to act. The human of today wants to see truth and does not want to let it only be demonstrated to him/her, touch it unaffectedly, and only gain a remote idea about it."[22]

Blondel thinks that the conceptual demonstrating of the Christian faith (or God's existence) must be balanced by the personal experience of faith, because only this may possibly encompass not only the limits of our knowledge of God but also its conditions, roots, and genesis within concrete human life.[23] Therefore, he proposed the concept of "integral apologetics," which attempts to harmonize "thinking," "acting," and "being" into coherent reflections of reality. In other words, to be able to think, we must act (thinking is a kind of acting), and if our acting (as well as thinking) could become meaningful, it must be related to reality. But how can we discover what is real? Blondel comes out of the human experience of acting. He suggests that each act has its limits and thus asks for its surmounting. The consequence of human acts ends up in the open arms of death. Human acting would be meaningless if there was nothing more to come after death. He thinks that true reality transcends our experience of reality. In other words, our experience of reality is just a distortion of true reality.[24]

For Blondel, the emptiness of human being senselessly floating through life towards its own termination awaits its fulfilment: transformation of contingent, immanent, and imperfect humanity into the transcendent, complete, and perfect humanity. Blondel finds this fulfilment in Jesus Christ, who alone can uplift humanity to its perfection. He changed the way of traditional methodology, which tried to prove transcendence through its own transcendental self-manifestation in miracles and proposed a way from immanence (thinking and acting) to transcendence (fullness of being). Therefore, his method is also often called "apologetics of immanence." For that matter, he had problems with the official teaching of the Catholic Church of that time. He was accused of cancelling the widely accepted difference between the natural and supernatural orders

---

22. Říha, *Filosofie konání*, 78.

23. Štěch, "Integrální apologetika," 61.

24. "A true fundament of Christianity is the possibility to reach an actual realization of humanity (unity of our thinking, acting, and being) through the incarnated, crucified, and resurrected Lord Jesus Christ. With him and in him, the emptiness of human being may come to its fulfilment." Štěch, "Integrální apologetika," 68.

(generally from "modernism"), and he had to defend his thesis for the rest of his life. Prophets are never welcome in their homeland.

Nevertheless, Blondel's thought was rehabilitated through the course of the time. It became an important source of inspiration for the *nouvelle théologie*. It even could be said that through persons like Joseph Maréchal, Henri de Lubac, and Karl Rahner, Blondel's thought influenced (albeit indirectly) texts of the Second Vatican Council. It may be perceived especially in its Pastoral Constitution on the Church in the Modern World, *Gaudium et Spes*.[25] Direct rehabilitation of Blondel was pronounced only later, by the pope John Paul II, who considered Blondel a truly Catholic philosopher and claimed his own work to be inspired by Blondel's philosophy.[26]

The first half of the twentieth century was marked by the discovery of "context" and "hermeneutics" as highly relevant themes for theology. Theories of interpretation brought about the notion of a "hermeneutical circle" into theological debates, and theologians became aware that Christians interpret fundaments of their religion (the event of Jesus Christ, Scripture, etc.) from contextual points of view. They approach them with their own level of knowledge, understanding (pre-understanding), and expectations. They project themselves into the tradition and biblical narrative. But they are also being influenced by them in return. When we apply the hermeneutical circle onto Christian revelation, we see that only Christians claim the event of Jesus Christ as revelatory. "Revelation does not exist as revelation in such a way that it compels recognition by all in the way an experiment in the natural sciences can. This realization undermines the apologetics of the Age of Reason completely. It demands a new kind of foundation for theology—a foundation acceptable to reason and experience in our times."[27]

In the second half of twentieth century, the Second Vatican Council represents a milestone for fundamental theology as an independent theological discipline. Even though council documents did not explicitly mention fundamental theology, they contain rich material for its constitution and development. It is especially the Dogmatic Constitution on Divine Revelation (*Dei Verbum*) where we may find numerous impulses

---

25. Štěch, "Integrální apologetika," 71. This may be compared for instance with the GS 22: "The truth is that only in the mystery of the incarnate Word does the mystery of man take on light."

26. Dulles, *Splendor of Faith*, 6.

27. Hellwig, "Foundations for Theology," 9.

for further study of Christian foundations. It is important to remember that the theology of revelation from *Dei Verbum* is still decisive for any contemporary fundamental theology. In the rhetoric of this constitution, revelation is newly understood in terms of the economy of salvation. Revelation is salvific because it is realized in the concrete historical and contextual event of Jesus Christ. Revelation is personal because it is a person! It is Jesus Christ. Contrary to a one-sided portrait of Jesus Christ (as attesting to God's revelation, the highest miracle, or a messenger delivering God's revelatory message to humankind) suggested by apologetics, the council offered a more balanced perspective of Jesus Christ as Revealer and revelation at the same time. "By this revelation then, the deepest truth about God and the salvation of man shines out for our sake in Christ, who is both the mediator and the fullness of all revelation" (DV 2).

Jesus Christ is an invitation for people to enter a personal relationship with their God. Such a fundamental shift in understanding revelation was accompanied with a new understanding of the relationship between faith and reason. They are not in opposition to each other but encompassed within a concrete human personality. The act of faith has three dimensions: cognitive, volitive, and affective, as we can read from the conciliar documents (DV 5). A certain priority is given to revelation over the "light of human reason" (DV 6). I think we can say that human experience is gaining priority over reasoning within this perspective. From my perspective, the traditional teachings about revelation revealed to people through Scripture and tradition is re-actualized in DV 9. The Scripture is the first source of revelation. But tradition has a very important hermeneutical role in interpreting the content of revelation within a particular historical and sociocultural context.

However, the Second Vatican Council surprisingly brought not a boom of fundamental theology but rather its crisis. It was a time of searching for a new discipline's identity. While classical apologetics focused more on fighting against unbelief and philosophical convictions challenging Catholic theology in the nineteenth century and first half of the twentieth century, fundamental theology turned its focus towards the inside of the Christian community.[28] It maintains an apologetic function.

---

28. It is necessary to note that apologetics simply does not vanish with the emergence of fundamental theology. It continues to do a good service to the church community wherever it is needed to defend the faith against various adversaries in a polemic way. Gerald O'Collins offers some good examples of such a contemporary exercise of apologetic polemics against new atheism. O'Collins, *Rethinking*, 5. At the same time, apologetics and fundamental theology share a common ground. It yet

It yet attempts to seek and explicate foundations of Christian belief to Christians. Fundamental theology today is understood not merely as a tool to prove the truthfulness of the basic Christian message but rather as a continuous endeavor to search for signs of the God's presence in the world. It does not want to simply replace former classical apologetics. It aims to bring its traditional notions into new light—the light of the gospel reflected in modern and postmodern times. However different, contextualized, and still re-actualized throughout history, fundamental theology is still dealing with the reflection of the grounds for Christian faith. Sometimes with more emphasis on an external apologetics, giving an account of the hope of Christians in Christ, and sometimes more internal, reminding believers of what they believe and why. Thus, fundamental theology today shall create a new theological background for apologetics advising it not merely to mentor or oppose, but to dialogue and discuss to become what John Milbank calls, "a mode of apologetics prepared to question the world's assumptions down to their very roots and to expose how they lie within paganism, heterodoxy or else an atheism with no ground in reason and a tendency to deny the ontological reality of reason altogether."[29]

However, fundamental theology today undergoes transformation, because the whole style of doing theology slowly shifts to the fully blooming postmodern period. Such transformation may seem to some as if fundamental theology is today "threatened with non-existence."[30] This may have been true for the last couple of decades, but recently, in the freshly unfolding third millennium, fundamental theology receives a new swing. Gerald O'Collins suggests that fundamental theology as a discipline "needs to be relaunched."[31] It seems that this call has been heard across denominations. In the Catholic environment, Neil Ormerod

---

moves in different ways and maintains different tasks. O'Collins names three differences (O'Collins, *Rethinking*, 4–5):

1). Apologetics deals only with defense of the faith in the Christian God; fundamental theology keeps this function but also "embodies the study of various central Christian doctrines, like divine revelation and human faith." O'Collins, *Rethinking*, 5.

2). Apologetics is usually aimed at well-specified audiences. Fundamental theology speaks to broad audience.

3). While apologetics employs only polemical language, fundamental theology must operate with much more inclusive language to explain and not mentor or oppose.

29. Milbank, "Foreword," xx.

30. O'Collins, *Rethinking*, vii.

31. O'Collins, *Rethinking*, vii.

and Christiaan Jacobs-Vandegeer made considerable steps forward with their extensive (450 pages!) book entitled *Foundational Theology: A New Approach to Catholic Fundamental Theology*.[32] Two major renewal impulses also came from the Protestant milieu. First, it is necessary to mention the Protestant perspective on fundamental theology written by Matthew L. Becker.[33] Second, there is Hans Peter Geiser and his splendid book entitled *The Community of the Weak*. Encountering this book (and Geiser's way of thinking) encouraged me to proceed with an attempt to interconnect fundamental theology with youth theology out of the environment of practical theology. Reading Geiser, my last doubts vanished, and I decided to answer the call of O'Collins to investigate what could happen when fundamental theology meets youth theology; what will happen when academic (fundamental) theology embraces the everyday theology of ordinary believers; what will happen when young people are recognized as sources of inspiration for fundamental theology.

In *the Community of the Weak*, Geiser proposes a new fundamental theology written in a "new key,"[34] considering all possible conversation partners from the realm of science but also ordinary people and their experiences. New fundamental theology, according to Geiser, understands theology as fundamentally "autobiographical"[35] and must be surprised (and surprising) or else it is not "jazzy" enough.[36] Reading Geiser, I was thrilled because it resonated so much with my own concept of theology and the way I always tried to teach theology, no matter if it was at the university or in a "milder mode" in high school. When I discovered his

---

32. The book of these two authors aims at writing a new fundamental theology from the perspective of Bernard Lonergan, whose work is its main resource (Ormerod and Jacobs-Vandegeer, *Foundational Theology*, xii). It also echoes the above-mentioned call of Gerald O'Collins, who inspired the authorial tandem to write this book. He also provided its preface, where he writes, "I have found it a significant contribution not only to Lonergan studies but also to the development of fundamental theology. It has grown out of the conviction that conversion, in its various forms, is the foundational reality of theology." O'Collins, *Rethinking*, vii–viii.

33. Becker puts himself in the tradition of Protestant fundamental theologians such as Wilfred Joest, Gerhard Ebeling, and Wolfhart Pannenberg. His aim is to provide a comprehensive, up-to-date, study and research resource for fundamental theology from the Protestant perspective. Even though it is relevant to professionals, Becker's book is designed as an introductory textbook aimed primarily at college students and general readers.

34. Geiser, *Community of the Weak*, 437.
35. Geiser, *Community of the Weak*, 438.
36. Geiser, *Community of the Weak*, 441.

references to Ann Pederson and his call for theology to be done or played as jazz, I just rejoiced.[37] Such soulmates, constantly trying to connect and interweave the old with the new and the classical with the progressive, may be found all around the globe and across denominations. Here is a hint of Geiser's understanding of fundamental theology: "Fundamental theology could be a place in the encyclopedic landscape of the many and various theological disciplines where new things, new themes, new tunes and new chords can be tried out, experimented with, improvised and newly arranged."[38]

Fundamental theology, for Geiser, is truly postmodern. But yet it strives to "lay down the ground for doing theology, both thematically and socially."[39] That means, fundamental theology shall not resign on its own task to provide reasonable grounds for faith but must change its style or method. Fundamental theology must not only be autobiographical, but as a proper theological discipline, it must put God at its very center as well. And I suggested above, any biography is not a story isolated from other stories. As we are not separated from our fellow human beings, as believing Christians; we are not separated from our God, the Triune One, either. (I will come back to Hans-Peter Geiser and his proposals for contemporary fundamental theology later in this work when discussing the possibilities for rethinking fundamental theology today, and when proposing a wedding between theoretical and practical in theology as the last chapter unfolds below.)

At this point we may sum up that the basic difference between apologetic and fundamental theology would be in their styles and orientations. While apologetic is convinced that it knows truth and wants to defend this truth against adversaries (evidentialist style), fundamental theology refocuses its orientation from outside to inside. Fundamental theology suggests going back to the roots of one's own faith, going back to basic revelatory experiences, and going back to the church's origin. In this way fundamental theology focuses on the basics of Christian faith and is not busy proving them right to anyone outside Christianity. Yet fundamental theology does not lack a missionary aspect. It is just different in style. The one who meditates through and experiences the foundations of one's own faith, both by heart and reason, is better equipped for dialogue with others than anyone who thinks in propositional truths as ammunition

---

37. Geiser, *Community of the Weak*, x, 428.
38. Geiser, *Community of the Weak*, 430.
39. Geiser, *Community of the Weak*, 438.

against all possible opponents. Fundamental theology is, in my opinion, a reformed apologetic, leaving behind its medieval armor and weapons by getting involved in the common quest for better humanity in the public spaces of contemporary times.

However, trying to place myself in line of the discipline's development sketched above, I should return to the metaphor used in the introduction. It seems to me as very apt for fundamental theology. Fundamental theology is like playing jazz inspired by the already-quoted conviction of Hans-Peter Geiser and Ann Pedersen. I intend this text to be an invitation by which youth theology and youth ministry can join a common jam session with fundamental theology to see what happens if we play together. The best way to start jamming is by showing what you play and how. It is a welcome. "Look, this is my music, this is my song. Would you like to join with your own?" This is what follows within the rest of this chapter—an autobiographical improvisation in fundamental theology interpreting three theological jazzmen (Boublík, Skalický, Dulles) who influenced my own sound.

Perhaps this is the right place to unveil my further intentions to discern where it all goes. Chapter 3 will be a break in playing fundamental theology, because after inviting others to play with us, we need to listen to what they play and sing. Invitation means making our own place available to others, creating a generous and hospitable space for encounters and giving, as well as for receiving and mutual enrichment. This will start with chapter 3, where I describe my experience of listening and reflecting on my relatively fresh (and thus also still a bit premature) perception of what music is played by youth ministry and youth theology. I will start making music again in the concluding chapter 4, where I hope to identify some pieces of common ground for fundamental theology and youth ministry, from which youth theology springs and comes out to search for partners across (and beyond) the spectrum of theology. This, I believe, will eventually inspire and enable both disciplines to encounter each other and start a new jam session of doing theology together.

2.2 ALONG THE PATHS OF FUNDAMENTAL THEOLOGY

We are all parts of certain traditions. When we decide to walk some way, we are never completely alone. We should consider those who preceded us on the roads and paths we walk. We have contact with those who walk with us. And finally, we must think about those who will follow our footprints. In the process of our own education and growth we encounter those who teach us to read maps. And we meet others who initiate us into the rules of traveling. Some present theories (maps) show us how to dwell in the labyrinth of the world and the landscapes we eventually decide to travel and walk. Some skillful globetrotters know that maps are not the same as actual landscapes. They know that theories are not identical with practice, but both are necessary for us to have a complete picture of our surroundings. In other words, maps usually tell us that there is a river or a bush. But they do not tell us how deep the river crossing is or how thick bushes are at the time we need to go through them. For this information we need someone who knows, who made and experienced. We need a local scout, an authentic insider. However, even the most skillful tracker cannot see the landscape in its wider context, as cartographers are able to see it. Connecting theory to praxis; reading maps and walking through landscapes; learning to understand map signs and getting to know corners and streets, forests, and rivers; roads and paths, local people, plants, and animals—that is what we need to search for; that is what we need to learn from those who are settled on local grounds as well as from those who travel a lot; from those who know places as well as from those who draw maps. Yet, there is always a danger of being too narrow-minded and thinking our (or my) map is the only one, that my reading of the landscape is the only one possible. We need to read our landscapes (theological traditions) "widely"[40] to maintain the balance between the general and the contextual and avoid abstract generalization on the one hand and exclusive contextual interpretation on the other. We need to pay attention to context, so we do not fall into the trap of ignoring the context of the other.

During my theological journey, I've met several "local scouts" who have never left their homelands. I've met some cartographers who have never left their office. I've also met a few who were able to draw maps and read them, and who also enjoyed scouting different landscapes themselves. Three of them were particularly influential on my own theological and personal formation: Vladimír Boublík (1928–74), Karel Skalický (1934–) and Avery Cardinal Dulles (1918–2008). All three were Catholic priests. All three traced a long and adventurous path to their priesthood. All three mastered their theological craft surfing on the great wave heaved by the last council of the Roman Catholic Church. All three

---

40. Budden, "Necessity," 61.

became theologians and served as educators and scientists. All three influenced my own theological thinking more than any others.[41] It was not only their theological writings that inspired me but also their life stories. A special place among the three mentioned theologians belongs to Karel Skalický, not only because he is the only one of the three still living, while the others have already concluded their life journeys and works, but primarily because he made my encounter with the other two theologians possible. He opened to me the writings of his teacher and friend Boublík and recommended that I read the works of Avery Dulles. Later, Skalický encouraged me to go meet Dulles, personally, in the United States. That means it is only Boublík whom I did not meet in person, because he died before I was born. Nevertheless, his story and texts moved my heart and mind with no less strength than the other two. When I started to study theology and, more precisely, fundamental theology with Karel Skalický, I realized that it was not only a matter of my profession. It would require the whole of my life.

As I already suggested above, theology seems to be a way of life. It is a way for us to live our relationship with God, other people, and the world. It helps us reflect upon God's revelation in human history and understand people as being part of it. Theology is a way to seek understanding of Christian faith, hope, and love, experienced in constant tension between humanity and the divine. Fundamental theology in particular helps us to search the grounds of Christian faith, understand Christian revelation, and interpret the Christian community. Fundamental theology, from the perspectives of these three authors, helps us to understand the world we live in, its past, present, and future, the world seen and unseen, and the physical and spiritual too. It helps us understand the multiple relationships in which we live. These include (1) one's relationship with one's own (often complicated) self; (2) one's relationships with other people (also often complicated); and (3) one's relationship with God (whom people have sometimes enormous trouble understanding)—the ultimate mystery Christians confess as the Triune Creator, Redeemer and

---

41. On my theological journey covered so far, I have met various inspiring thinkers: male and female, Catholic, Protestant, evangelical, and Orthodox as well. It is not possible to name them all. But they were European, African, Asian, and North American, as well as Latin American, theologians. Some of them I met in person during my studies in the Netherlands (Nijmegen, Amsterdam) and United States (New York). Some others were mediated to me by my three "key theologians" named above. Theology truly became an inseparable part of my life, and thus I would say my life became theological as well.

Savior of humankind and everything that was called by him into being and development (directed towards "becoming"). This kind of theology is not only an academic effort. It is not only about drawing maps. It is also about *doing* at the same time. It is a matter of scouting the actual landscapes, wherever they are. Theology from the perspectives of Boublík, Skalický, and Dulles is existential. It touches upon the remaining of human existence, which can be found in relationship with Jesus Christ. Their theologies try to be understandable and accessible to the broadest public possible. Yet they remain properly academic. They have an evangelical and mystagogical undertones and want to drive people's attention towards the question of their lives' meaning and purpose. They point towards Jesus Christ as a viable way to answer these questions of human life and death. This calls those who read and listen to the path of continuous conversion, which is, from my perspective, the fundamentally theological way of life—life that is constantly trying to understand our relational engagement in this world where God is not absent but very much present instead; God, with whom people may have a personal relationship and thus also a proper share in his life. And that is why it could be said that fundamental theology helps to set up a life perspective and seeks to define human identity.

During searching for my own personal identity (including my professional one), life orientation, and meaning, I discovered that due to accepting Skalický as my teacher and mentor, I connected myself to a particular theological tradition. Skalický developed his own fundamental theology on the grounds laid down by his teacher and friend Vladimír Boublík.[42] Skalický continued what his predecessor was unable to finish saying due to his untimely death. However, Boublík remained a key author for Skalický's independent and original fundamental-theological conception. Studying with Skalický, I was also naturally introduced into Boublík's thought. Furthermore, Skalický was also influenced by Avery Cardinal Dulles[43] and his theology, especially his theology of revelation and his thinking in models. For that reason, Skalický wanted me to know Dulles as well, and he even convinced me to write my doctorate on his theology. This encounter opened new horizons for me again and enabled me to traverse the tradition of Boublík and Skalický, which became my own theological background. During the time of pursuing my doctorate

---

42. Skalický, *Za nadĕji*, 233.
43. Štĕch, "Fundamentální teologie," 27.

I started to think about theology overall. I found myself at home in its concrete tradition[44] and came to realize that theology should become a mode of my life as it was for all three of my source theologians.

All in all, Skalický disclosed some maps to me and taught me how to read them. He directed me to search for more. At the same time, he encouraged me to get out of my office and scout the streets and landscapes, to get to know people and their environments. He told me many times that if I wanted to do theology I need "to get my hands dirty." Only those who have experience on the ground (liberation theologians would say "grassroots") and learn to read the maps can become good future cartographers and scouts for others who seek their own paths, orientations, identities, and meanings of life. From this perspective, it may be said that fundamental theology is a story to be continued. It is a sequence of life stories that emerge and are recorded in the writings of concrete people/theologians encountering and experiencing (Christian) mystery in their lives and even wrestling with it sometimes.[45] There are always lives of concrete people behind these stories. Therefore, I decided to structure the following exposé of Boublík, Skalický, and Dulles in a way that would first introduce their life stories and then link them with their distinctive theologies. I am convinced that none of their theologies would be the same had they lived different experiences. With such a narrative background, it is possible to highlight aspects of their theologies which I consider most important for my own attempt to rethink fundamental theology in conversation with youth ministry and the concept of youth theology (later in this text). It is naturally not possible to make a comprehensive introduction into the wide theological works of these theologians, but let them entice us to take paths within our discipline accompanied by the most competent guides—experienced and respectful elders, who walked ways of fundamental theology probably even before most of us were born.

2.2.1 Vladimír Boublík and a Fundamental Christology

Vladimír Boublík (1928–74) was a Catholic priest, theologian and a professor at Pontifical Lateran University in Rome (1959–74). In 1972 he became the dean of its faculty of theology. His life journey was quite

---

44. Štěch, "Od věrohodnosti," 85.
45. Skalický, *V zápase s posvátnem*.

adventurous, and it would not be an exaggeration to say that the same is true of his theology. For Boublík, theology was a way of searching for the meaning of life, facing its inevitable termination in (physical) death. His time was marked by flourishing existentialism seeking the meaning of human existence experienced by people as being towards death—"Sein zum Tode," in Heidegger's words. Therefore, in his work Boublík sees theology as an (existential) adventure of searching for life's meaning. He is convinced that theology can help us to find out (1) who we are as human beings; (2) what our specific place in this world is, and (3) what the purpose of our existence is, directed and slowly floating towards death. According to Boublík, answers to these questions may come from the relationship with the transcendent, personal, and triune God of Christianity. This kind of relationship is modelled on the life and story of Jesus Christ. Human life is an adventure of love.[46] Love seeking not only understanding but also its own fullness within the ahistorical completeness of Love. This Love, however, became part of history in the event of Jesus Christ. The ahistorical became historic. Yet it remained ahistorical; transcendent became immanent while nevertheless remaining fully transcendent. This paradox reveals the true nature of God and sets up the possibility for human beings: that their love as a particular and historical act can connect to God, the transcendental, personal, and everlasting source (and fullness) of love. In his spiritual diary, Boublík writes, "And love—it never ends after all. Thus, each moment of our life, ever full of vanity, finality, uselessness, as soon as it is revived by love—connected to the deeds and plans of God, must immediately thwart the terror of vanity, because it becomes endless, follows us. It never ends; it does not stop."[47]

Thus, for theology it is crucial to focus on anthropological questions (e.g., love, beauty, sin, grace, predestination, human freedom, etc.) and relate them to God. Boublík interprets theology not only as love seeking its understanding and fullness but also as hope searching the same, resisting the sneaky hopelessness of our daily lives. Finally, theology from the perspective of this theologian seeks also understanding faith and its source. Christian faith is an adventurous way of living our lives between humanity and the divine. It is an adventure of nothing less than an interpersonal relationship.

---

46. Boublík, *Duchovní deník*, 147–48.
47. Boublík, *Duchovní deník*, 148.

One may object that existentialism as a philosophical orientation reached its peak in the late twentieth century and today is far beyond the horizon, that this kind of theology is out of date—and if this is the case, why deal with someone whose theological reflections seem decades old? It is a serious objection, but not everything that is old is necessarily out of date. It appears to me that existential questions did not diminish when existentialism retreated from the primary interests of philosophers and theologians of the last century. They are still relevant and urgent to our humanity, as it was a few decades ago. People still have their own existential questions. They search for life's meaning and strive to discover their identity, albeit that historical, cultural, and social conditions contextualizing these processes have considerably changed, of course. Despite all of this, I still consider Boublík's theology relevant today, because it strives for orientation and ultimate fulfilment. A Christocentric orientation is characteristic (and fundamental) to the theology of Boublík overall. He suggests that we may understand the world we live in through theological optics. Thus, theology is for him not only an academic study of God and God's traces in the world but a way of life, a way or relating to God also. "It is most important to prove . . . that theology is not a science for science, but that it is the science of life."[48] Theology is the adventure of Jesus Christ and everyone who believes in him and decides to follow his path (as Boublík decided to do). This was maybe the first lesson Boublík taught me. I realized theology was going to be a life adventure and not only a struggle to understand the meanings of terms and logical arguments.

When we take a brief look at Boublík's life, we may see that it corresponds with the way he writes and does theology. It is an adventure. He grew up as the first born of three sons in a poor, rural family in southwestern Bohemia. He responded positively to his mother's wish that one of her three sons become a priest. He entered the seminary in České Budějovice straight after he finished his high school education in 1947.[49] He concluded the first year of his theological studies as one of the best students, and the local bishop sent him to Rome. There, he was supposed to continue his studies and priesthood development at Nepomuceno, a Czechoslovakian theological college, starting in September 1948.

But this never happened. Boublík did not receive a travel visa, and in mid-August, he was arrested and imprisoned because he got involved in

---

48. Boublík, *Duchovní deník*, 29–30.
49. Žůrek, *Prolegomena*, 12–13.

an illegal group helping people escape abroad after the Communist party took power in the former Czechoslovakia in February 1948. Instead of becoming priest, he became an outlaw and a prisoner. After two years in a Communist lager, he was released and started working in the Škoda machine factory in Plzeň. According to the biography compiled by Žůrek, he found a girlfriend amongst the workers in the factory. At the same time, he continued studying theology, even though it was very complicated.[50] Boublík enjoyed freedom only for a few months. In October 1950, he was recruited by the well-known "auxiliary technical battalions."[51] Already at the beginning of 1951, he was arrested again for falsifying holiday permissions for Christmas. Sadder but wiser (from his previous stay in a Communist jail), he managed to escape before he was taken into prison.

The problematic soldier became a deserter. Boublík knew that now he had to leave the country and thus made several attempts to cross the border. All of them failed, mainly due to bad weather and a lot of snow. He searched for help in various places, usually in parish houses or monasteries. But no one wanted to be linked with a fugitive and deserter of the priesthood. Finally, one of the priests he asked for help betrayed him to the state secret police, and Boublík was caught and escorted to the military jail. During interrogations, "standard methods" were used, and he suffered a severe dental injury. This made his desire to escape again even stronger. A chance occurred in 1952, when he was asked by a prison guard to deliver food to his fellow prisoners. The kitchen was in a less-guarded area of the prison. In that unguarded moment, Boublík walked out the rear entrance, climbed the fence, and disappeared into the woods.

Under various dramatic circumstances, after ten days and a few hundred kilometers (traversed mostly on foot), he arrived in West Berlin totally exhausted.[52] There, he received new documents as a Czechoslovakian refugee, and soon after obtained an Italian visa. The way to Rome and to the priesthood was open again. In Rome, Boublík enrolled in the Czech theological college and continued his studies. However, it was not easy for a prisoner, worker, deserter, and refugee to become a student

50. Žůrek, *Prolegomena*, 18–19.

51. The former Czechoslovak People's Army created special battalions called "auxiliary technical battalions." These were practically labor camps where "politically unreliable" young men were sent to fulfil their conscription service. It was one of the tools used by the Communist regime to oppress "class enemies." All clergymen, including candidates for priesthood, were counted among them.

52. In 1952 Berlin was not yet divided by the famous Berlin Wall, and so our refugee had a chance to get there through the line of military guards. Žůrek, *Prolegomena*, 22.

and seminarian again. His experience did not harmonize with the rigid environment of the institutional church espoused by Nepomuceno College. Much of formative priesthood seemed to him merely empty, pious talk. His diary entry from June 9, 1952, reads:

> So, I don't know, what was happening a long time ago in the seminary of České Budějovice is happening again. When I got there, I had the impression that here, people live in a holy way, that God is the first concern of all, that to study (although a bit exaggerated) is viewed from the perspective of God and one's own perfection, that a certain unity exists, although it perhaps feels shame to be expressed by direct love.
>
> And after a month of my stay here the same questions from five years ago return to life: What sort of Christianity is the one which gives to the heart only phrases from the Holy Scripture, a multifarious pious piffle, and repulsive filth to acts? What sort of education is the one (for now I only met its pharisaic, ugly face in all church institutions),which persists as naive trifles on the one side and ignores basic principles, not merely of Christianity but also of humanity—obvious even to ordinary people—on the other? And what priests are we going to be when after six years of first-class spiritual formation, after knowledge of different ultra-ascetics and different theological sentences, we make such foolish things that everyone who is normal today considers immoral?
>
> True—I cannot find the error in Christianity, but in us. But I can think about throwing in the towel. It may be better, since I know my own way of pharisaic mentality, although different—but it is pharisaic as well and repugnant too, in a way. I lack the example of a saint. But precisely because I am not a saint, there are only two solutions: either avoid the filth or resignation. One is to leave this field—and this would mean, under the given circumstances, to leave a field completely and scrape along somewhere with only one advantage (would it be small advantage?): that I live poorly, but without the pharisaic mask. The second alternative is to put an end to my own filth, take up own thoughts, my own strengths together and with true confidence in God's omnipotence and the strength of his love, fight and not step back. And prevail? I think not—maybe only personally. So what?—It seems to me that if these workmen/ guys[53] would see in what environment I persist to live, they

---

53. Boublík most probably refers here to his former workmates in the Škoda machine factory.

would spit contemptuously (and rightfully) in front of me. If I had the moral right, I would even spit twice.[54]

Boublík fought many battles on his long way to Rome. He went through factories, prisons, labor lagers, and military camps. But he would have to fight many more battles during his priest formation at Nepomuceno College. These were maybe even harder, because they took place inside his soul, mind, and heart. There are many more records, such as the one quoted above in Boublík's diaries. I chose this one because it illustrates well what shaped his theology. Boublík wanted a true Christianity, not a pious church made of empty phrases and formalist ritual—a true Christianity, existentially oriented on and rooted in the personal experience of meeting Jesus Christ. Although aware of his own weaknesses, he wanted to fight to become a true priest and wanted to contribute to the improvement of church education, despite his constant doubts about himself. Theology was for him an adventurous attempt to understand the actual world we live in and the purpose of all human activities.

His theology always goes to the ground (at times, it even goes underground). He asks himself what workers would say about his theological ideas—how academic theology could reach them and not only other academics. In one of his personal letters to a friend, he writes, "Tell me, how to get to these great (although oafish, rude) blackened boys, to these great girls (although sentimental, not exemplary regarding the sixth commandment) in a new style? How to get to the workers? How to get to farmers a Christianity truly living?"[55]

Nevertheless, Boublík continued his studies and concluded them with excellent results. He also finished his spiritual formation and was ordained a Catholic priest in 1955. The new priest was sent to the South Tyrol. After two years of service as chaplain in different Tyrolean parishes, he was called back to Rome. His former professor of dogmatic theology, Monsignor Antonio Piolanti, chose him as an assistant, and Boublík started working on his doctorate under Piolanti's supervision. In 1959 he defended his thesis entitled "Predestination: St. Paul and St. Augustine,"[56] and in the academic year 1959–60, he started to teach the Introduction to Theology and Apologetics course at Lateran University,

---

54. Boublík, *Duchovní deník*, 40–41.
55. Schreier and Skalický, *Česko-římský*, 2.
56. Boublík, *Predestinazione*.

newly promoted (17 May 1959) to the rank of the Pontifical University.[57] The young theologian received an enormous opportunity to design his own way to teach and research fundamental theology—a new discourse in apologetics, and maybe more.

So, the fundamental theology of Vladimír Boublík was developed in turbulent times, when classical apologetics were reborn into fundamental theology within the Roman Catholic Church. As we have seen above, theologians of that era wanted to keep the merits of apologetics on the one hand but equally suspected its inability to reflect relevantly on Christianity's credibility in the context of modernity. A new model for fundamental theology was sought, and it also often included apologetics. As did other great theologians of that time, Boublík worked out his own model for a newly forming discipline. He wrestled with the classical, manual approach which dominated his own theological training as well as with his personal (theological) difficulties, including no less than his loyalty to the church and prophetic theological intuitions.

Even though Boublík was in favor of the new fundamental theology, he was convinced of the continuous importance of apologetics at the same time. He thought apologetics rightly identified an ever-relevant theological topic (the credibility of the Christian message and Christianity itself as such) but that it had lost its capacity to present the objective truth of Christianity in an understandable and relevant way. Therefore, the newly emerging fundamental theology, according to Boublík, had the potential to restore this capacity in a way more apt for the late 1960s and early 1970s. In these decades Boublík observed that the mentality of the modern world was preoccupied with reality rather than objective truth. Contrary to Boublík's experience, I believe that I again observe a certain turn towards the search for objective truth amongst contemporary youth and, consequently, attempts to escape reality by taking recourse in virtual spaces. On various occasions when I theologized with young people during the past few years, I always tried to help them see particular things from different possible angles. I assumed that if they are young, they must be open-minded. When I was young, open-mindedness was a synonym for being young. But soon I learned that this is not necessarily the case. During my work with young people, I encountered lots of comments like "don't tell us possible interpretations—say how it really is." And when I said, "I do not know for sure, but I can share my experience

---

57. Schelkens, *Catholic Theology*, 111.

with you and present you with my convictions and faith," they seemed to be dissatisfied. They demanded a clear answer. When these reactions started to appear regularly at these meetings, I tried to consider where they were coming from. Why do contemporary young people want to receive clear and readymade objective truth (the best in a prepositional way) instead of taking up their own quests to search for reality? Do they fear uncertainties? Or are they "fed up" with relativism? Why are they so quick to adopt fundamentalist positions? While working on a joint article together with my colleague Ludmila Muchová, we made an important observation:

> In the Czech Republic, we strongly feel the fundamentalism of youth supported by official Catholic Church authorities through the latter's focus on developing and perceiving exclusively Catholic identity. At the same time, we observe a similar fundamentalism among secularized youth, who live with societal prejudices towards everything Catholic and Christian. They are often left alone with uncertain feelings of the sacred, without the means to discover a coherent answer to their questions of the divine. Both groups can hardly meet. To overcome this gap, and fight all kinds of fundamentalisms, we suggest a return to fundaments.[58]

But let us return to Boublík. He also wanted to discover fundamental principles of Christian faith. Concerning fundamental theology, he distinguished between its theological and apologetic aspects. The former focused on Christian revelation as the source of theological knowledge. The latter maintained the topic of credibility. Boublík was convinced that in terms of its credibility, Christianity (and its apologetics) must emphasize the sincerity of Christian life and the practice of faith, considering these anthropological foci of each Christian theology. Boublík suggested a plan in "three steps: philosophical, historical and semiologic."[59] In the first step, Boublík identifies questions of existential philosophers as highly relevant for ordinary people. According to him, all people expect the future to come. But their expectation necessarily hits the limit of death. In the second step, Boublík offers a solution. If people meet the historical Jesus in Scripture or proclamation and recognize him as Christ, the ultimate future of humankind and their expectation of the future will transform into awaiting Christ. Recognition of the historical Jesus as

---

58. Štěch and Muchová, "Sustainable Youth Ministry," 65.
59. Žůrek, *Prolegomena*, 97.

Christ—the Messiah brings us to the third, semiologic step of Boublík's theological plan: the human expectation of the future as awaiting Christ and the eschatological fulfilment of our humanity from a Christian perspective. A specific meaning is attributed to the historical event of Jesus. It may be useful to add that meeting Jesus may occur principally in two different ways. First, Jesus may be encountered in his humanity as our alter ego, as a respectful and respected other, as a friend or as a fellow human person. Second, Jesus may be encountered in his divinity as the aim and limit of all human expectations. Both ways are complementary, and one leads to the other.

However, meeting the historical Jesus in everyday life has a crucial (theological) importance for Boublík. It results in his fundamental Christology. Recognizing Jesus as Christ is central to Boublík's fundamental theology. It is the ground for each Christian theology. According to Boublík, Christians bear witness to holiness (even though they are not completely holy) and thus are able to recognize God within the human world. The role of theologians is to guide people on their way to Jesus Christ, to remind them that they can believe, that faith is not impossible. If people expect the future with hope, they are also able to love and believe. But human faith, hope, and love search for meaning and understanding. Expecting is possible if people see meaning in their expectation as well as in the expected future. This theory will be used further in discerning who young people are, from a theological perspective. According to Boublík, Christian faith can provide an answer to each human search for meaning because it proclaims Jesus Christ as the principle of human history and the ultimate future of humanity, as the completion (and source) of all the meaning. The fundamental theology of Vladimír Boublík is a fundamental Christology.

Boublík was convinced of the possibility of meeting Jesus Christ (as well as his message and teaching) within this world. Therefore, he addressed his theology to everyone—Christians and non-Christians alike—who seek the future, to all who want to understand the content and meaning of their lives[60] and true humanity. Therefore, the fundamental question of Boublík's theology is: Who is Jesus of Nazareth? The following quotation may well illustrate it: "During the twenty centuries, this question appeared in the lives of many people—scholars and common people, sinners and saints, believers and non-believers—(they all)

---

60. Boublík, *Teologická antropologie*, 9; Boublík, *Setkání*, 16; Boublík, *Člověk*, 6.

would want to know who Jesus of Nazareth is, what his significance for world history and for the personal life of each of us is."[61]

In his theology, Boublík wanted to present a vital Christianity for his contemporaries. Like some other theologians (e.g., Teilhard de Chardin), he held that Christ is "realized" within human history.[62] He developed an intuition that history consists of three phases of Jesus Christ. First, it is the past of the Jesus of Nazareth, whom Christians believe is the incarnated word of God. Second, it is the presence of the resurrected Christ, whom Christian faith meets within the lives of believers. Christ's presence in each moment of history continuously prepares for the final future in cooperation with human beings, expecting fulfillment of the future in hope. A third aspect of Boublík's account of "Christified" history is the future of Christ expressed in eschatological terms. In the future of the Christ's second coming, the whole of creation will be transformed into the perfection of God's kingdom, the whole Christ (*Christus totus*), where God will be all in all.[63] "For 'God has put all things in subjection under his feet.' But when it says, 'All things are put in subjection,' it is plain that this does not include the one who put all things in subjection under him. When all things are subjected to him, then the Son himself will also be subjected to the one who put all things in subjection under him, so that God may be all in all" (1 Cor 15:27–28).

For Boublík, Jesus Christ is a fascinating and mysterious interplay between humanity and the divine, between God and creation. Because of Jesus Christ, people are predestined to be introduced into the everlasting mystery. Therefore, it is possible to meet Jesus in our lives and expect Christ as the ultimate fulfilment of the future of humanity.[64] Boublík's fundamental theology is based on the expectation of a fundamental Christology. It reminds his readers that meeting God is possible, even in times when the simple meeting between human beings becomes difficult. However, the message is important: it is possible to remember the time when God was one of us. Boublík's existential concern and fundamentally Christological perspective opened the way for his student and successor, Karel Skalický, who continued to develop his own fundamental theology along the lines set by Boublík.

---

61. Boublík, *Setkání*, 25.
62. Boublík, *Setkání*, 95.
63. Štěch, "Od věrohodnosti," 88–89.
64. Štěch, "Od věrohodnosti," 89.

2.2.2 Karel Skalický and Fundamental Theology in the Existential Horizon of Thinking

"Therefore, understand this, O beloved: The mystery of the Passover is new and old, eternal and temporal, corruptible and incorruptible, mortal and immortal."—Melito of Sardis, Peri Pascha 2

Karel Skalický (1934–) was born the only son of a forest engineer in Hluboká nad Vltavou, a small town in the South Bohemian region. After he finished high school and a short working practice, he decided to study at Charles University in Prague. He enrolled in the agricultural faculty to study the mechanization of agriculture in 1953. Despite the technical orientation of his study, he appreciated music, dance, and reading. During his university studies, a desire to become a priest started to mature. In this respect, Skalický was influenced by Vladimír Třebín—a Premonstrate priest candidate whom he met during Easter 1955. Soon they became friends, and Třebín gave him a book: *The Following of Christ, in Four Books* by Thomas à Kempis. Skalický started to read and meditate on his vocation. Slowly he decided to give his life fully to the service of Jesus Christ as a priest in the Catholic Church. But it was rather impossible to realize such a vocation in the context of the early 1950s in Czechoslovakia, ruled by the Communist party and administered by Soviet counsellors. In the whirl of uncertainties and ruminations about what to do, a clear impulse again suddenly came from Třebín, who unexpectedly invited Skalický to join him for an escape to "the West," where they could both study freely for the priesthood and reach ordination. Skalický was shocked because he knew about the military-guarded electric fences and barbed wire barriers freshly built along the Czechoslovakian border separating the Eastern block from the free Western world.[65] Friends of his father, workers in the border woods who lumbered trees in the "forbidden zone," told him stories about its impenetrability. "Do you want to join me?" asked Třebín. Skalický remembers that he started to fudge the issue. He first told his friend that he had to finish university, that

---

65. Such barriers were parts of the broader concept of the so-called "Iron Curtain," a complex effort of the former Soviet Union to seal itself and other countries off under its political influence (including Czechoslovakia)—ideologically, politically and even physically—from the (non-communist) West. While it is common knowledge that the Berlin Wall assumed the symbol of the Iron Curtain, particular post-communist countries have their own symbols as well. In the contemporary Czech Republic, the forbidden border zone and so-called "wires" function as symbols of the Iron Curtain.

he was not the kind of person who escapes works in progress, that he could not leave his parents behind. But deep down he knew that the die had been cast, that he had already decided—and these were just excuses. "Okay, fine, I'll go," answered Skalický in the end. During the dark and rainy night of June 15, 1956, their desire to become priests led Skalický and Třebín to the southern border of Czechoslovakia. They managed to get through the guards and barbed-wired barriers (including the electric one). After crossing the swollen river, they arrived in Austria. The road to Rome was open to the fresh (overnight) refugees.[66]

After this inner (deciding to go) and outer (journey itself) adventure, and after a few months spent in Austria (Vienna, Geras), both refugees arrived in Rome safely and enrolled in the Czechoslovakian seminary. While Třebín was eventually dismissed from Nepomuceno College for aggressive behavior,[67] Skalický completed his spiritual formation and was ordained a priest in the Lateran Basilica just after Christmas 1961. Soon after, in 1962, he finished his theological studies and defended his licentiate. After that, Skalický started working as a youth minister in Saint Peter's oratory in the Vatican City. Simultaneously, he continued to study philosophy and was invited to take part of the last Second Vatican Council session as an *assignator locorum* (usher). Skalický of course did not miss the unique opportunity to witness the council's *aula* atmosphere. Later he cast this experience into a commentary on the *Gaudium et Spes* conciliar document, which soon became a prominent reference point for everyone in Czechoslovakia who wanted to deal with the council and its pastoral constitution.[68]

In 1966 the communist regime of Czechoslovakia expatriated Cardinal Josef Beran, who retired to Rome in exile. Very soon after his arrival, Karel Skalický became his second secretary. Meanwhile, Skalický

---

66. At this point it is necessary to note that the story has another dimension revealed to Skalický only a few years ago from newly discovered archival materials. Třebín and Skalický's escape was not really illegal. In fact, Třebín was already an agent of the StB (State Security—plainclothes secret police serving as intelligence and counter-intelligence service for the communist regime in former Czechoslovakia), and Skalický served as proof (a young idealist) of their escape's authenticity and Třebín's mission abroad. Třebín was sent to the Czechoslovakian seminary in Rome (Nepomuceno College) to collect information about the site, people, and life there.

67. When the undercover agent finished his mission at Nepomuceno College, he made trouble (slapped a cleric colleague in the face publicly) and for that reason was expelled from the college. With the mission accomplished, the agent was free to return undiscovered.

68. Skalický, *Radost a naděje*.

finished his theological doctorate and together with his secretarial duties became the editor-in-chief of the famous Czechoslovakian exile journal, *Studie*. He served as such until 1990, when the journal ceased publication. In 1968 Skalický officially became an Italian citizen. It was again possible for him to travel freely with an Italian passport. In the same year he was appointed assistant professor at Lateran University, where he became a colleague of Vladimír Boublík. Skalický had already met Boublík as a seminarian. Boublík was his teacher and mentor and eventually became his friend. Their friendship and collegial cooperation lasted until Boublík's death in 1974. After Boublík passed away, Skalický took over his job at Lateran University and became full professor of fundamental theology,[69] assuming the responsibilities of the Theology of Religions program that had been established by Boublík.

From being a student, youth minister, and council's usher, Skalický went on to become secretary to the cardinal, editor-in-chief, and later, professor at Lateran University. Skalický knew that if his university teaching career was to be fruitful, he had to keep contact with daily life and praxis. Therefore, despite his university commitments, he served as both chaplain in the house general of the Marist Brothers (1970–85) and spiritual administrator of Czechoslovak refugees in Italy (1970–79). His university activities were not limited to the city of Rome. He travelled a lot and lectured in most European countries, the United States, Zambia, Ecuador, Guatemala, and Puerto Rico. In 1987, he was named "Monsignor" by Pope John Paul II as a reward for his excellent service to the church. His illustrious career as respected professor and prominent clergymen was in full bloom when the communist regime in Czechoslovakia collapsed. This was the second time this evil ideology of the twentieth century turned Skalický's life upside-down. At the instigation of his long-time friend and confrere, Monica Schreier, he relinquished his post at Lateran University, left his commodious, sunny Vatican flat, and, at the age when most other university professors retire, relocated to the town where he was born and started working at full throttle once again.

In 1994 he became a local priest in Hluboká nad Vltavou. At the same time, he became professor at the newly established University of

69. As his successor, Skalický builds on the fundamental theology developed by Vladimír Boublík. It is especially obvious from the extensive introduction he wrote for Boublík's fundamental theology, which was discovered in the estate of the deceased Monica Schreier (a close friend of Boublík and Skalický) in 2014 and published two years later. Skalický, "Saggio Introduttivo," 11–85.

South Bohemia, Faculty of Theology in České Budějovice—a town nearby. From 1996 to 1999, he also served as its dean. In the year 2006 Skalický received the highest state distinction—the Order of Tomáš Garrigue Masaryk—from the president of the Czech Republic for his merit to the state in democracy, humanity, and the development of human rights. In the year 2010, he received an honorary doctoral degree from Palacký University Olomouc. In 2013 Skalický became professor emeritus of the University of South Bohemia. Nowadays, Skalický is still active, despite turning 91 in 2025.

At this point I should note that I joined the story of Karel Skalický in 1999 as one of his students in České Budějovice. Soon I became his student assistant (2000), and therefore (naturally), he served as consultant to my master thesis and later, also as promotor of my doctorate. After completing my doctoral degree in theology, I became a colleague of Skalický's and took over his responsibility for teaching fundamental theology at the University of South Bohemia. We worked together until the summer of 2016, when I moved to Prague and became a researcher at Charles University. Since that time, we have kept in close contact. His theology and exemplary lifestyle continue its formative influence on my own theology to this day.

In what follows I would like to summarize his fundamental theology. There are two main difficulties. First, Skalický's work is still in development, and it will be the task of future research to assess properly the whole corpus of his work. Second, because of the limited scope allowed by the genre of this text, I can only present a brief sketch rather than an in-depth study of his fundamental theology. But I have attempted this elsewhere.[70] Due to these limitations, I am going to introduce here only what is important for the development of my own thoughts on fundamental theology.

Skalický's first comprehensive text on fundamental theology was published in 1979. He wrote a textbook in Italian for his course at the *Instituto superiore di teologia a distanza: Ut Unum Sint*. He used this text for his lectures at Lateran University. Skalický's textbook so on became popular among students, and a second (corrected) edition was published by the Ut Unum Sint Institute in 1980. A third edition was published by the Lateran University Press in 1987. Finally, a fourth expanded edition

---

70. Štěch, "Fundamentální teologie a křesťanská identita," 23–38.

of Skalický's *Teologia fondamentale* was published in 1992.[71] Even though we may find in his "fundamental theology" a certain structure, Karel Skalický denies that he proceeded strictly systematically while writing it.[72] Despite this, its first version already consisted of ten didactic units (and Skalický decided to keep this structure in all future editions of the book), proceeding from the study of general religious phenomena (religious studies), through philosophical reflection of religion, to a theological interpretation of the crucial event of Christianity—that is, according to Skalický, the resurrection of Jesus Christ. After careful study of various concepts of the idea of God and its origin,[73] Skalický holds that the idea of God is born only from the need for orientation and meaning. Human beings need a plausible concept of meaning for their elementary residing in the world. However, he does not build this argument as another "proof" of God's existence. Rather he shares his own expertly reflected experience, his own explanation of the origin of the idea of God in the human mind.

Skalický shows that a religious fact (or phenomenon) is always somehow ambiguous. It oscillates between humanity and the divine while both elements are interconnected in their formations. After all, "each questioning for God always finally leads to questions for humanity."[74] But religious studies alone cannot answer Skalický's further question, if something in reality corresponds with the idea of God.[75] In the effort to answer this question, Skalický leaves the field of religious studies and turns to philosophy. After considering two traditional philosophical argumentations for God's existence, one of Saint Thomas and the other of Anselm of Canterbury, he considers the axiological argument of Albert Lang, popular in those years.[76] Skalický is neither satisfied with Lang, nor Saint Thomas, nor Anselm. Consequently, he attempts to work out his own argument, which would best be called "comparative." In this effort, he was inspired by Claude Trésmontant and Avery Dulles (especially by

71. Skalický, *Teologia fondamentale*.

72. Skalický, *Za nadeji*, 229.

73. Skalický concentrated his interest on different hypotheses about the origin of the idea of God provided by different scholars like Edward B. Tylor, Albert Lang, Wilhelm Schmidt, Sigmund Freud, Raffaelle Pettazzoni, Emile Durkheim, Carl Gustav Jung, and Peter L. Berger. Skalický, *Teologia fondamentale*, 230.

74. Skalický, *Po stopách*, 19.

75. Skalický, *Za nadeji*, 230.

76. Lang, *Wesen und Wahrheit*, 236–53.

his thinking in models). Skalický strives to prove the relative character of humanity and the world in relation to the absolute, which for him chiefly means to prove the createdness of the whole "worldly-human reality."[77] In his opinion, classical arguments for God's existence presuppose the relative nature of the world; thus logically they must reach the conclusion that the absolute cause of the relative world must exist. But is the world relative as such?

This question leads Skalický to a methodological approach different from those applied by Saint Thomas, Anselm, or Lang. He suggests human being in its humanity as a criterion[78] for the truthfulness of various non-biblical "universal" or "total" systems. Skalický identifies together six of them: 1) It is the system of chaotic-evolutionary myths, (2) the onto-static system of Parmenides, which has (according to Skalický) a parallel in the cosmology of the Upanishads, (3) the emanationist system of Neoplatonism, followed by (4) the substantial system of Spinoza. The fifth considered system is the (5) dialectical-spiritual one of Hegel, and the last "total" system of the world interpretation is (6) the dialectical-materialistic concept of Marxism-Leninism. In all these systems, the humanity of human being is always somehow reduced, while only in a framework of the biblical understanding of God and creation are all aspects and values related to humanity preserved. Therefore, Skalický concludes that this biblical understanding (or at least the concept of God), the creator of the world and all human beings as introduced in the Bible, is truthful because it is the only system that substantially and explicitly enhances the humanity of human beings and does not deny any of its aspects.

But this argument is the result of typically objectivistic way of thinking, very clear and accessible yet more probabilistic than apodictic. Skalický is aware of this and thus gradually resigns to all attempts to give another proof of God's existence. He points out only the rationality of religious faith in the (1) absolute, (2) transcendental, and (3) personal (and thus immanent) God. He presents this rationality in contrast with (and as an alternative to) the six ideological rationalities named above. The first step of Skalický's fundamental theology aims at presenting a credible concept of transcendence and emphasizes the rational aspects of religious faith open to more concrete formulations in human lives. In

---

77. Skalický, *Za naději*, 231.

78. "But it would be misapprehension of this idea to see it in the sense of the Pythagoras's 'pantón metron anthrópos.'" Říha, "Fundamentální teologie," 139.

short, he starts his fundamental theology with a firm conviction that the God of Christianity demands human love instead of any proof of his own existence. God does not need people for any manifestation of his own existence. But God nonetheless appreciates them as partners in relationship. Skalický presents this conviction in the form of a "Cartesian dream":

> I had a dream that soon after Descartes gave perfectly irrefutable and strictly apodictic proof of God's existence, God revealed to him and said, "Excellent! Your proof of my existence turned out well. You will surely enter the history of human thought with it. But consider what you have done to me by your proof. Actually—if I may say so—you force me to exist. From this moment, when you irrefutably proved that I am, I cannot presume to pretend as if I would not exist. Can you see what this means? Probably not. Thus, pay good attention: in order that you understand, I am not a God of reign and hegemony, who always needs scientific ideology for his own justification, proving undeniably the existence of such a super-ruler, but I am God of freedom who can do without such ideology very well. I reveal to you today that I will confuse all human thinking. I will confuse it in such a way that you will search for me but you won't find me if you say: not our speculating, but our love to him, love exceeding each other's love, is the highest proof of His existence. Thus, do not say that God exists because we strictly-logically proved him as a necessarily existing Being. But rather say: He exists, because we love him more than anything else. Take account that I do not want to exist alone out of my own power of independent Being. I want to exist also—and primarily—through the power of your love, your will to God. Thus, give existence to my Being. Make an endeavor that I will exist not only because of your logical considerations, but that I will exist through the power of your active and creative love."[79]

But in Christianity people are exposed not only to the question of God's existence (or non-existence) but also to the question of Jesus Christ (the God who has been born and died; the God who became human). This point was already central to Skalický's predecessor at the Pontifical Lateran University in Rome, Vladimír Boublík. Skalický naturally builds upon Boublík's thought and further develops the resurrection, especially of primary importance for any kind of theology, and for fundamental theology above all. The Czech Jesuit philosopher Karel Říha affirmed this

---

79. Skalický, *Po stopách*, 182.

position in his review of Skalický's *Teologia fondamentale*: "Possibilities and tasks of fundamental theology can be only measured on the unique character of this problem (of resurrection)."[80] For Skalický, the phenomenon of resurrection points out the mysterious unity of the full deity and full humanity in the person of Jesus Christ—God who has been born, has lived, and has died, while (mysteriously) not losing anything from his divinity. Therefore, he rejected the common argumentation of classical apologetics that consider resurrection as a kind of "peak miracle" (the Miracle among other miracles) as one-sided and too evidentialist. From that perspective, Jesus functions as a mere bearer (messenger) of God's revelation. Skalický is looking at the theological problem of resurrection in a more complex way. In the revelation of Jesus Christ, there is an identity of the Revealer with the mystery of salvation (with what is revealed). "The deepest truth about God and the salvation of humanity shines out for our sake in Christ, who is both the mediator and the fullness of all revelation" (DV 2). With explicit reference to the Dogmatic Constitution on Divine Revelation of the Second Vatican Council, Skalický sees resurrection as 1) inseparable from revelation, 2) a concrete and visible manifestation of God in human history (from below), and 3) *mysterium salutis* (from above) at the same time.[81]

In his theological investigations of resurrection, Skalický starts searching for data already available. What do we know about resurrection? What texts do we have available? What are their differences, and what do they have in common? After an extensive and careful analysis of biblical narratives dealing with resurrection,[82] Skalický goes deeper in his linguistic investigation. What language is employed to present the paschal event? What words, terms, and expressions are used? Skalický finds four different styles (languages) which are together used in the Bible to describe resurrection[83] and thus concludes that for human language, it is an extremely difficult challenge to speak about the event, which is real and eschatological at the same time.[84] Is it possible to share reality (both historical and trans-historical) and the (continuous) radical

---

80. Říha, "Fundamentální teologie," 146.

81. Skalický, *Teologia fondamentale*, 195–202.

82. Skalický highlights 1 Cor 15:3b–5 as the most important text for interpretation of the paschal event from theological as well as historical point of view. Skalický, "Třetího dne," 17.

83. Skalický, "Třetího dne," 24–31.

84. Skalický, "Třetího dne," 31.

newness of such an event at once? Skalický thinks it is only possible through the "combination of various languages which complement one another, and yet it seems they oppose each other,"[85] as expressed for instance by Melito of Sardis in his famous work, *Peri Pascha* (*On Pascha*). These different languages unveil different aspects of the paschal event and drive our attention to the level of its truthfulness and meaning. Yet they never exhaust all the possibilities to express the mystery so close and yet far away too.

What does it mean for us that Jesus was born, lived, died, was buried, and rose from dead on the third day? If it makes sense for us, is it true? Did it really happen? And how? "What actually happened that night in Jerusalem?"[86] These questions are, for Skalický, "an urgent invitation to the decision of faith."[87] They challenge the human ability to believe, which is closely related to the human ability to receive and give love. There is always a desire to receive and give love at the baseline of each human faith in resurrection. Yet such a desire is not anonymous because it is grounded in concrete historical events and the particular experiences of certain historical personalities who loved (e.g., Rom 13:8; Eph 5:2; 1 John 4:10–11, 19, etc.) and were loved (e.g., John 11:5, 36; 13:1, 34; 15:12, 17; etc.). Skalický sees Christian faith as way of exercising love, which is inseparable from confidence:

> When you think of it, the Christian faith is inseparable from confidence in the truthfulness of the personal witness of the apostles. Whoever is not willing to be confident to the other, in principle, is not actually able to believe in the true Christian way. Faith in God and the willingness to trust people are uniquely interconnected in Christian faith in a way that has no equivalent in any other religion. . . . In Christianity, it is not possible to separate faith in God from confidence in people.[88]

With confidence in the witness of Saint Paul (especially to 1 Cor 15:3b–5), Skalický provides an excellent exercise of what fundamental theology should be: an art of reflected confrontation of the various ways of thinking, knowledge, and understanding (empirical, rational, intuitional, creative, provisional yet informative, improvisatory, and

---

85. Skalický, "Třetího dne," 31.
86. Skalický, "Třetího dne," 41.
87. Říha, "Fundamentální teologie," 147.
88. Skalický, "Třetího dne," 43.

spiritual). In other words, while remaining within a thorough scholarly discourse, Skalický's fundamental-theological account of resurrection meets the call that theology must be "beautiful, compelling, engaging,"[89] as well as "understandable, and existentially relevant."[90] Fundamental theology shall respect specific competencies of all possible approaches to theology and its themes and look for good values they may offer[91] to our complex theological investigations—similar to what Saint Paul says in his first letter to the Thessalonians: "Test everything (and) hold fast to what is good" (1 Thess 5:21). Consequently, we may say that Skalický does not want to exclude (*a priori*) any possibility for understanding love, the basic principle of our humanity and of human relationships (including the one with God). He uses hermeneutics as well as the metaphysical principle of *analogia entis*.[92] He always attempts to mediate both theory as well as praxis.[93] In the fundamental theology of Skalický, there is a principal of openness to all expressions of faith as relationships to the divine or "sacred." But at the same time, there is a firm confession of the particular faith in Jesus Christ, who is, according to Skalický, the only one who reveals the true meaning of humanity and who actually is the only true (incarnated) answer to the mystery of humankind: the way, the truth, and the life (John 14:6).

In claiming this, Skalický invites his readers to track with him the "unknown" God,[94] the initially anonymous "sacred" perceived and experienced in human lives. In his theological endeavor he wrestles with the sacred,[95] motivated by a desire to fill the term "sacred" with progressively more accurate content or meaning in a way by which the face of Jesus Christ—the Resurrected One—slowly appears in clearer contours on the canvas of Skalický's fundamental theology. For Christianity, Jesus Christ is the concrete content, shape, substance, and meaning of the sacred. It is already obvious that emphasizing resurrection and its inseparable link to revelation plays a significant role in Skalický's fundamental theology. At this point it is possible to conclude that the initially apophatic start of Skalický's fundamental theology turns cataphatic. It satisfies rational

89. Roach and Dominguez, *Expressing Theology*, 19–22.
90. Štofaník, "Popularization and Autobiography," 68.
91. Špidlík, "Skalického fundamentální teologie," 608.
92. Skalický, *Po stopách*, 28.
93. Říha, "Fundamentální teologie," 134.
94. Skalický, *Po stopách*.
95. Skalický, *V zápase s posvátnem*.

minds with arguments pointing towards the credibility of Christian faith but at the same time reminds us that the more we think we know God (*Deus Revelatus*), the more mysterious, hidden, and "unknown" (*Deus Absconditus*) God appears. Precisely this kind of interplay of cataphatic and apophatic moments in Skalický's theology discloses the need to choose a horizon in which to think (and live) theology. In which mode of thinking do we approach the experience of revelation and the reality of resurrection? In which mode of thinking do we reflect upon our theological life?

Skalický distinguishes two horizons of thinking: intellectualistic and existential. The latter he prefers as a principle for his own fundamental theology, because he holds that only within an existential framework can an authentic Christian faith be born. In the former horizon we ask and answer. But questioning and answering are not enough! In the second horizon we search and create, we fight for the meaning of one's own existence in this world.[96] In other words, the reality of resurrection must relate to a radically existential experience of and with the Resurrected One. Such an experience is certainly also an experience of revelation (or revelatory experience as such). The search for the meaning of Jesus' resurrection is the main and specific task of fundamental theology for Skalický. In an interview with Jan Regner for Radio Vaticana, he says, "I regard as the primary task for fundamental theology today that which my predecessor at the Lateran University, Vladimír Boublík, started to work out and what I attempted to do in my Italian fundamental theology—that is, to point out the credibility and deep meaning of the resurrection of Jesus."[97] But where is this meaning? And how could it possibly become credible (and existentially relevant) for contemporary people?

The hypotheses of a transcendental God might be only a matter of reason and respond only to the question of the rationality of the world's origin. The real idea of God can only arise in the context of faith. If we search for the meaning of human dwelling in this world and, thus also, the meaning of this world as such, it is necessary to leave the path of searching for solely a hypothesis of God and, further, to find the courage to enter into relationship with him. Karel Říha thinks that "the meaning of life as a whole . . . is not only an active relating . . . but a relationship of the (human) spirit as such to transcendence."[98] In this sense, meaning is

96. Říha, "Fundamentální teologie," 150.
97. Regner, "Víra a fundamentální teologie," para. 12.
98. Říha, "Fundamentální teologie," 148.

the unity of discovering and creating and is characteristic of all human relationships. If I pin meaning into some relationship, simultaneously, I find it there as well.[99] But religion from a Christian perspective is rather an interpersonal relationship between a personal God and created persons who relate to God as individuals (and as groups or communities of faith). There is God on the one side, who relates himself to human beings through his Word (*Logos*), and this Word is God, who says "human"—fervidly and lovingly insofar as he himself became human—he incarnates. On the other side there is a human being who relates to God through his/her calling of faith "God, Father!" It is a very simple yet deep meaning of the word "Theo-logy."[100]

For Skalický, this interpersonal communication between humanity and the divine is possible only because God reveals himself in human history to confirm his promises of a new life for a humanity wrestling with and foreseeing its own physical termination (death), in fear and trembling. Karel Říha summarizes Skalický's emphasis on resurrection as follows: "Anticipation of death and new life is the meaning that was revealed in history, which is the life, sacrifice, and resurrection of Jesus, in its radical way. Since then, the decision of faith, the decision towards fullness of life, has been carried by unification with Christ. To become open to life in Christ means to have a deal on his life, death, and resurrection. Therefore, the question of resurrection is crucial for fundamental theology."[101]

Skalický's emphasis on resurrection enabled through experiences of revelation sheds light on the mystery of life and death (those of Jesus, as well as of our own). Through understanding resurrection and the experience of revelation, people can see at least a glimpse of meaning of their own life, historically framed by birth and death. Skalický's focus on questions regarding the meaning of life and death (existential questions) marks and implies the new understanding of fundamental theology and a new conception of metaphysics understood as an "open system of correlativity of the acts of the mind—knowing and wanting—in the necessity of being and freedom of love."[102]

As such, Skalický's fundamental theology offers a clear and concrete (Christian) vision of the absolute horizon of humanity which we are not

99. Říha, "Fundamentální teologie," 148–49.
100. Štěch, "Fundamentální teologie a křesťanská identita," 30.
101. Říha, "Fundamentální teologie," 150.
102. Říha, "Fundamentální teologie," 148.

only able to experience, but through faith, with "it," we are also able to enter a personal relationship. Precisely because the absolute horizon of humanity is, from a Christian perspective, not a blurry vision but rather a particular person. It is not "it" but "the person" instead. It is Jesus Christ, the God with whom we may become friends;[103] the God with whom we cooperate on the constant improvement of our humanity and the world in which we live. Following Boublík, Skalický's fundamental theology maintains not only theological but also anthropological focus. Quite simply, we cannot love God unless we love our fellow human beings and the world. I think this is what fundamental theology may offer Christians as well as non-Christians (to all those who search the mysterious meaningfulness of the world and our being in it)—a reflection of the God-human mutual relationship experienced within the scene of this world and its particular (contextual, sociohistorical, geographical . . .) landscapes. According to Skalický, emphasizing and enhancing humanity could be used as the criterion to assess the truthfulness of one's world view (*Weltanschauung*) because (at least in Christian terms) everything that improves humanity and preserves it in all its aspects directs us and leads us to God—who became one of us in order to reveal that human being shall be nothing else then human being heading towards its completeness and fullness offered by God as salvation.

2.2.3 Cardinal Avery Dulles, SJ, and the Dynamics of Christian Life

"When he was at the table with them, he took bread, blessed and broke it, and gave it to them. Then their eyes were opened, and they recognized him; and he vanished from their sight."—Luke 24:30–31

When I was about to start writing my master thesis in theology, I wanted to work on the theme of power. It seemed to me that Christianity as such didn't have much to do with power. But the Catholic Church learned well from history how to work with power and how to use it in both good and bad ways. I wanted to discover the fundamental, theological mechanisms of power and authority in Christianity in general and in the Catholic Church in particular. I proposed my topic to Skalický and had a few long discussions with him about it. In the end he convinced me that I should wait and learn its theological grounds a bit more before dealing with the

103. Boublík, *Setkání*, 126–27.

theme I proposed. I remember that I felt discouraged and dejected at that time. My proposal got rejected as too complicated, and the deadline for master thesis was looming. But Skalický did not leave me without a suggestion: "Why don't you take this book and learn something about the different models of the church first?" The book to which he was referring, and which subsequently gave me, was Dulles's classic *Models of the Church*.[104] A new path opened, and I set off upon it. After the successful defense of my master's thesis on Dulles's ecclesiology, I continued to elaborate his theology during my doctoral studies. In due time, the Jesuit cardinal became for me one of the most important theological points of reference. This was also due to my personal encounter with Cardinal Dulles, in whom I found a welcoming, generous, and critical mentor during the concluding phase of my theological training. Therefore, Dulles embodies the last exemplary theologian with whom we will investigate further paths for fundamental theology.

Avery Dulles was born in 1918 to a very important Presbyterian American family who made history in the United States. His father was a diplomat and later served as secretary of state during the presidency of Dwight D. Eisenhower.[105] Avery's uncle (Allen Welsh Dulles) pursued a career in the Secret Service and became the director of CIA (1953–61). Avery Dulles was raised in the Presbyterian tradition. But his family was secularized, and religion did not play a big role in the family. Young Avery completed his basic education at the prestigious private school, Saint Bernard in New York, and was sent to Switzerland to start his high school education. After two years he returned to the United States and graduated at the prestigious Choate School in Wallingford, Connecticut. The road to university was open, and the excellent student had several options. He opted for Harvard, "but unlike many of his peers, he had no career goals in mind when choosing a college."[106] He started to study politics, (medieval) history, art (especially literature and painting), and later, philosophy. During his early Harvard years, he was a fully secularized young man living in the typical tempo of the era. The world was for him an original, uncreated reality explained conveniently by physical laws.[107] In his autobiography, he writes:

---

104. Dulles, *Models of the Church*.

105. John Foster Dulles (1888–1959) was an American statesman and anti-communist and served as secretary of state between 1953–59.

106. Carey, *Avery Cardinal Dulles*, 22.

107. Dulles, *Testimonial to Grace*, 4.

> Every notion of God was in my opinion a sort of deus ex machina, an invention of the human mind to explain away facts which could not be otherwise accounted for. Man having been produced by chance, it seemed illusory to hold that he had any ordained end or was subject to any moral strictures not of his own making. Morality, then, could be interpreted as a texture of conventions woven by the ingenuity of men for reasons of convenience. Revealed religion I dismissed as a vain attempt to find sanctions (where none in truth existed) for such conduct and mental attitudes as proved conductive to social well-being.[108]

Consequently, Dulles considered happiness the aim of all human endeavor. This kind of happiness, however, was deeper than a simple sensual delight. It went hand-in-hand with struggle. Dulles was fascinated by the figure of Prometheus whose destiny he found as a "more valid conception of heaven than did the eternal bliss of the angels."[109] Dulles characterizes his first year at Harvard as wild and chaotic, completely in consonance with his skeptical and materialistic worldview.

> Desisting somewhat from artistic pursuits, I took up at this time the cult of what is called "experience." As a result, my freshman year was a wild and chaotic year, marked by an excess of drinking and a corresponding deficiency of sleep. My room, distinguished by the possession of a percolator, became a center of nocturnal revelry. Whole nights were passed in aimless jocularity either here or in shoddy Boston bars; my attendance at classes was casual at best.[110]

Dulles dramatically changed his lifestyle when he began to study philosophy during his second year at Harvard. Among others, Aristotle and Plato engaged his interest the most. Both ancient philosophers attracted him by their "sounder outlook on the universe than the narrow mathematicism of Descartes and Spinoza or the sterile skepticism of Hume and Kant."[111] From Aristotle, he learned that reality is not chaotic but structural. He also learned a respect for final causes that restored his confidence in reason as the best link between one's personal self and the outer world. In his memoirs Dulles writes, "The chaotic world in which I had been living yielded place to the hierarchic universe of Aristotle. . . .

---

108. Dulles, *Testimonial to Grace*, 4–5.
109. Dulles, *Testimonial to Grace*, 6.
110. Dulles, *Testimonial to Grace*, 8.
111. Dulles, *Testimonial to Grace*, 11.

On apprehending the dignity of reason and its true relation to reality I all at once felt at home in the universe. It is impossible for me to exaggerate the sense of joy and freedom which came from this discovery."[112]

Further, Plato convinced Dulles that moral values could have an objective basis and showed him that there are some objective standards of beauty. Dulles sensed that Plato's concept of goodness is very close to his own intuitive idea of beauty. "Both were self-contained and supreme; each was to be sought for its own sake."[113] Besides reading Plato and Aristotle, he also studied (modern) Catholic Aristotelians like Jacques Maritain and Étienne Gilson. During this time, he also met with Paul Doolin, a charismatic Catholic convert who was assigned to him as tutor. Later, Dulles expressed that Doolin had a great influence on his own conversion because he presented him with a vivid picture of Catholic faith.[114] However, the more immediate role in Dulles's conversion had been (maybe quite paradoxically) his own political reflections.[115] Dulles studied Marxism and fascism and refused both ideologies as false and even dangerous. He was not strictly persuaded by democracy and did not consider it an ideal system either. At the end of his political considerations, Dulles concluded that regarding questions of state organization, it is necessary to accept the authority of qualified leaders. Here, we see Dulles stepping out of his former liberalist positions (dominating the Harvard milieu at that time) towards the acceptance of authority not only in politics but also in faith and morals. However, all his attempts to find some political ideal failed, and he faced the same failure with regards to the eternal question about the aim and purpose of human being. A hostile silence spread out in the soul of the young, searching student, and emptiness entered his heart. He expressed it as follows: "In the darkness of my inner world the highest human instincts were confronted with a vacuum. Into that vacuum stepped the grace of God. The barren desolation of my materialist philosophy, its utter falseness and my humiliation at discovering it so, gave God His chance."[116]

God's gracious act of giving the self to Avery Dulles came in a very simple way. His witness continues in the melancholic scene of a cold, rainy, and grey February day when he could not concentrate while reading

---

112. Dulles, *Testimonial to Grace*, 14–15.
113. Dulles, *Testimonial to Grace*, 17.
114. Dulles, *Testimonial to Grace*, 22.
115. Dulles, *Testimonial to Grace*, 33.
116. Dulles, *Testimonial to Grace*, 35.

Augustine's *City of God*, assigned for a course of medieval history. He left the library and ambled along the Charles River towards Boston town, enjoying the rain and the atmosphere of that day. Suddenly he stopped in front of a young tree. "How could it be . . . that this delicate tree sprang up and developed and that all the enormous complexity of its cellular operations combined together to make it grow erectly and bring forth leaves and blossoms?"[117]

In this moment God's grace forcefully entered the life of the future cardinal. From that simple encounter with a tree, the evidence of order sprang. It became clear that there was something behind it, something that determines the order, the order which has beginning and end. There must be a kind of intelligence that determines the order of things. Where there is intelligence, there must be also some kind of free will. Intellect and will are constitutive moments of personality. Such an unexpected eureka moment penetrated everything that Dulles read and lived so far. All his previous intuitions suddenly converged together, and at that very moment, his new life begun. He writes in his autobiography:

> I was conscious that I had discovered something which would introduce me to a new life. . . . That night, for the first time in years, I prayed. I knelt down in the chill blackness at my bedside, as my mother had taught me to do when I was a little boy and attempted to raise my heart and mind towards Him of Whose presence and power I had become so unexpectedly aware. I recited the Our Father. The words came slowly, and I had to make many new starts before the whole prayer unfolded itself in my mind. Our Father Who art in Heaven. Hallowed by Thy name. Thy will be done on earth, as it is in heaven.[118]

Dulles's conversion started when he responded by an act of faith (prayer) to the revelation he experienced during his walk on the riverbank. This first (conscious) touch of God's grace was accepted, and he responded in faithful prayer. Communication was established, and this experience motivated Dulles to search for community, a denomination, where he could live his newly born Christianity. But it still took a lot of time before he confessed Jesus Christ in the Catholic Church. Because of his family tradition, he first searched for a Protestant denomination. But, according to his own words, the Catholic Church attracted him most,

---

117. Dulles, *Testimonial to Grace*, 36.
118. Dulles, *Testimonial to Grace*, 38.

especially for the consistency of its doctrine.[119] The inner drama of the development of Christian faith took place during the Second World War. After Pearl Harbor, Dulles joined the Navy and served as an officer until 1946. Only after the war could he continue to follow his vocation and become a Jesuit, priest, and theologian. The voice of Avery Dulles was significant in theology (especially systematic and fundamental) from the 1950s until he passed away in December 2008. His monumental work (twenty-nine books and more than eight hundred articles and book reviews) still enjoys the attention of many contemporary fundamental theologians. For instance, Gerald O'Collins, in the preface to his *Rethinking Fundamental Theology*, writes that today it is necessary to preserve and renew the legacy of various great fundamental theologians of twentieth century. He names Dulles first among them.[120] Dulles is mentioned in a few references in his latest book on revelation as well.[121]

Dulles's story is rich and adventurous indeed, but for the purposes of this chapter, I decided to tell only its beginning.[122] It is because there are three crucial elements clearly present, which, according to my estimation, sets in motion the dynamics of Christian and theological life (as they did for Dulles). It is revelation (a young tree); faith (born in the night prayer); and community, the church (searching for a community in and with which to live one's own faith in fulness). These three notions represent pylons on which Dulles's life and theology rest.[123] In what fol-

119. Dulles, *Testimonial to Grace*, 61–62, 84.
120. O'Collins, *Rethinking*, vii.
121. O'Collins, *Revelation*.

122. To those whom I disappointed by not continuing to tell the story of Avery Dulles and want to learn more about his life and work, I recommend Dulles's autobiography, *A Testimonial to Grace and Reflections on a Theological Journey*, as well as the extensive biography by Patrick W. Carey (Carey, *Avery Cardinal Dulles*) and the exhaustive bibliography of Cardinal Dulles, including witnesses from many who worked closely with him during the last years and days of his life: Kirmse and Canaris, *Legacy*.

123. Reflections on revelation, faith, and the church are fundamental to every theology. If we have a random look at different books on fundamental theology, we find that this triad represents key elements from each of them (Becker, *Fundamental Theology*, xvi–xviii; O'Collins, *Rethinking*, 15; O'Collins, *Fundamental Theology*, 22; Fries, *Fundamental Theology*, 389; Bulst, *Revelation*, 12; Dulles, *Revelation Theology*, 10; etc.). Although we may see certain links between the aforementioned terms in these books, their authors usually treat them separately. But it is the mutual interconnection of these terms that is of great benefit when we think about the ground for contemporary fundamental theology. The ways people practice their beliefs are deeply rooted in the theoretical concepts of the church, faith, and revelation that they have in mind while living their (theological) life. These concepts are also parts of their religious identities.

lows, I would like to offer a basic mapping of mutual interconnections between revelation, faith, and the church, which were treated by Avery Dulles separately in different sets of models.[124] Together they represent a basic structure of Christian life and theology. When I realized that the experience of revelation is that to which one responds by faith and, at the same time, searches for its communal anchorage, the whole of theology started to make sense to me. The pieces of the puzzle started to fit together. I began to see theology as holistic endeavor, attempting to balance unity with a plurality of discourses, the one faith of the church with a legitimate theological pluralism. I converted to theology again, and since that time I've had to do it many times, hence as much as I had to continually convert and reconvert in my Christian life. Converting to Christianity is not something one does once and for all. It is an everyday adventure, and it is so also for theology. We need to continually challenge ourselves by questioning its very nature time and time again.

As we have seen, conversion was important for Dulles in his private life, and consequently it projected itself into his theology (especially fundamental). In his view, fundamental theology and conversion are closely linked. It is necessary to note that Dulles does not understand conversion as an initial decision to believe in Jesus Christ and become a Christian. From his perspective, conversion is a lifelong dynamic process of communication between people and God. It is a process of practicing the inner dynamics of Christian religious life in the space between the human and the divine. "Conversion is a dynamic process demanded at every stage of the Christian life, and . . . fundamental theology is therefore of existential import to all believers. Being a Christian is not a static condition, for no believer has faith fully and securely in hand."[125]

Continuous conversion is a *modus operandi* in the search for Christian religious identity, which is not set up once and forever (e.g., by primary conversion or baptism). It is rather a lifelong learning process. Learning to live in community with our fellow human beings, in community with all creation, and learning to live in the presence of the Triune One, God the eternal Creator, who rests and dwells within and beyond of everything. If there is such a thing as Christian religious identity, it is certainly not only belonging to a church. Church-belonging is rather a natural consequence of a dynamic process of encountering and

---

124. Dulles, *Models of Revelation*; Dulles, *Testimonial to Grace*; Dulles, *Models of the Church*.

125. Dulles, *Craft*, 54–55.

experiencing revelation, expressing and living faith (continuous conversion), and attempting to live in community (with fellow human beings, the world, and God). The community of people living in this world with God and heading towards his kingdom to come may be called "church," in the broad sense of the term.

The notion of continuous conversion corresponds well with Avery Dulles's conviction about the necessity of re-actualizing the understanding of revelation, faith, and the church in every epoch. On an institutional level, this was undoubtedly an attempt of the Second Vatican Council, to which Dulles was a committed interpreter. He "became one of the most creative interpreters, supporters, and promoters of the council and an advocate for reforms in theology and church structures."[126]

Although Dulles advocates the progressive spirit of the Second Vatican Council and holds that conciliar emphasis on ecumenism and religious freedom clearly surpasses earlier teachings of the church, he still thinks the church of the Second Vatican Council is the same church as it was in the times of Nicaea, Chalcedon, Trent, and First Vatican.[127] To be honest, I am sympathetic to such an approach. I have learned from Dulles that when one would like to start doing good theology, it is better to start by interpreting and reinterpreting the tradition of understanding the fundamentals of Christianity (already existing theological interpretations), rather than refusing all that was done in the field before and starting everything anew. It is about the creative acceptance of tradition. I hold that it is all too easy to throw old things away and buy or get new ones. But this kills creativity. A more creative approach is to accept old things and think about how or in which way we may use them anew. It is about the whole idea of material recycling. Let us use old material again. Let us use old things anew—and why not in a completely different and surprising way? According to my conviction, creativity is one of the skills most needed for theologians, since they are literates, poets, and storytellers above all. On this issue Cardinal Dulles notes, "History, of course, does not stop. . . . Progress must be made, but progress always depends upon an acceptance of prior achievements so that it is not necessary to begin each time from the beginning."[128]

I would like to add that progress does not necessarily mean recycling in terms of remaking the same thing. In other words, plastic from a

126. Carey, *Avery Cardinal Dulles*, 212.

127. Guarino, "Why Avery Dulles."

128. Dulles, "Vatican II," 11.

recycled bottle does not have to become material only for making another plastic bottle. That material might appear again in rubber shoe soles, for instance. Theologians, from the perspective of Dulles, contribute a significant deal to the constant reformation and appropriation of the church and its teaching. They are workers in a religious and symbolic recycling factory.[129] Creativity, however, brings a diversity of perspectives, positions, and conceptions, which may not always be in consonance. On the contrary, it often brings disagreements, tensions, and conflicts too. Therefore, it must be balanced with genuine dialogue and a loving attitude among those who theologically elaborate revealed truths.[130] Perhaps because he was a convert, Dulles was always interested in the problematic linked to discussion about unity in diversity. Thomas Guarino, in his article on Dulles, formulates the central question this way: "How could a variety of positions be understood as complementary rather than as contradictory?"[131] It was most probably this ecumenical disposition of his personality, accompanied by an imperative of inner and outer dialogue suggested by the Second Vatican Council,[132] that drove Dulles to study different perspectives on revelation, faith, and the nature of the church and organize them into models.

Perhaps the most famous are his *Models of the Church*. This book, originally published in 1974 and subsequently republished several times, was well received and soon became one of the classics in ecclesiology,[133] enjoying attention even to this day. The same method he used for his ecclesiology, Dulles applied again when writing on revelation and faith. Using the method of models in theology has several merits,[134] but at the same time, we must also acknowledge some disadvantages which has been (some rightly) criticized by Dulles's opponents, for instance, Joseph

---

129. Sanks, "Homo Theologicus," 530.

130. "All in the Church must preserve unity in essentials. But let all, according to the gifts they have received enjoy a proper freedom, in their various forms of spiritual life and discipline, in their different liturgical rites, and even in their theological elaborations of revealed truth. In all things let charity prevail. If they are true to this course of action, they will be giving ever better expression to the authentic catholicity and apostolicity of the Church" (UR 4).

131. Guarino, "Why Avery Dulles," para. 8.

132. Especially in its constitutions *Lumen Gentium* (dialog within the church) and *Gaudium et Spes* (dialog with the world). Štěch, *Tu se jim otevřely oči*, 268–69.

133. Carey, *Avery Cardinal Dulles*, 255–56.

134. Štěch, *Tu se jim otevřely oči*, 62–63.

Komonchak and Christoph Schönborn.[135] One of the objections against using the method of models in theology is that it is too bookish and uncreative.[136] Well, it may seem like that (and perhaps it is), but I benefitted from this method both in my own theological training as well as in my teaching. I used both *Models of the Church* and *Models of Revelation* as textbooks for my students to motivate them to read in English and because of the clarity of their positions, masterfully defined. Despite that, I never forget to warn my students that these are just models and that reality is always more complex and colorful. Yet it is worth studying models because they give us a first clue about the topic under scrutiny. Perhaps creating models is not super creative, but it certainly awakens curiosity and provokes one's own creativity. In this way I am grateful and indebted to Avery Dulles, who taught me to focus on my students more than on my own creativity. I must say that the basic courses were a bit boring. But more interesting were the discussion seminars because in them, students gained a certain level of knowledge, which enabled them to be more creative in their own attempts to theologize. Study and discussion are vessels for communication. Study without discussion remains impotent and discussion without study is a shallow waste of time. Only well-informed discussion makes sense and has the potential to change positions, lives, and practice. Only such discussion may become transformative—and if theological, also ecclesial-transformative.

In general, Dulles's whole theology could be characterized as ecclesial-transformative, and as such, it rests upon a "kind of symbolic realism in which reality is held to have a symbolic structure."[137] That can be perhaps best illustrated by Dulles's account of revelation. He holds (and the vast majority of theologians today would agree) that revelation comes to the human being in a symbolic way and is symbolically mediated by a certain set of religious (Christian) symbols embodied in Christian religious practice.[138] Religious symbols have hermeneutical as well as instrumental traits[139] and therefore might be perceived as both signs available to semiotic practice (an activity of interpretation) and instruments of transformation (personal, social, cultural). This allows for being outside the symbol (to interpret it) and, at the same time, inside the

---

135. Carey, *Avery Cardinal Dulles*, 482–84.
136. Dulles, *Craft*, 52.
137. Dulles, *Craft*, 20.
138. Dulles, *Craft*, 17–39.
139. Neville, *Truth*, 1–2.

symbol (to encounter a reality signified by it). But the questions remain as to the proper interpretation (if there is such a thing) of the religious symbol (i.e., the semiotic perspective) and the participatory engagement with and within it, because this has a potential to lead persons into salvation. While semiotic practice (often limited to textual interpretations) may fall short of indwelling, understanding a symbol as an instrument of transformation allows for participatory engagement with realities behind or beyond the symbol. (It allows one to enter the symbol.) According to Michael Polanyi, participatory engagement with a symbol is crucial for symbolic meaning-making, and as a matter of example, he mentions religious rituals and worship as "the highest degree of indwelling that is conceivable."[140] It is necessary to note that despite Polanyi's symbolism and emphasis on personal engagement in the process of making meaning, Dulles's conception of revelation is also largely inspired by Rahner's symbolic ontology and the notion of symbolic being. It also influenced by Lindbeck's approach to religious doctrine.

Dulles himself understood a symbol as different from a simple indicative sign. A symbol contains the reality to which it points and, as such, functions as an access point or open door to that (transcendental) reality. For Dulles, a symbol is an "externally perceived sign that works mysteriously on the human consciousness so as to suggest more than it can clearly describe or define . . . a sign pregnant with a plenitude of meaning which is evoked rather than explicitly stated."[141] Being quite a definitive understanding of symbol, this is acceptable. But according to Michael McGowan, it must be extended if a symbol is supposed to become a variable designating "an open space to house anything through which God decides to reveal."[142] For McGowan, this extension should be carried out in three ways: (1) a symbol should be perceived not only externally but internally too; (2) there must be space left for the possibility that a symbol does not evoke any emotions; and (3) revelation must be given the possibility of stating exactly what it clearly states. It might be the case that revelation expresses more than it states, but it may not always be the case, argues McGowan.[143] However, revelatory symbols are for Dulles

140. Polanyi, *Personal Knowledge*, 198.
141. Dulles, *Models of Revelation*, 131–32.
142. McGowan, *Bridge*, 120.
143. McGowan, *Bridge*, 120.

those which "express and mediate God's self-communication"[144] and as such, they "carry a spiritual power able to convert and save."[145]

In sum, revelation as symbolic communication is always mediated through experience in the world. It includes what is communicated but also more than that, because it is generally open to any interpretation. In other words, symbolic communication is an encounter of free, personal beings where the symbol plays an indispensable, mediating role. God's revelation as an interpersonal communication has a symbolic structure because human life is symbolic.

> The human person is essentially symbolic, a being that is both material and spiritual and hence constantly expresses itself in symbolic acts. Human beings reveal themselves to others and to themselves when they perform properly human acts which are always symbolic: speaking, working, dressing, eating, lovemaking, travelling, worshipping, falling ill, and dying. . . . If God wishes to communicate with homo symbolicus, this revelation must take a symbolic form or road. God the revealer is necessarily God the symbolizer.[146]

From the perspective of Christian theology, God immerses himself into immanence to such an extent that he mysteriously becomes immanent (in Jesus Christ) and thus present (as both symbol and symbolizer, message and messenger, communication and communicator—a true agent of mediation) in the material world, culture, and history, while remaining fully transcendent at the same time.

Together with the rediscovery of experience and (auto)biographical narrative as a source for theology (theological thinking and living), the speculative nature of theology started to shift its form to participative. Revelation as symbolic communication requires participatory knowledge to develop its transformational potential into effect. While speculative knowledge is merely a result of human reason, participatory knowledge is a confluence of the free divine gift and its free, grateful acceptance. God gives the person a share in his own revelation. God enables people to gain participatory knowledge of Godself. God offers revelation as a gift. Thus, we cannot perceive revelation only as a process of sending a message (through a particular channel) and its acceptance but also as an

---

144. Dulles, "Symbolic Structure," 56.
145. Carey, *Avery Cardinal Dulles*, 311.
146. O'Collins, *Rethinking Fundamental Theology*, 40–41.

active, engaging, and challenging relationship motivating (and stimulating) human imagination and activity. Participatory knowledge results in wisdom, which transforms its recipients, changes their behavior, and gives insight into the mystery that the human mind is not capable of understanding on its own.[147] At this point we may conclude together with Ros Shecterle: "Revelation because of its inherent quality of, and tendency toward, 'symbolic' communication, is foundational for all of theology."[148]

This account of revelation as symbolic communication must be accompanied by proper reflection on faith and community (church), because from the perspective of Dulles, "fundamental theology . . . must ask not only how we get to God but how God comes to us. It must maintain a theological as well as an anthropological focus."[149] Dulles's typologies are notoriously known, so I need not repeat them in this short chapter. But I would like to highlight the more important point that revelation, faith, and the church alike are, for Dulles, not static categories but highly dynamic processes by the very nature of their content. Together they create a dynamic of Christian life, as I suggested and argued for in the conclusion of my book on Dulles's fundamental theology.[150] In what follows, I will now present briefly the mutual interplay between the human and the divine (the anthropological with the theological) within revelation, faith, and community (church). When closely related to each other and applied in a general grid of history, they result in dynamics of Christian life which may provide the argument for a dynamic, yet firm concept of Christian identity. In this I was inspired by Avery Dulles and would like to offer this theory here, as a matter of conclusion for the present chapter in which I wanted readers to encounter Dulles as one of the three most important source-theologians for my own theology.

Revelare (Lat.) means "to remove a veil,"[151] and the semantics of this word points toward the dynamic charge of the term itself. After the veil is removed, we see something that we had not seen before. It is the reality of divine revelation, the mysterious, intimate self-disclosure of the divine to the human being on the one hand (from above) and the mysterious, utterly human, inner experience of the divine (from below), on the other hand—and both at the same time. Most of the Christian denominations

---

147. Dulles, *Models of Revelation*, 136–39.
148. Shecterle, *Theology of Revelation*, 7.
149. Dulles, *Craft*, 56–57.
150. Štěch, *Tu se jim otevřely oči*, 341–51.
151. Dulles, *Revelation Theology*, 9.

would probably agree that revelation requires faith as an appropriate response. Despite that, revelation also means an awakening of reason, which, together with faith, works toward the evidence for the existence of the divine and one's own relationship with it. Therefore, the dynamics of revelation take place within a mysterious encounter between the human and the divine. Revelation as a free divine activity is an objective category. But it is also a very subjective category of the recognition of revelation in human experience that decides whether the free offer of divine grace will be accepted. The mysterious interplay between the human and divine is what sets Christian revelation up as a dynamic concept that happens both globally and locally—on a personal as well as a communal level every day—while being firmly grounded in the history of salvation in the event of Jesus Christ, the peak of revelation and the Revealer, at once and for ever. "Revelation is God's free action whereby he communicates saving truth to created minds, especially through Jesus Christ as accepted by the apostolic Church and attested by the bible and by the continuing community of believers."[152]

The dynamic of revelation is closely related to that of faith. But dynamics of faith involve reason as well, because faith and reason are integral parts of each human mind. Even if one is not a person of religious faith, one has a kind of faith, confidence, or thrust to one's own sensual perception, to related persons, to experts, etc. Without faith we cannot exist in community; we would not be able to function in society. At the level of religion, an intertwining and constant dialogue of religious faith and reason is what is going on when an individual as well as a community searches for God's face, when people do theology. It was the encyclical letter of the late Pope John Paul II, "Fides et Ratio," where the Roman Catholic church acknowledged with enormous clarity the importance of religious faith for reason and vice versa. In words of Fides et Ratio, "It is faith which stirs reason to move beyond all isolation and willingly to run risks so that it may attain whatever is beautiful, good and true. Faith thus becomes the convinced and convincing advocate of reason" (FR 56).

Since "Fides et Ratio," faith and reason haven't stood in opposition anymore but rather have supported one another in mutual service. Like revelation, the dynamics of faith (where reason plays an indispensable role) include two inseparable moves: ascending and descending. Faith includes the human aspect, as it is a human response to revelation (from

---

152. Dulles, *Models of Revelation*, 117.

below—ascending) but also a divine aspect, as it is also gracious gift of God (from above—descending). Probably most Christians, if you ask them about their faith, would affirm these two aspects. Faith happens inside believers and involves reason as an active agent of making decisions to respond to revelatory experiences. But one of the crucial experiences for Christians is also the constant and critical deficiency of human faith, which may be surpassed only by the generous activity of the One in whom Christians believe. God alone is perceived as the donor of faith, which our limited human powers can accept and possibly maintain. The decision to believe is thus nothing more and nothing less than the acceptance of the divine gift of faith in response to revelation, which in general is always the offering of that gift.

Because of its nature, faith cannot simply be a requirement or demand of the human longing for God, even when God is desired. Such desire must not be the desire of a spoiled child screaming until it gets what it wants. Rather, it must be an obedient desire (*potentia oboedientialis*), as Karl Rahner puts it, in the sense that *Dei Verbum* understands it:

> The obedience of faith (Rom. 13:26; see 1:5; 2 Cor. 10:5–6) is to be given to God who reveals an obedience by which man commits his whole self freely to God, offering the full submission of intellect and will to God who reveals, and freely assenting to the truth revealed by Him. To make this act of faith, the grace of God and the interior help of the Holy Spirit must precede and assist, moving the heart and turning it to God, opening the eyes of the mind and giving "joy and ease to everyone in assenting to the truth and believing it." To bring about an ever deeper understanding of revelation the same Holy Spirit constantly brings faith to completion by His gifts. (DV 5)

But obedient desire describes faith mostly from below. To describe it from above, we may use another Rahnerian term, "supernatural existential" (Ger. *übernatürliches Existential*), which speaks about the divinely given dispositions of human beings that enable them to accept divine revelation. Fundamental theology should always reflect on both characteristics of faith, since it is truly something that happens between the human and the divine.[153]

In searching for God's face (who is the one revealed?), one meets other seekers who share their experiences. Some of them, of course, have very similar experience to one's own, and it is with these that one usually

153. Knauer, "Potentia," 79–90.

comes to share the dynamics of faith. In this sharing of faith and theologizing together, our personal recognition of God and its expression in our personal response of faith meets its communal dimension. *My* faith searches for and becomes *our* faith. Groups of believers and worshipers are formed. They tend to become somehow institutionalized. Through this process, the church as we know it today is born. From the Christian perspective, the church is an ordinary human society, organized like an association of beekeepers or a motorcycle club (from below—ascending). But also, it has its sacramental character, where it is described as the *mystical body of Christ* or the community of saints (*communio sanctorum*) (from above—descending).[154] In line with the dynamics of revelation and faith, we find that the dynamics of the church also happen between the human and divine.

If we consider all these three dynamics together, we can see that they are relational above all because they are only possible from the perspective of a relationship between free persons. The personal God reveals and offers a gift of faith that calls the one who accepts it into community with Godself. People recognize revelation as an invitation to relationship, respond by faith (which is fundamental for any human relation to the sacred), and create spiritually powerful communities to mirror God's promise of salvation to all humanity (and to the entire world). The church is an environment which anticipates the eschatological promise of the kingdom to come (Matt 6:10). Based on such relationality it is possible to create an intellectual construction which describes the dynamics of Christian life and allows one to place one's own life of faith in a particular context (geographical, social, and historical), into the historical framework understood as the history of salvation. Let me note at this point that if we understand history in Christian terms as the history of salvation, we may also understand the spaces in which we live as environments or landscapes of salvation. This conviction is supported by the famous claim

---

154. I am aware that this is predominantly a Catholic-sacramental approach towards the church. The Son is the sacrament of the Father, and the church is a sacrament of the Son. De Lubac, *Catholicism*, 29. The Second Vatican Council was very much in favor of this concept as well (Cf. LG 1, LG 9, 48; SC 26; AG 5; GS 42). The sacramentality of the church is certainly a disputable question. But I believe many denominations may agree that the church is not only a matter of the people in it but is also a matter of their God. The church may be also sacred when it embodies and treasures the meeting of the human with divine.

of Edward Schillebeeckx, that there is no salvation outside the world—*Extra mundum nulla salus*.[155]

The dynamics of revelation, faith, and community (the church) happen or evolve in time and space. History is perceived by Christians not as a Godless flow of time but rather as an existential framework where God is not a passive entity. The same could be said about the world and its places. The Christian God is certainly the God of places. He abandons his placelessness and reveals in places. He becomes temporarily present "here." For instance, in the prophet Isaiah, God speaks of himself as being "here" (Isa 52:6; 58:9; 65:1–3). In the New Testament, Jesus came to this world because he was sent here by his Father (John 8:42) and because Mary recognized and accepted this "here" of the One who still is "there." Through Jesus Christ, the incarnated, crucified, and risen (Luke 24:5) *Logos*, God revealed himself as being eternally present in places "here," yet paradoxically remaining in the far numinous (timeless and placeless) "there" (eternity). True divinity meets true humanity in Jesus Christ, "where" they become one, still discernible, yet inseparable in the plan of *Heilsgeschichte*—the history of salvation.

From this perspective, we may find that the dynamics of Christian life in all places and in each moment of history, from creation to its eschatological fulfilment. Let me demonstrate this with the five following (paradigmatic) examples:[156]

1. At the *time and place of creation*, it is creation itself which might be called revelation. God reveals himself as the Creator of creation. The relationship of the first people, Adam and Eve (men and women being together is a complementary principle of humanity), can be understood as the prototypes of faith, in both its strengths and weaknesses. Their partnership with God, each other, and all creation in the garden of Eden can serve as a model of the primordial community.

2. At the *time and place of the chosen nation*, God reveals through his words and mighty deeds (e.g., Pss 111:6; 118:15–16), interpreted

---

155. Schillebeeckx, *Church*, 12.

156. I elaborated these paradigmatic categories more into depth in the conclusion of my book on Cardinal Dulles's fundamental theology (Štěch, *Tu se jim otevřely oči*, 341–50) but do not yet include with the notion of place. I consider my earlier understanding of the dynamics of Christian life only according to the paradigm of time as one-sided and incomplete. It appears more complex if the paradigm of place (and space) is also included.

by the forefathers and prophets of Israel. God also offers covenant to the people of Israel (Gen 17:4; 17:13; Exod 19:5; Lev 24:8, etc.), where he reveals his will to have a relationship with them. Israelites respond to such revelatory experiences by their faith because they saw themselves as a community of people who wanted to walk the paths of God (Ps 25). Yet their faith often falls short of the promised faithfulness. The chosen nation continues to misbehave, according to the previously accepted covenant at many times and in many places. Despite that, God always wants to restore the community with his chosen nation and continues to do so at many times and in many places in history. There is no time in history and no place in this world that would be exempt from God's salvific searching activity towards human beings.

3. At the *time and place of the new covenant*, it is Jesus Christ who is the Revealer and revelation at the same time. The Logos incarnates at a particular place when time comes to its fullness (Gal 4:4) and calls people to faith through announcing the kingdom to come—the kingdom which is his, as it is his father's in heaven. Those who believe to and in Jesus form a community of disciples which represents the first model of the church from a Christian perspective. The community of disciples follows Jesus' life story all the way up to Calvary, where only the most faithful stand under the cross. What seems at the beginning as a promise for revolution in Jerusalem is replaced by the depression of the Good Friday. The community of disciples falls short of faith and is dispersed in crowds until it is reformed and transformed by a renewed post-paschal faith in the Lord risen. The time that matured in Christ at that place of Palestine is where the substantial was revealed in the mysterious interplay and identity of Revealer and revelation. But the history of salvation running through the places of this world has not yet come to its eschatological conclusion.

4. At the *time and place where we are*, the dynamics of revelation, faith, and community continue to unfold. Even though Christians consider the event of Jesus Christ (incarnation, birth, life, death, and resurrection) to be the peak of revelation, God has not stopped since then to reveal himself in other places during time (*revelatio continua*).[157] God continues encountering people and calls them to

---

157. It is perhaps better to call continuous revelation a "dependent revelation,"

faith in all places and times. This faith is kept and maintained in Christian communities (churches) which await the second coming of Jesus Christ.

5. At the *time and place of the eschaton*, the revelation of the eschatological Christ's second coming will take place, according to the faith of Christians. This revelation, however, could be perceived in line with other paradigmatic times and places within the theoretical plan of the history of salvation as having both timely and spatial dimensions. As we do not know about the time, we also do not know about the place. But we know that there will be an end of time (e.g., Matt 24:14) and that the holy town of the heavenly Jerusalem will descend on the earth (Rev 21:2). Despite this eschatological or final revelation, there will be both the faith of human individuals in its eschatological excitation (the faith radically opened by hope for salvation) and also the collective faith of the eschatological community of disciples facing the momentum between the darkness of the last judgement and the light of the morning of new creation, when God will be all in all; in particular places which will be transformed by God's presence into something we may perhaps call saved placelessness.

I hope that this little theological exercise can help illustrate what learning from the past masters in drawing theological maps could do to your theology. It becomes more speculative, but certainly it can maintain its focus in practice. In this case it is possible to understand the dynamics of revelation, faith, and community, or the church to which we belong,

---

following the terminology of Paul Tillich. Tillich, *Systematic Theology*, 126–27. Tillich's distinction between original and dependent revelation is helpful, but Gerald O'Collins suggests adding a category of eschatological revelation for having a complete terminological clarity on different aspects of revelation. "Whatever precise form it takes, we need a terminology that adds an essential third point and distinguishes between (1) revelation inasmuch as it reached an unsurpassable, once and for all fullness with Christ, his apostles, and the outpouring of the Holy Spirit, (2) inasmuch as it continues today and calls people to faith in a living encounter with God, and (3) inasmuch as it will be gloriously and definitively consummated in the life to come. In one sense revelation is past (as 'foundational'), in another sense it is present (as 'dependent'), and in a further sense it is a reality to come (as 'future', 'final', or 'eschatological'). The Book of Revelation witnesses to God revealed as 'the One who is, who was, and who is come' (Rev. 1:4, 1:8; 4:8). As foundational, revelation 'was'; as 'dependent', it 'is'; and as final, it 'is to come.'" O'Collins, *Revelation*, 103. Thus, it is possible to speak about continuous revelation but always from the perspective of the above-mentioned distinction, which includes the past, present and future to come.

within a larger, theoretical plan of history, understood as the history of salvation. At the same time, it is possible to see one's own place and role in concrete contexts defined by concrete time and space, defined by the here and now. From this perspective, we may come to see our small personal stories as indispensable parts of the larger narrative of the God-human encounter. This little theological exercise helped me, at least, to understand my own life as meaningful. Through it, I became aware that through my faith I participate in the eternal movement of Christ's realization throughout time and space. If that is true, everyone who believes in him has a particular share in the whole of history and the universe. From a theological perspective, people are meaningful because time and space is meaningful. I am meaningful because the time and places in which I live are meaningful. All this is meaningful because, through Christ, with him and in him, we are pilgrims on the way to the mystery of life, to the completeness and fulfilment of our spatial-temporal humanity. That is the dynamic of Christian life, which is fundamentally theological.

At this point I shall stop introducing the three outriders of theology who influenced my own present scouting of this territory of rugged terrain. In the following section, I would like to continue a brief meditation on how the discipline of fundamental theology could move forward. What are the most important impulses that came to me from my theological predecessors, and how (or in which way) might they be used to meet the task of rethinking fundamental theology today? Where are the possible links of youth ministry and youth theology? Concerning the last question, I will try to make these links more explicit in section 2.3, preceding the larger part 3, in which I will describe my encounter with youth ministry and share my interpretation of the story of youth theology.

2.2.4 Rethinking Fundamental Theology

When I set myself the task to try and rethink fundamental theology from my own auto/Theo-biographical perspective, I followed the advice of Gerald O'Collins. The first step one must take in pursuing this kind of a task is to go back to the great masters of the discipline, remember them, and try to further develop their legacy.[158] I deeply resonated with such a call and asked myself: Whose legacies should I remember, rethink, and perhaps develop a little? Then, I started to write down my list of

---

158. O'Collins, *Rethinking*, vii.

inspirations, the list of those who influenced me on my (fundamental) theological journey. I came to conclusion that Avery Dulles, Karel Skalický, and Vladimír Boublík were the most inspiring sources for my own theological endeavors. I must confess that, for me, the theology and life of Karel Skalický was and continues to be not only informative but also formative in terms of thinking theology as an integral part of my own life.

Theology is an exercise of the Christian life, as well as the pondering of experiences experienced through this life. These may even take a form of a scholarly reflection. But the very fundament of theology lies in its own complexity of interconnecting personal human being with God and other human beings, allowing it to form human communities and bring people into unity with all that exists upon the earth and beyond. The theological nature of Christianity makes it possible to anchor one's own life in the universe. That suggests living and thinking in two generic plans: 1) according to time and 2) in relation to place.

It seems to me that since the time of the great scholastic masters, much of theological living and thinking was done primarily according to the first generic plan of time. The second generic plan of place was a bit downplayed or often remained subsidiary, if not altogether ignored.[159] This was not the case in biblical times. Attention to place is coming back in some recent theological concepts.[160] However, emphasizing one over the other leads to an imbalance. Thinking and living according to the plan of time leads to abstraction. This is because time is the abstract category par excellence. Time is a conceptual idea worked out by the reflecting mind. To the contrary, thinking and living in relation to place emphasizes (radical) human embodiment. People dwell in places. This way of perceiving reality is less abstract and more concrete. It suggests more practice then theory. While the demands of places make people more practical, the demands of time make them more theoretical. Yet both emphases must be in balance to avoid undue abstraction on the one side and unreflected being, here and now (resulting in a cult of enjoyment and consumption), on the other.

In times of struggle with secularism, abstract and theoretical focus on time helps theology remain present in academia and defend its own "scientific" character (as discussed above). However, this kind of achievement resulted in an imbalance, to which many reactions came from many

159. Bergmann, *Religion*, 369.
160. Štěch, "Here I Am," 148–59.

different sides during the twentieth century. At least within the Catholic Church, more attention was given to the context of the world in which Christianity lives and, consequently, to the concrete and the practical. The conciliar document, *Gaudium et spes*, bears clear witness to it. But a practical refocusing of theology was present in Christianity throughout the spectrum of diverse denominations. The emergence of theological attempts, like the theology of the world,[161] theology of earthly realities,[162] contextual theology[163] and many others, tried to overcome the traditional division of theology into systematic and pastoral (practical). All these trends suggested many things and drew attention to many problems with which we must deal in our lives on this earth (and theologically too). They kept the dimension of time in their respectful theologies, yet they brought our attention back to the places where we live. They helped us see the artificial distinction between thinking and acting for the sake of taking both seriously and uniting them together once again.[164]

Both styles of thinking and living, according to the generic plan of time and the generic plan in relation to places, have their merits. But if they remain isolated from each other in separation, they suffer from considerable weaknesses. Therefore, their unity is desirable because of that unity's ability to balance our theologies to equally maintain the abstract and the concrete, the theoretical and the practical. Theology, if done this way, can become what Terry Veling calls "practicing theology"[165] and what I would call "holistic theology." All three theologians with whom I was discovering the fundaments of theology were already pointing in this direction. Thanks to them I am now convinced that this paradigm shift has great potential for rethinking fundamental theology today. Thinking and living time (and in time) must be paired with thinking and living in relation to place. The inner dynamic of Christian life (suggested above,

161. Metz, *Theology*.

162. Thils, *Théologie I & II*.

163. A leading figure of the Taiwanese Presbyterian Church in the late 1960s, Shoki Coe, is commonly understood as pioneer of contextual theology. Coe, "Preliminary Word." His "new conceptualization and terminology triggered a massive reorientation of Christian thought, both East and West, North and South, truly a paradigm shift. In the following years, all the major Christian traditions have grappled with the implications of *contextualization*, the term used by Protestants, and *inculturation*, the term preferred by Roman Catholics." Shenk, "Contextual," 193. Contextual theology started to develop with names like Luzbetak, Schreiter, Stackhouse, and many others throughout Christian denominations.

164. Veling, *Practical*, 5.

165. Veling, *Practical*, 4.

because of my study of Cardinal Dulles's theology) shows how time and place might be connected in dealing with traditional notions of fundamental theology like revelation, faith, and community.

All in all, fundamental theology is traditionally very sensitive to the environment in which religious experience takes place. This environment consists of time and space (and consequently also places), yet for conceptual purposes, this environment is commonly called "context." All theology today is (and ought to be) contextual[166] and public at the same time,[167] because contemporary theological thinking takes place in a specific time, characterized by a fragmentation of formerly universal interpretative frameworks. One such interpretative framework is that by which Christian civilization, or perhaps better Christendom, was largely ideologized into a form of dominating the world. At this point I need to clarify that by Christian civilization, I understand a close link between Christianity and European cultural heritage. Consequently, the term "Christendom," in my way of interpretation, emphasizes the fact that this form of Christianity exercised its sovereignty and decisive (cultural) power beyond its original geographic borders. In Christendom, theology was used to justify power claims of Christian civilization. The Roman Catholic Church in the Baroque period was especially often presented as a fully visible and hierarchically organized community equal to the kingdom or republic (e.g., Robert Bellarmine), where the supernatural was clearly manifested. Theology provides clear and distinct evidence of such a manifestation.[168] This is not a true picture of the world anymore. Any attempt to rethink fundamental theology today must more likely confirm that Christians are living after the collapse of Christian civilization (or Christendom, if you prefer the term launched and better maintained by chiefly Protestant authors).[169] Catholic authors do not speak much about post-Christendom, but their reflections on Christianity living in the globalized world (e.g., Bevans, Schreiter) correspond to the concept of post-Christendom to a certain extent. "As modern culture is evolving toward a new stage—usually called postmodernity—increasingly it is recognized that Western theology, developed in response to the realities

166. Bergmann, *God*, 1.
167. Moltmann, *God*, 1.
168. Dulles, *Models of the Church*, 8–9.
169. Hauerwas, *After*; Murray, *Post-Christendom*; Murray, *Church*; Hall, *End of Christendom*; etc.

of a Christendom that no longer exists, must adapt to this changing culture if it is to serve the church."[170]

It is characteristic of such a context that, while Christianity in the Global South flourishes today,[171] European Christianity experiences disorientation and decline—it loses members, property, power, and influence in society.[172] In my opinion, what has changed is not only the way Christianity is lived but also the way people understand its (doctrinal) content. Therefore, the future task for theologians could be defined as threefold: (1) actively participating in intra-denominational discussions about the development of doctrine, facing immense social and cultural changes of the world today; (2) connecting theology into the interdisciplinary nature of thinking characteristic to contemporary times; and (3) constantly emphasizing to the public the relevance of theology as a service to thinking and to the sustainable development of life on both a local as well as a global scale.[173] Note that each of the three tasks encompass both dimensions of time (past, present, future) and place (particular and general). Fundamental theology has the potential to serve us well for the purposes of dealing with the above-mentioned tasks. In fact, they can define the future understanding to fundamental theology in return.

These tasks were, however, already somehow present in the theology of Dulles, Skalický, and Boublík. Attentiveness to contextual situations, especially in terms of time (but not so much of places), was significant to Boublík. He wanted to present a vital Christianity for his contemporaries, and thus he was focused on the mutual interplay between humanity and the deity in history, with a special focus on his contemporary era. Such an encounter between humanity and the divine, from Boublík's perspective, finds its summit in the person of Jesus Christ. Therefore, each theology deserving to be named Christian should have a Christological foundation. This was a departure point for Skalický too. From his perspective, the study of resurrection is tightly bound with incarnation, and revelation is fundamental to all theology. Both Boublík and Skalický agree that in Christ, human beings are most likely to find completion and the fullness of their humanity. This makes Christianity attractive as a comprehensive answer to existential questions people face in each epoch of human history. Daily life is, for them, the source for theology, with which it must never loose

170. Shenk, "Contextual," 193.
171. Jenkins, *Next Christendom*, 1–14.
172. Geiser, *Community of the Weak*, xi.
173. Štěch, "Teologie," 65.

contact. Boublík and Skalický were in their time members of a pioneering generation which attempted to bring (Catholic) theology back down to earth from the abstract heights of metaphysical speculation and return it to ordinary people to make it understandable, applicable, compelling, and life-transforming again. Much of this theology was lost during the time of Christendom and in the long fights of the Catholic Church against modernity, especially during the nineteenth century. To sum up, the study of the fundamental story of Jesus Christ in terms of time (preexistent Logos, incarnated Logos, and Logos risen) and place (Where is Jesus Christ?), actualized for each generation and living in a certain time and place, contextually set up what seems to me to be the greatest impulses of Boublík and Skalický for rethinking fundamental theology today.

Avery Dulles was somehow a different kind of personality than both Czech theologians. He was also very different in his theology. Yet I loved his theology for its conceptual clarity. For me it was like an invitation to visit a blooming meadow. Dulles introduced me briefly to all the kinds of plants and delicate fauna growing there. He also suggested ways by which I might continue studying that meadow as such and in a concrete way too. He left me alone in the meadow of theology to deal with all that was around me. I realized that I am also part of that scenery. I am not detached from the little creatures living secretly under the leaves or the tiniest plants growing near the earth's surface in the shadows of the bigger ones. Dulles helped me to assemble intuitions and findings derived from the works of Boublík and Skalický. He taught me the craft of theology. Based on the study of my three apostles of fundamental theology, I would define (or better, describe) the discipline of fundamental theology as the Christ-centered, existentially relevant reflection on the dynamics of Christian life, consisting of the dynamics of revelation, faith, and the Christian community.

After I finished my theological training, my attention was drawn to the context of distinguishing and holding both the generic plans of time and space together, as well as learning to rethink fundamental theology from my three necessary and prerequisite master predecessors today, in the time and place where I am at home. But all that seemed to incomplete to me. Something was still missing. What else did I need? To master the craft of theology, one always needs creativity and invention. These qualities are certainly coming from inside the person (they are gifts to be discovered and developed) but not alone. Both creativity and invention come from dialogue with others. They need to be exposed to the constant and ongoing dialogical process of encountering others, the world, and, in theology, God. Fundamental theology used to be done chiefly from a confessional perspective, no matter if it were Protestant[174] or Catholic.[175] Even though all three of my masters of fundamental theology were highly open and dialogical, their visions of the discipline always remain confessionally limited. Their points of view are defined by the traditions from which they come. Only quite recently did I discover two attempts to rethink fundamental theology from a programmatically ecumenical perspective. One is Ivana Noble's *Tracking God*; the other is Hans-Peter Geiser's *Community of the Weak*. Both are quite creative and innovative, each in their different and respective ways.

While Noble's *Ecumenical Fundamental Theology* is written in the more traditional code and style of academic writing, Geiser's *Community of the Weak* is truly a postmodern *bricolage*—creative and daring to reframe the future. Surely both books are masterpieces attempting to write theology in a new way, as more appealing to contemporaries. It is noteworthy that both Ivana Noble's and Hans-Peter Geiser's books represent important contributions to the field, and after reading them I became convinced that the only relevant way forward for fundamental theology is in this direction. This is not to suggest that doing confessional fundamental theology is wrong. On the contrary, there is indubitable value in denominationally exclusive perspectives, especially for interdenominational dialogues about the foundations of faith. But following the expression of Avery Dulles (already quoted above)—that fundamental theology is properly theological yet pre-dogmatic because "it does not rest on a finished theory regarding revelation and its mediation through tradition and ecclesiastical pronouncements,"[176]—I think that real progress in fundamental theology may come only if constructed in an ecumenical way and perhaps with an openness to world religions as well.

An ecumenical orientation to the discipline of fundamental theology rests upon theology's foundational relationality,[177] and consequently

---

174. E.g., Becker, *Fundamental Theology*.

175. E.g., Ormerod and Jacobs-Vandegeer, *Foundational Theology*.

176. Dulles, *Models of Revelation*, 15.

177. "Theology is not an isolated subject, finding its fulfilment in an isolated God. Some form of community is needed, where the relationships that are reflected are lived as reality, and not only thought as ideal modes of being. Likewise, there needs to be an access to the wisdom accumulated in tradition, and its symbolic forms of meaning that allow the reading of one's life journey as a journey with others towards God's kingdom." Noble, *Tracking God*, 235. See also Geiser, *Community of the Weak*, 388.

its invention and creativity cannot be *only* based upon individual personal qualities (even though this is certainly important). But they are essentially nurtured from relationships as well. Rethinking fundamental theology must therefore start with embracing essential relationality, with a focus on creativity. Such orientation has the potential to help maintain and treasure what is true and good while approaching theology in terms of the neo-scholastic tradition, on the one hand, and yet still allow theologians to be creative in terms of a post-critical approach to theology on the other. According to Dulles, postcritical theology is to be conceived as an art rather than a science. Thus, theology might be defined as the art of correctly articulating Christian symbols,[178] because it tries "to reunite the creative with the cognitive, the beautiful with the true."[179]

A post-critical understanding of theology as art implies that it is not just an art of abstract thinking but a complex art of living instead. This notion was taken up by some postmodern theologians like Roger Haight, for instance. In his seminal book *Dynamics of Theology*,[180] Haight argues for a dynamic understanding of theology not only in conceptual terms but also in terms of a life dynamic. From Haight's perspective, theology is a reflexive way of life, constantly flowing and undergoing change and transformation and facing novelty. Dynamic theology as a dynamic way of life has a historical consciousness, which is "the condition for the possibility of creative theology."[181] I am very much in favor of Haight's dynamic concept of theology and his creative effort to present theology anew. At the same time, I think proper creativity in theology comes when a historical consciousness meets with a proper awareness of place, since relational dynamics do not happen only through an abstract projection onto the screen of history but rather in concrete places instead. Awareness of places is included in Haight's fundamental theology rather implicitly through discussions of context (which is understood in sociohistorical terms, though the geographical dimension is not discussed explicitly). It also applies a concept of action (action always takes place somewhere) within both human life and theology. Following the French philosopher Maurice Blondel, Haight understands human life as a project,[182] and each project is a creative action indeed. This is well noted by Geiser, who

178. Dulles, *Craft*, 8.
179. Dulles, *Craft*, 15.
180. Haight, *Dynamics*.
181. Haight, *Dynamics*, 5.
182. Haight, *Dynamics*, 8.

develops this notion further and speaks about a "creative ecology of living,"[183] forming a context for contemporary fundamental theology. According to Geiser, the task of theology in general and fundamental theology in particular is twofold: (1) social living (living with historical consciousness) and (2) ecological living (living in the geographically perceivable ecosystems of places).[184] Through performing and striving to fulfil this twofold task, theology becomes a project and a creative activity—a life-transforming endeavor and ground for *biocentric* spirituality.[185]

> Making theology into a project . . . could mean getting out of the classroom into the environing ecology of the close and farther surroundings of our world in order to develop a concrete project with local people in the neighborhood or our personal communities who want to see theology walk and work, compose and paint, craft and construct, model and sketch, empower and change the globe. This could be a community action, an educational program, a church meeting, a peace project, a shelter facility, a youth cellar, a cultural event, an artistic performance, a political campaign, or a global initiative, all translating and incarnating theology into the concrete and visual, local and experiential places of people's homes and houses, habitats and communities in theology's environing surroundings of an ecology of life.[186]

Geiser is attempting to form a new style of fundamental theology. He uses traditional themes in new contexts and suggests new themes of culture, postmodernism, ecology, and power. He sees fundamental theology in the twenty-first century as "confronted with the issues of culture, postmodernism, ecology, and power. Within the parameters of these four themes a contemporary fundamental theology will have to be developed in the future."[187]

His patchwork fundamental theology is motivated by public engagement and is intentionally designed as artistic and personal.[188] Geiser's fundamental theology in *The Community of the Weak* appears to me as one of the most (if not *the* most) interesting, creative and challenging of the

---

183. Geiser, *Community of the Weak*, 383.
184. Geiser, *Community of the Weak*, 384.
185. Geiser, *Community of the Weak*, 391.
186. Geiser, *Community of the Weak*, 385.
187. Geiser, *Community of the Weak*, 447.
188. Geiser, *Community of the Weak*, 444.

fundamental theologies published in present decade. Geiser introduces one of the possible ways forward in rethinking fundamental theology. This is especially the case in his balanced treatment of traditional and new themes within fundamental theology, his innovative approach to its method and style (using personal narrative), and the way he connects theology to other disciplines, as well as to praxis and daily life. Geiser's fundamental theology is global and local at the same time. It allows for the compression of time and space in terms of seeing the problem of wounded people throughout history and across places, across the globe. In this sense, his theology is truly postmodern, reimagining the task of Christian theology today, as theology rising from the personal windows of lived experience (as stated on the back cover of Geiser's thick book).

If I were to summarize what I have learned from his fundamental theology, I would say that if theology should respond to the calls of life, it must become life itself. It sounds easy, but it is extremely demanding. Theologians must recognize that they are not neutral observers within the realities that they study and interpret. Only when they unlearn what they think they already know and open themselves up to new ways of understanding, presenting, and interpreting theology will they be able to respond to the challenges of contemporary life. Rethinking fundamental theology requires not only different mode of thinking but also and primarily new mode of life. It involves "metanoia"—repentance (2 Pet 3:9) from all previous theologies and a complex conversion to theologies we either are trying now or will be doing in the future. As Jungian *wounded healers*,[189] we must know and be sure that we must repent from each present theology we do and each future theology we will do. Our theologies will be judged together with all what we are, were, and will be. Our theologies are inseparable from our auto/Theo-biographies.

2.3 FROM FUNDAMENTAL THEOLOGY TO YOUTH MINISTRY AND BACK AGAIN: THE ROAD TOWARDS YOUTH THEOLOGY

In his vision for rethinking fundamental theology, Gerald O'Collins distinguishes between three styles of doing theology: 1) academic, 2) practical, and 3) contemplative.[190] Each of them is specific in its own way.

189. Sedmak, *Doing Local Theology*, 9.
190. O'Collins, *Rethinking*, 323–25.

But only together, says O'Collins, are they able to contribute towards a well-balanced and healthy Christian theology. The complementarity of disciplined reasoning, transformative action, and sincere prayer is that for which O'Collins calls. From his perspective, rethinking fundamental theology means rethinking theology as such, including its styles and methods.[191] Rethinking fundamental theology involves rediscovering the nature of human relationships with others, with the world and the revealed God. Rethinking fundamental theology is an invitation to reconsider our complete worldview and renew our faith ever again. Rethinking fundamental theology requires openness to Christian revelation (dynamics of revelation) calling us constantly to convert our minds and hearts (dynamics of faith) and change the ways of our personal as well as social lives (dynamics of community).

My personal effort to rethink fundamental theology brought me to youth ministry, and I found there a profound source of inspiration. This is especially the case in youth ministry's recent endeavor to make up its own theology, which is sometimes called the theology of youth ministry (and sometimes also youth theology). The lack of clarity in labels and terms used for describing emergent concepts is significant for the phase of searching the road towards youth theology. It seems to me that designing youth theology from out of experiences in youth ministry is a way of designing a contextual fundamental theology of its own kind. Therefore, to engage fundamental theology with youth ministry (i.e., in its effort to design youth theology) seems to me to be potentially beneficial for both. While fundamental theology may offer theoretical expertise and tools for designing intelligible concepts, youth ministry may offer, in return, enormous practical and empirical experiences from an environment in which faith is being born and its subsequent Christian identities are being formed in their earliest stages. A mutual dialogue between youth ministry and fundamental theology could be fruitful for designing youth theology, which would be recognized as a theological discipline. More broadly, it has the potential to contribute towards practicing theology as a holistic dynamic between personal and communal auto/Theo-biographies. To see whether this potential is real or illusory, we must cross the bridge from fundamental theology to youth ministry and hear the stories of youth ministry's search for theological foundations on the road towards youth theology. This chapter is therefore a bridge. A bridge from

---

191. O'Collins, *Rethinking*, 322.

an extensive treatment of fundamental theology to youth ministry and youth theology, presenting my point of view on its origins and history, conceptualizing it, scouting its landscape with my three apostles of fundamental theology and, finally, suggesting some impulses for the future rethinking of that discipline).

Bridges are very interesting places in this world. We can use them to cross small and big rivers, chasms, and ravines, or to move between individual buildings of shopping malls. Bridges allow us to go back and forth. They connect riverbanks, boroughs (in New York for instance), and even whole states (like the bridge between Oberndorf by Salzburg in Austria and Laufen in Germany). Physical bridges connect riverbanks. They connect landscapes divided by water hard to cross. More importantly, they connect people from both sides—people able to cross the bridge and meet. Bridges are relational, strategic objects, making it possible for people to reach others in a relatively easy way. Bridges make connections and relations possible. In addition to physical bridges, there are also virtual bridges with the capacity to connect different opinions, worldviews, and, of course, theologies as well. Bridges can connect a variety of approaches within one single academic field of theology—particularly, fundamental theology and youth ministry/youth theology, for our purposes. But at the same time, they maintain their function of connecting particular people, their lives, bodies, hearts, souls, ideas, beliefs, and thoughts.

Much more can be said about bridges. But at this point I would like to emphasize the essential bi-directionality of bridges. We may walk to and fro. We may experience and explore both sides of the bridge. We may cross from fundamental theology to youth ministry and back again. That bridge is, however, tiny and perhaps also a bit dilapidated. There seems to be a common conviction that, even though the disciplines with which I am concerned in this text are part of the same realm of Christianity, they have very little in common (if anything at all). However, I think there always was a bridge: a bridge of common interests in the re-actualization of the Christian message and faith, in particular contexts of time and place and a common sensitivity to changes of cultural environment and new ways of thinking.[192] Together, a sensitivity to and interest in youth ministry and fundamental theology give me hope that the decrepit bridge might be replaced, widened, and modernized (or directly postmodernized). But that requires a readiness and principal openness to

---

192. Říha, "Fundamentální teologie," 146.

collaborative learning. Only by learning from and about the other can we possibly learn more about ourselves too. Therefore, standing on the bridge between fundamental theology and youth ministry and trying to take careful steps forward, ready to learn something about others and from others also about myself, I see the absolute necessity of struggling for a hermeneutical reciprocity and inclusiveness between these two disciplines (if their genuine encounter around the table of collaborative learning shall ever come true). This cannot happen if it does not start from a particular person, from a particular life experience, inspiration from, or fascination by others. Personal stories motivate our theology. Yet they cannot become a universal interpretative tool. Reality consists of constant dialogue and a process of collaborative learning—an ongoing discernment of what is valuable, true, and good for the sake of the whole of humanity. Ivana Noble elucidates this in the conclusion of her ecumenical fundamental theology:

> If we are able to learn from each other, such a process requires a genuine openness and reciprocity, and cannot be organized by any tradition, denominational or ecumenic institution, or by any theologian, as if from above. To be within this process of learning and teaching and common search, we need to take seriously that within the common journey our personal life-story is important. Its messiness, relying on finding life where life is to be found, its letting go of what is dead, and its often-multiple belonging, where life can be shared, is of an indispensable value. Our life-stories ground our theology, but at the same time, make generalizations very difficult.[193]

That is precisely the reason why this text claims no authority whatsoever. It is rather construed as a personal narrative of a particular life story which is at the stage of searching for partners with which to learn collaboratively. It is like the metaphor of a jam session that I adopted from Ann Pedersen and Hans-Peter Geiser (already evoked a few times above). I would like to show what kind of music I play and invite others to join me. I want to hear what they play, and I want to play with them together. Perhaps during common jamming, something new, beautiful, compelling, understandable, and even existentially relevant could be found, not only in the product (common music) but also—and maybe chiefly—in what comes to blossom behind the scenes, in each of the genuine encounters with the other, each partnership established, and

---

193. Noble, *Tracking God*, 243.

each relationship found. We are shaped through encounters. I already explained the side of the bridge from which I come from. Now, it is time to set off to the terrain of youth ministry and youth theology. I would like to investigate that landscape before returning back to begin reforming my own disciplinary background in a way that hopefully becomes more open to dialogue and collaborative learning within the complex body of the one Christian theology—beautiful in its inner diversity yet striving for a unity of multiple voices of people addressing their Creator and Savior, the Son who is One in three persons. Fundamental theology is far behind, and the road towards youth theology through the domain of youth ministry lies open ahead.

3

The Story of Youth Ministry and Emerging Youth Theology

THE FOLLOWING PRESENTATION OF the story of youth ministry and youth theology does not come from the computer of practical theologian or a practicing youth minister. It is written by someone who was inspired by meeting with young people and still remembers his own youth making a continuous effort to practice theology in everyday life. I am constantly undergoing conversion as a Christian and as a theologian too. I try to live in a theological way—having weak and strong moments on my way of faith, hope, and love seeking understanding. This text is the fruit of a pausing (fundamental) theologian, allowing himself time to stop and reflect upon: (1) his own academic discipline—its past, present, and possible future developments; (2) impulses received from my own engagement with the youngest generation of Christians, as well as with secular youth searching for life orientation, identity, and meaning; (3) and his encounter with youth ministry performing its ongoing theological turn and creating youth theology.

In previous chapters, I've explained my personal journey, theological development, and disciplinary background, including some sources of my thought. Now, I am entering into territory in which I am not fully at home. Therefore, I would like to ask for indulgence from those who are at home in youth ministry and youth theology research. Furthermore, I would like to kindly ask anyone who may feel inspired or outraged by this text to react and engage in debate with me. Let us start the debate, once again, about what theology is and how it should be done. Let us discuss youth ministry, youth theology, and all their related themes and topics in an open dialogue for those who are ready and open for collaborative learning. Let us combine our perspectives to progress in our theological lives towards a more intensive and intimate encounter with the first and last "Theo-Logian" who speaks about himself, the Triune God, alone.

This text is offered as my input for that kind of potential discussion, including questions about the origin of youth ministry and youth theology, their nature and development, as well as the central question: Is it possible for youth theology to truly grow and benefit from a theological turn in youth ministry? Other fundamental questions will be asked during this chapter, especially those concerned with the theological nature (or specificity) of youth, the theological capabilities of young people, and the relevance of their voices in theology. What could young theologians possibly learn from those established in academia? What can they teach academic theologians in return? Let us now listen to the stories of youth ministry and youth theology (while keeping in mind those of [fundamental] theology from the previous chapters).

3.1 YOUTH MINISTRY AS A SOURCE OF YOUTH THEOLOGY

"Let no one despise your youth but set the believers an example in speech and conduct, in love, in faith, in purity." —1 Tim 4:12

Youth ministry[1] is generally a problematic term to define. Usually, it serves as an umbrella term "that refers to ministry to, with and for adolescents and their families, focusing especially on young people from the onset of puberty through emerging adulthood."[2] An official document of the United States Conference of Catholic Bishops from 1997 defines youth ministry in a slightly different way: "Youth ministry is the response

---

1. Roebben provides us with standard translations of the term "youth ministry" into various languages. In German, it is *Jugendseelsorge*; in French, *pastorale des jeunes*; in Spanish, *pastoral de juventud*; and in Dutch, *jongerenpastoraal*. Roebben, *Seeking Sense*, 261. In the Czech language, youth ministry is usually translated as *pastorace mládeže*, and it is closer to the French, Spanish, and Dutch translations.

2. Dean, *OMG*, 26.

of the Christian community to the needs of young people and the sharing of the unique gifts of youth with the larger community."[3] Youth ministry, from this perspective, has an intrinsic ecclesial dimension, and, as such, asks for deep theological grounding. To provide theological foundations for youth ministry, ecclesiology is at hand. But ecclesiological reflection on the place where youth ministry has not been enough to encompass the whole scene, as it should in a practicing Christian community. The definitions given above presuppose not only the theology and praxis of the church responding to the needs of young people but also their own ability to share their unique gifts and their theology to the larger community of the church. Therefore, it traffics on a two-way street. Youth ministry is an environment and practice of empowering young people to live their lives as disciples of Jesus Christ. It should invite them into full participation in the life of the church and help them create and foster their Christian identities. "Youth ministry . . . relates to the activities of churches and faith communities to support young people and young adults in their moral and religious identity development."[4]

Even though youth ministry refers primarily to Christian churches and their concern for youth, some authors, like Kenda Creasy Dean for instance, call for extending the reach of youth ministry beyond ecclesial boundaries: "Churches can no longer afford to limit youth ministry to teenagers who gather in the church basement. The research on adolescence, and our citizenship in a global village, requires us to extend our reach."[5]

Following Dean, I would distinguish between intra- and extra-ecclesial youth ministry in terms of a new evangelization that is honest, deep, and refrains from proselytizing, as suggested by Roebben: "We cannot and should not attempt to convert whole groups of postmodern young people by merely adaptive strategies of the church. Young people are very sensitive to, and critical of, hidden proselytism. This experience in youth ministry serves as a sort of warning: we must go deeper and become more authentic; we must focus on the real aspirations of young people in the global era."[6]

Thus, youth ministry is neither social work nor a leisure time club, nor is it exclusively a mission, nor a prayer community. Youth ministry is an environment created by a community of faith, where all things

3. United States Conference of Catholic Bishops, "Renewing the Vision," 1.
4. Roebben, *Seeking Sense*, 261.
5. Dean, *OMG*, 26.
6. Roebben, *Seeking Sense*, 222.

(ordinary and sacred, natural and transcendent) have their own time and place for mutual permeation (cf. Eccl 3:1–15). Only through exploring everything with the possibility of avoiding evil and sticking to the good (cf. 1 Thess 5:21–22) is it possible to live a genuine Christian life—to recognize oneself as a disciple of Jesus Christ. In other words, youth ministry encourages young people to create "playgrounds of transcendence"[7]—or maybe better: youth ministry encourages young people to theologize to create, design, and redesign such playgrounds.

But before reaching convictions like the one just mentioned, we must recall that youth ministry has covered much territory, starting from traditionally organized, institutionalized, programmatic, and mostly instructional concepts of ministry with youth conducted by churches before the 1960s. First (rather hesitant) statements recognizing the youth as not merely objects of the church's pastoral care but as carriers of the apostolate appeared in the Roman Catholic environment in 1965, when the Decree on the Apostolate of the Laity, *Apostolicam Actuositatem* (further abbreviated AA), was issued by the Second Vatican Council. Young people, in the words of this document, have a considerable influence in society, which "demands of them a proportionate apostolic activity, but their natural qualities also fit them for this activity" (AA 12).[8]

A similar concern with the integration of youth into the complex missionary task of the church was observed also in the World Council of Churches at this time.[9] From the 1960s to the 1980s, youth ministry was seen mostly as a junior partner to Christian religious education[10] and largely irrelevant for any kind of proper theological reflection.[11] Today, it is a self-confident, self-reflective, independent, and interdisciplinary field

---

7. Roebben, *Seeking Sense*, 214.

8. It is necessary to note that such conviction is not characteristic of all Second Vatican Council documents. In the council's declaration on Christian education, "*Gravissimum Educationis*" (further abbreviated as GE), issued less than a month (October 28, 1965) prior to AA (issued November 18, 1965), young people are praised as "hope for the Church" (GE 2). But, at the same time, they are still understood merely as object of pastoral care and Christian education. "The Church is bound as a mother to give to these children of hers an education by which their whole life can be imbued with the spirit of Christ and at the same time do all she can to promote for all peoples the complete perfection of the human person, the good of earthly society and the building of a world that is more human" (GE 3).

9. Dean, *OMG*, 108.

10. Dean et al., *Starting*, 19.

11. Dean, *OMG*, 108.

of study based on and rooted in practical or pastoral theology.[12] As youth ministry gradually became aware that its own proper theological reflection was needed, it engaged with the closest theological partner it could find in practical (or pastoral) theology, although today some attempts to relate youth ministry with other theological disciplines (moral, systematic, and biblical theology) strengthen their voices. Their main question is: How might a youth hermeneutic be developed with respect to moral, scriptural, or systematic theology? Root and Deans's book *The Theological Turn in Youth Ministry* is a representative example of this with regards to systematic theology. Ron Becker's texts[13] on the relation between exegesis, biblical scholarship and youth ministry are likewise representative with regards to biblical (and practical) theology.

Despite this, youth ministry is commonly conceived to be closely linked with practical theology and perceives other theological disciplines in the wider context of youth ministry.[14] (Some even consider youth ministry to be a practical theology of its own kind.) The last couple of decades have shown that Christian youth ministry has remained entrenched in praxis. At the same time, it reached the world of academia, experts, and scientific reflection. Today, it has its own professional journals (e.g., *The Journal of Youth and Theology*; *The Journal of Youth Ministry*). Youth ministers, pastors, priests, theologians, and other professionals involved hold conferences at which they design their own research agenda for the discipline in general. There are now study programs on youth ministry at colleges and universities. People can receive a special training, obtain a university degree (including a PhD), and start their professional careers in youth ministry, not only as practitioners (youth ministers) but also as theoreticians (experts on youth ministry). Churches and their legal bodies installed positions in youth ministry, and the position of "youth minister" became a possible profession—a career opportunity—in some places in the world.

All this means that something has changed. Youth ministry has come far from the time it was a matter of volunteers and particular enthusiasts. It has become professionalized,[15] with all the good and bad that entails. Be that as it may, one thing is certain. There is an increasing interest in research on youth and youth ministry worldwide, but it is "not

---

12. Dean, *OMG*, 109; 115–16.
13. Becker, "Beyond"; Becker, *Reading*.
14. Dean et al., *Starting*, 31–32.
15. Jones, *Postmodern*, 216; Dean, *OMG*, 121–22.

always free from the instrumental concerns of adults."[16] Youth ministry research is often lacking the capability to genuinely hear the authentic voices of young people, and it often does not give the youth a chance to speak out for themselves and express their theology. What do they think youth ministry is and should be about? Unfortunately, sometimes we find youth ministry practiced in such a way that it assumes little more than the role of an institutional tool trying to possess and impose control upon what is perhaps essentially uncontrolled. The same is true for youth ministry research. Young people simply cannot be conceptualized merely as objects for any kind of research, not even a theological one. On that matter, Roebben remarks, "In order to understand what young people really believe, hope, and love, they should be invited to become the real agents of perception, interpretation and change (see, judge, act), in other words, to become real researchers themselves!"[17]

3.1.1 The Research Agenda in Youth Ministry

As youth ministry becomes professionalized and a matter of scientific reflection, it also develops its own research agenda. In the beginning, youth ministry borrowed research methods and techniques from other sciences like pedagogy, psychology, sociology, etc. These were adapted for the specific needs of an emerging academic field. It was during the last decade of the twentieth century that youth ministry widely discovered its connection to theology and started reflecting upon itself from this point of view. Youth ministry research was interdisciplinary since the very beginning. The inclusion of theology into its scope led to the discovery "that theology contributes to the interdisciplinary discussion as well, and that youth ministry has its own contributions to make to theology and social science."[18]

At this point, I would like to review the contemporary youth ministry research agenda according to the late chair of the IASYM, Bert Roebben, and find a place for my own research interests within his taxonomy. During the 2009 US Youth Ministry Conference in Louisville, Kentucky, Roebben introduced six points defining the research agenda for youth ministry.[19] Four years later, he condensed these into four categories of research

---

16. Roebben, *Seeking Sense*, 261.
17. Roebben, *Seeking Sense*, 262.
18. Dean, *OMG*, 124.
19. Roebben, "Youth," 247–52.

activities (research tracks) for youth ministry in the second edition of his book *Seeking Sense in the City*.[20] Comparing both of these two iterations, I find the earlier one more approachable and transparent. I address it here first (before moving to its latter and reduced formulation below):

1. **Empirical research on youth.** Roebben begins by steering contemporary youth ministry research in an empirical direction. In his perspective, youth ministry builds on a long tradition of attempts that churches have made to understand their youth with the help and through lenses of different disciplines in the humanities. It certainly makes sense to study young people from sociological, psychological, and pedagogical perspectives. Thus, Kenda Creasy Dean remarks, "Thanks to the high percentage of youth ministry professors who are sociologists, psychologists, and educators, nontheological empirical research still dominates youth ministry."[21]

   Empirical research within youth ministry employs various quantitative as well as qualitative methods to gather data useful for further reflection on the character, needs, and specificity of contemporary youth in relation to religion and religious phenomena. It is a response to the lack of knowledge about youth, especially in terms of how they relate to religion (if at all). While from the side of Christian churches, this kind of research was usually motivated by the simple need to understand secularization (Why are we losing the youth?), from the side of general research on youth conducted by different humanities, the spiritual and religious dimension was often simply excluded. "It is a well-known secret that lots of youth research does not encompass the spiritual or religious dimension. And it is also a well-known secret that precisely practitioners and scholars in religious education and youth ministry are on the forefront of new developments in educational research, praxis and theory."[22]

   Empirical research into youth ministry, however, remains important because it has the potential to facilitate contact, dialogue, and exchange with other humanities. As such, it may still emphasize the often-neglected spiritual and religious dimensions of youth and

---

20. Roebben, *Seeking Sense*, 263–65. The earlier version of Roebben's research agenda appeared in Roebben, "International," 192–206.
21. Dean, *OMG*, 124.
22. Roebben, *Seeking Sense*, 266.

further relate them to other dimensions investigated by standard research methods. Gathering data about young people remains interesting and necessary. But at the same time, any kind of empirical research of youth and religion must be also accompanied by thorough theoretical reflections by which to place such empirical findings into appropriate frameworks. Other research directions attempt to fill this gap.

2. **Models of youth ministry in the church.** The second research option for youth ministry, for the earlier Roebben, focuses on the discernment of the actual models applied in concrete church youth ministry practice and further ambitions to develop new ones. The model of a particular youth ministry depends greatly on the ecclesiology characteristic to the church in which it is found. With this kind of focus, contemporary cultural changes related to faith and religion are discussed in the contexts of both youth ministry and community-building. Roebben asks, "Can we simply continue our traditional efforts and methods of approaching young people in their search for personally reflected meaning and authentic commitment to the community of the future? Can our pastoral strategies remain the same against the background of the radical change that young people's environment, and society as a whole, has gone through?"[23]

These questions are crucial when thinking of newly developing contemporary models for youth ministry. The context of youth is traditionally a laboratory of new trends and places in which each tradition is being tested (and, eventually, accepted or rejected) by the forthcoming generation. In words of Root and Dean, "In every corner of the globe, youth ministry acts as the church's 'research and development' department, an unofficial laboratory where youth and adults alike try to figure out new ways of being the church for our surrounding cultures."[24]

At the very least, this singular reason for attending to the voices of young people for the sake of their own stories must be adopted by each generation as it matures into adulthood and steps or proceeds beyond their youthful status. Within this second research area, "different models of presence of youth—and their ministers!—inside and

---

23. Roebben, *Seeking Sense*, 219.
24. Root and Dean, *Theological Turn*, 16–17.

outside the church are discussed."[25] This links youth ministry with ecclesiology and a systematic theological reflection on the church. Consequently, the formulations of youth ministry rely deeply on the ecclesiological models applied by different churches. This approach to youth ministry research prompts further questions: What is the influence of a particular ecclesiology (i.e., its conception of "church") on the actual reality of the youth ministry it produces? Could it be that youth ministry inspires ecclesiological revisions in particular denominations? Questions such as these dominate the present research focus on youth ministry. It is necessary to note that the conversation between youth ministry and ecclesiology may also link youth ministry to contemporary concepts of public theology, since it is concerned with the public relevance of Christianity today.[26]

3. **Youth churches and liturgical renewal.** The third research area for youth ministry defined by Roebben considers the actual participation of young people in the liturgical services of the church. It also refers to the contemporary phenomena of "youth churches,"[27] or emerging youth congregations, on both the factual and virtual levels.[28] Young people tend to experiment in the liturgical platform, trying new things as well as old things anew. Experiment is a key word. Liturgy and church rituals become the platform by which youthful ideas are tested in confrontation with the broader church community. Young people invent and reinvent the church by/through their (liturgical) explorations. They remind the church that it must remain always open to its own inner renewal. Tradition and renewal dialectics are at the center of this research focus,[29] asking questions like: How do young people understand traditional symbols and rituals? Do they create their own? What are these new symbols and rituals? How are we to interpret them? Do they contribute to the development of Christian praxis and doctrine? If so, how?

---

25. Roebben, "Youth," 249.

26. Even though it does not specifically or overtly link youth ministry to public theology, I find the following article by Yolanda Dreyer relevant and very inspiring for the context under discussion: Dreyer, "Public," 919–45.

27. Ward, *Participation and Mediation*, 16–17.

28. Roebben, "Youth," 250.

29. Roebben, "Youth," 250.

4. **Critical church work with youth.** What is the right mode of working critically with youth within the church? This could be one of the possible ways to formulate a leading question to those who would adhere to the fourth research area in youth ministry proposed by Roebben. Critical church work with youth does not simply mean finding out what young people like and adapting the gospel and church practice accordingly. It is the opposite. Critical church work with youth means presenting religion, faith, and church praxis as reasonable options in the contemporary world and society. Youth ministry maintains its constant emphasis on praxis, in the light of the gospel (practical orientation). It maintains its critical potential and awareness about its own undeniable contextuality as it relates to global conditions of the contemporary world.

Youth ministry indeed has the potential to become a place for "slowification," a safe environment for the exchange of auto/Theo-biographies. To live up to this potential is, however, quite demanding on those who run or organize youth ministry, because it requires programmatic and long-term work with the whole community or congregation, constantly asking this question, formulated by Roebben: "How should the (Christian) praxis in the congregation look, so that it can bear witness in a reliable and open way to salvific coming of God to humankind, to which only a free and personal commitment can correspond?"[30]

The ways by which youth ministry appear and function are not just the concerns of youth ministers. They are conditioned results from the whole community and its environment, in/from which they appear and function. This works both ways. (Like the traffic on our particular "bridge," it is bi-directional, not unilateral.) Youth ministry is relevant not only for actual youth but also for the whole community, in which everyone shall have a place and a contribution to the common practice of the community and its theological reflections.

5. **Theology for youth ministry.** Roebben's fifth research direction springs out from of the previous four. It is the domain of theologians, who realize that youth ministry cannot be only or exclusively interpreted and reflected upon through the eyes of the humanities (psychology, sociology, pedagogy, etc.). As a part of religion-, faith-,

---

30. Roebben, *Seeking Sense*, 225.

and church-based phenomena, it also requires a proper theological reflection. This is precisely what this research area in youth ministry brings into the discussion. Different theological conceptions are constantly tested within the environment of youth ministry. That alone makes it relevant for all "classical" theological disciplines, because it relates youth ministry to the traditional body of (academic) theology. In youth ministry, theology (systematic, fundamental, biblical, moral, etc.) is used as a tool for interpretation and reflection of reality, with special focus on young people and the contexts of their lives. This focus considers all theological disciplines as specifically relevant to the theory and praxis of youth ministry. It also works vice versa. Through contact with youth ministry, different theological disciplines are called to reflect upon themselves, to consider and reconsider their own developments and changes. In contact with young people, theological reflection (academic and ordinary alike) may receive fresh impulses and eventually new vitality as well. Along these lines, Dean Borgman reminds us that those who work with young people are theologians, because the work they do "demands theological reflection."[31] He concludes, "We cannot expect excellence in youth ministry without effective research and theology of youth ministry."[32]

6. **Youth theology and its impact on theology.** Engaging theology in youth ministry has an interesting consequence: the emergence of *youth ministry theology* or *youth theology*. In his sixth research area (model of research), Roebben is convinced that youth ministry is not only nurtured by theology, but in fact it produces its own theology. A theologian is not only a professional who is supposed to deliver the theoretical background for youth ministers. Let me use a metaphor. The theologian is simply not a "food supplier," and the youth minister is not simply a "blender" mixing the appropriate amount of salt, pepper, and spices; even less is the youth minister a waitress or waiter serving dishes to young people. Finally, young people are by no means mere "consumers" obliged to accept, eat, and give thanks to the "food provider." I am sure some would still like it this way. But the reality is a bit different. Together with Bert Roebben, we may observe the "emergence of a specific and original

---

31. Borgman, *Foundations*, 10.
32. Borgman, *Foundations*, 10.

youth theology. Young people not only devise their own churches, rituals, and morals, but also create their own theologies."[33]

This last, and relatively new, direction in youth ministry research brings the potential of youth ministry under scrutiny to create or design its own theology. Roebben believes in such potential, based on the conviction that we are all theologians, because theology (as a way that human beings principally relate to God) is primarily a way of life. Consequently, we may ask: What kind of theology could be found in youth ministry? What is youth theology? And how it is expressed by its authors? There is, no doubt, deep theological thinking among young people. But the primary question for this research direction is: How can it to be found (or discerned)? What can academic theologians, church leaders, and professional youth ministers, pastors, and priests learn from it? Do we pay enough attention to this kind of theology? Do we really hear it? From the perspective of this research direction, theology cannot be a monopoly of educated scientists and church leaders. Theology should be a communitarian practice and enterprise in which the voices of children and youth can be heard as equally as others. Theology is everyone's business . . . including young people, since all Christians are called to reflect upon their personal relationship with God (*Theos*), and all churches are consequently asked to do the same on the level of community.

As mentioned above, Roebben's youth ministry research agenda later shrank to four research tracks. Most probably it is because the six research directions presented above are sometimes very close to each other; they overlap and combine their interests, complementing each other. Thus, according to the later Roebben (2013), we need four research tracks, providing data "on (1) religious youth cultures, on (2) explicit YM initiatives, on (3) the presence of faith communities in the public realm and on (4) the spiritual and theological voices of young people."[34] Each facet of youth ministry research deals with one or more data sets coming from empirical as well as non-empirical reflections. It may be said that together they create a context for each youth ministry and a framework for its research. Both sets of Roebben's research trends can serve as useful tools for researchers to relate their own (theological) investigations to youth ministry.

33. Roebben, "Youth," 251.
34. Roebben, *Seeking Sense*, 265.

At this point it is necessary to mention an alternative to Roebben's view of the research agenda for youth ministry, as presented by Kenda Creasy Dean in her youth ministry handbook.[35] She also proposes six research directions for studying youth ministry in the twenty-first century. At first, she mentions the research of a youth ministry hermeneutics of biblical texts and church tradition. The second research area focuses on a life cycle paradigm. What does it mean to be young? Themes of youth, growth, and maturity need to be studied. Third, youth ministry must reflect on leadership formation. Fourth, youth ministry matters for church communities, and thus congregational cultures of churches must be studied in relation to youth ministry. Focus on intergenerational dynamics and inclusive participation is, here, at hand. The fifth research track aligns youth ministry with missiology. Finally, Dean's sixth direction opens youth ministry to a variety of new voices and impulses, including ecumenism, ethnography, new media, social networks, and communication models within church hierarchies. Youth ministry will always have to reassess its own purpose and foundations, yet still it must maintain its principal openness and passion for the uniqueness of each (young) person, with programmatic interdisciplinarity.[36]

The research agenda for youth ministry is by no means a finished one. It is widely open for new impulses and developments. It continues searching for new challenges and investigating new possibilities to interpret young people theologically, reflecting on their own theologies that arise from specific cultures and contexts. Despite this, the tendencies and trends (directions and tracks) in youth ministry research named and discussed above might serve as models for anyone wishing to engage with youth ministry research. Am I one who advocates the empirical approach to research on youth? Do I want to reflect upon youth ministry from a more theoretical and theological point of view? Am I more interested in the spiritual voices of young people or in the public appearance of youth activities within church and society? Is my focus local, or do I want to address the global issues connected to youth ministry? Are my considerations denominational, or are they general, ecumenical? Am I referring to praxis or theory in youth ministry, or both? Such questions can perhaps be better answered now, after the overviews of Roebben and Dean,

---

35. Dean, *OMG*.
36. Dean, *OMG*, 124–25.

as crucial discernment tools needed when considering how to engage with youth ministry research.

In this text, I mostly adhere to points 5 and 6 from the earlier set of research directions proposed by Roebben. What could be the basis for youth theology? What principles shall be emphasized or (re-)discovered by the classical theological disciplines to hear the theological voices of youth? However, other themes from the youth ministry research agenda are addressed throughout this text as well. But the focus remains theological. I encountered youth ministry as fundamentally theological, and my way of understanding fundamental theology searches for impulses from young hearts and minds. Fundamental theology seems to me to be the right starting point for opening a wider theological debate. It is necessary to discuss the fundamental principles first before we engage youth ministry with biblical, systematic, and moral theology. Fundamental theology and youth ministry must enter a mutual, interdisciplinary dialogue. Both disciplines refer to intrinsic and indispensable parts of Christian life and the identities of both believing individuals and communities. In other words, knowing *what to do* is equally as important as knowing *why to do it*. Searching and interpreting the past and present circumstances of one's culture and community is of the same importance as longing for the future and searching for meaning. Put simply, youth ministry has recently rediscovered its theological nature and raised its own theological voice to contribute to the broader theological conversation of the contemporary era. It was Andrew Root and Kenda Creasy Dean who labelled this shift in youth ministry a "theological turn."[37] In their perspective, theological awareness of youth ministry has grown from grassroots, from the praxis of youth ministry within churches of all denominations.

3.1.2 The Theological Turn in Youth Ministry

If we make a quick overview of the wide production of books and articles on youth ministry during last three decades, we find a growing number of titles claiming (some more explicitly than others) a theological approach to youth ministry. It seems that theology is becoming increasingly important in youth ministry. But this was not always the case. It was not long ago that youth were deemed unable to theologize, in a strict sense of the word, or it was assumed that theology was something in

---

37. Root and Dean, *Theological Turn*.

which youth were not interested at all. This was caused by a strictly delimited understanding of theology as solely a matter of intellectual effort (rational reflection on faith). For instance, in the Catholic environment, theology was reserved only for the clergy until the Second Vatican Council (1962–65). It is necessary to consider and remember that only five decades have passed since the Roman Catholic Church sanctioned and espoused *theology for all*.[38] A Catholic *theology for all* is still in its youth. (It may well still be in its infantile stage.)

The general absence of theological reflection within youth ministry is caused not only by decisions of official church authorities or the traditional reservation of theology (as a high discipline) to experts and clergy. Unfortunately, youth ministers also don't tend to regard themselves as theologians. Consequently, "the practice of youth ministry has been seen lightweight both intellectually and ministerially because we have failed to see ourselves as theologians doing a fundamentally theological task."[39]

During the last two or three decades, the tendency to return to theology can be identified within youth ministry worldwide (some places better than others), because it is increasingly realized that youth ministry is "enacted faith"[40] or "enacted theology."[41] This means that everything Christians do (regardless of age) is somehow rooted in faith, and faith is always accompanied by theology. Yet theology as such sometimes remains unreflected, unknown, unintentional, implicit, and so on. From

---

38. In the Czech Republic, the first laymen were allowed to study theology in theological faculties affiliated with the Roman Catholic church in the early nineties, since theology was reserved only for (male) priests or priest candidates prior to that time. The study of theology was officially opened to women as well (though some women still struggled to gain admittance to some theology programs). This was the case at the Catholic Theological Faculty at Charles University in Prague, at which women were unofficially not accepted to study theology until 2002! The reason behind this (unofficial) policy was the convictions of faculty leaders (all clergymen) that held it unnecessary or irrelevant for women to study theology simply because they were still not entitled to become priests. Public pressure and other problems that the faculty experienced in those days finally led to a change. Nowadays, it has become an open environment where priest candidates, lay men and women study together. The situation was better in other non-Catholic denominations. For example, women were allowed to study at the Protestant Theological Faculty of Charles University in Prague even during communism. Regardless of the gender issue, theology in the Czech Republic is still widely considered irrelevant for, and having nothing to do with, children or youth. It is reserved for adults and experts.

39. Root and Dean, *Theological Turn*, 37–38.

40. Bailey, "Enacted Faith," 25–39.

41. Root and Dean, *Theological Turn*, 17, 137–236.

this perspective, spiritual practices are enacted beliefs,[42] and the whole life of a believer is enacted theology—a processual worship of life, or a continuous, personal relationship with God—because its principle is faith, which is naturally seeking its understanding. Such conviction incited an enormous interest in theology among those who work with youth. They realized that

> the practice of reflecting theologically on youth ministry is becoming both normative and necessary. . . . Youth workers are pushing for theological depth in their practice, for lenses to help them understand what they do is essentially about navigating the sacred connection between God and humans. This palpable "turn" in youth ministry reveals our longing for something solid and deep on which to stand with young people, a way to move beyond the consumer habits and entertainment focus that too often consume youth ministry.[43]

As one would expect, practical (or pastoral) theology was the first theological discipline to which youth ministry turned to seek theological reflection of its own praxis. And it is widely agreed that practical theology is a parent discipline of youth ministry, perceived as a theological enterprise. Such theological awareness is today symptomatic of youth ministry, and thus there is no wonder that it searches for new ways to engage not only with practical theology but also with other theological disciplines. At the beginning of the twenty-first century, several scholars "made a plea for theology as leading discipline for youth ministry research."[44] However, it seems that in the present state of the theological turn in youth ministry, systematic and fundamental theologies are still neglected and most youth ministry research goes in the direction of empirical theology.[45] If present at all, they serve only as a presupposition for reflections in practical theology. Root and Dean, for instance, speak about revelation, Trinity, various aspects of Christology (the cross, resurrection, Christo-praxis, etc.), and even about conversation about actual youth ministry with "tradition."[46] They use various systematic or even

---

42. Root and Dean, *Theological Turn*, 32.
43. Root and Dean, *Theological Turn*, 16.
44. de Kock and Norheim, *Five Questions*, 7.
45. de Kock and Norheim, *Five Questions*, 10. Authors further argue that "empirical research is at the heart of youth ministry research." de Kock and Norheim, *Five Questions*, 243.
46. Root and Dean, *Theological Turn*, 95.

fundamental (or foundational) theological theories to support their claim that youth ministry is actually a way of (practical) theological reflection. Another practical theologian, Dean Borgman, starts with an account of theology as such before developing a practical theological reflection of contemporary youth ministry. He seeks theological foundations for youth ministry but does not enter conversation with fundamental or foundational theology at all. He mentions apologetics but only briefly.[47]

Pete Ward's experience as youth minister shaped his own theology.[48] For him, theology is a form of culture in which churches and their youth ministries live. But at the same time, theology is more than just culture. Theology, says Ward, "functions as culture or as a way of life and yet it cannot be reduced to culture."[49] Ward's (practical) theology comes from his own experience with youth work and theological questions coming out of his praxis. The same is true for my own fundamental theology. It springs forth from my experiences during several years of youth work within a church and mostly outside it, among high school youth, where I unexpectedly encountered theological questions (most often implicit, or not specifically Christian, yet very fundamental). In that environment I encountered genuine searching for the fundamentals of human existence and an inclusive approach to others on the one hand but also fundamentalism and exclusion of others on the other.[50] These questions and experiences awoke my interest in attuning it with fundamental theology in academia, which was also my job. Thus (like Pete Ward), I became both a "committed academic" and an "academic with commitments."[51] Even as an academic, I always understood theology as a way of life, because Christianity is not simply a garment we wear to Sunday services, which

---

47. Borgman, *Foundations*, 20.
48. Ward, *Participation and Mediation*, 6.
49. Ward, *Participation and Mediation*, 95.
50. I recall one high school student who took an interest in my presentation of Christianity as a kind of "ideal socialism," as is the perspective of some liberation theologians. I had just used it as an example during a discussion about economic issues. He asked how it was possible that Christianity is presented differently by different people— that he needs to know what Christianity really is. I replied (perhaps naively) with a short lecture about hermeneutics, different perspectives, point of views, contexts, and experiences and how these shape our perceptions of reality, etc. At the end of my "splendid" talk, he said, "I did not want to know what is possible. I wanted to know how it is." I was speechless for a while, and then I told him that I do not know how it is. I just search and hope that one day (and most probably not during my lifetime), I will know. He seemed unsatisfied, but at least I provoked his own search (. . . at least, I hope so).
51. Ward, *Participation and Mediation*, 6.

merely hangs in the entrance hall of our flats and houses during the rest of the week. Christianity is rather the clothes we wear from baptism ever after. We are clothed with Christ, in the words of Saint Paul (Gal 3:27).

Now, it is beyond doubt that theology is important for youth ministry both as a reflective tool and (maybe more significantly) as a product of youth ministry practice. Despite calling young people "intuitive practical theologians," Root and Dean still call for youth ministers ("proficient practical theologians") engaged in pastoring them.[52] I would rather opt for calling everyone an "intuitive theologian" by "virtue of calling."[53] From a Christian perspective, everyone (including young people and children) is called to be an intuitive theologian by being human, by being created in the image and likeness of God (Gen 1:26). Everyone is called to live theologically. Within this picture, some of us are called to become more proficient in theology simply because we are gifted and inclined to it. Some practice it more than others, just as those more skilled in playing the piano, vegetable gardening, or carpentry spend more time practicing those activities, respectively. But mastering one craft does not mean one cannot also be an intuitive theologian at the same time.

This became clear to me when tiling the floors of our house with the help of my friend, who also plays the organ in a cathedral nearby. When the job was done, some of our friends laughed and said, "Unbelievable that this was done by theologian and organist." Of course it was done, but it was not done professionally. For a while, we became intuitive tilers, as everyone can become (and is becoming) an intuitive theologian when encountering situations of existential importance in their own lives. Just as it is necessary to lay down some tiles from time to time, it is necessary to become a theologian when it is needed. This is the case during childhood, or youth, as well. But if we can do it ourselves, do we necessarily need professional theologians? Of course we do! We can sometimes do it ourselves, but still, we need professionals for the sake of community. We can lay tiles in our home and be proud of it, but most of us probably cannot help to lay tiles in the local bar, a new library, school, or the church. There we need professionals to employ the mastery of their craft. We need their advice if we want to try to do it ourselves and, more likely, we need their help and damage control once we eventually screw up the job as novices. However, just as the advice and service of professionals are

---

52. Root and Dean, *Theological Turn*, 76.
53. Root and Dean, *Theological Turn*, 76.

important, so too are the experiences and ideas of non-professional others when it comes to the overall process of living, which does not exclude theology and the life of the church.

Let us now return to the theological turn in youth ministry. It is something that is already widely happening, but it is also what has yet to happen. The process has only recently commenced. Therefore, we can only envisage its further development. What seems certain is that youth ministry is searching for sound theological grounds or fundaments. It has great interdisciplinary potential, because it is highly "informed by social sciences and liberal arts"[54] (yet it must not be reduced to them). In my perspective, youth ministry remains always theological, because it is relevant for the church and for the kingdom of God. It is precisely due to this that I am convinced that fundamental theology must contribute towards the theological turn in youth ministry by offering the expertise, insight, and experience of having found itself as the border discipline between theology, society, and other sciences. That is why I take the theological turn in youth ministry as a theological challenge not only for practical but also for systematic and fundamental theology too. In my opinion, the challenge for fundamental theology lies in reimagining, rethinking, and rewriting itself, namely in terms of its method, which should become more experiential and relational. For that purpose, I find the suggestion of Hans-Peter Geiser very helpful and even prophetic. He claims fundamental theology in the postmodern age should decide to put experience at the fore once again: "To put experience first is to allow the world to play with us the way children allow the world to come in and play with it. It follows the human way and method we use to know and discover this world around us. Maybe theology, in its ominous tendency to keep this world around us out, would be well advised to let experience come in again."[55]

From Geiser's perspective, experience refers not only to the "inner life of an individual"[56] but also to the social, cultural, and communal aspects

---

54. Dean, *OMG*, 115.

55. Geiser, *Community of the Weak*, 252–53.

56. Geiser quotes Alister McGrath, who deals with problematic usage of experience for theological research in his respectful *Christian Theology: An Introduction*. According to McGrath, experience refers to the "inner lives of individuals, in which those individuals become aware of their own subjective feelings and emotions. It relates to the inward and subjective world of experience, as opposed to the outward world of everyday life." McGrath, *Christian Theology*, 146.

of it.[57] Geiser concludes his call for putting experience first in theology as follows: "Theology coming out of our most personal and social experiences of human sin and human grace lives in a social landscape made out of relationships, stories, mutual dwellings, and personal and social recollections. Experience as the starting point in our theological beginnings is never simple but complex and multi-faceted. Nevertheless, it lays the ground and basis from which all our theologies are built and developed."[58]

From my point of view, theology operating in the theological turn in youth ministry is precisely a theology rooted in and based upon experience and relationality. It devotes itself to interpreting reality in the light of the gospel that is always contextual, actual, and new. As Roebben remarks, "True religion is always dialectically interwoven with human experiences—in line, but also in tension with them. True religion is about transcendence (clearly always in a human horizon of immanence), it is about de-centering the human story (clearly always in reflection on this story). True religion opens the living and learning space for the surprising coming of God, for His or Her radical alterity within diversity, immanence and self-reliance."[59]

In this light, connecting youth ministry with (fundamental) theology no longer seems obscure but rather an attractive way toward complex theological renewal, starting from a new theological grasp of human experience. Youth ministry has made this theological turn and has started considering itself as a form of (practical) theology.

3.1.3 Youth Ministry as a Form of (Practical) Theology

In one of the first "programmatic" books dealing with the theological understanding of youth ministry, Kenda Creasy Dean writes:

> Practical theological reflection—reflection that connects what we believe about God with how we live as disciples of Jesus Christ—is the first task of ministry with young people. By first, we do not mean that practical theological reflection on youth ministry necessarily precedes everything else. All decent theology begins and ends in practice, so sequence matters little in the ongoing cycle of practical theological reflection. Such reflection

---

57. Geiser, *Community of the Weak*, 254.
58. Geiser, *Community of the Weak*, 255.
59. Roebben, *Seeking Sense*, 216.

comes "first" in the sense that it is primary, fundamental—basic to everything else we do and to who God calls us to be.[60]

In one of her later books, she expresses her conviction even more precisely: "Youth ministry—or adolescent discipleship formation, if you prefer—is first and foremost an expression of practical theology for and with young people and the church."[61] Elsewhere in the same book, it reads: "As practical theology, youth ministry focuses on practices that allow us to perceive God with and through young people."[62] From this perspective, youth ministry is always contextual, having a personal as well as a communal character, ever oriented towards Christian practice and action in terms of *imitatio Christi*. Most contemporary authors dealing with the theological reflection of youth ministry agree (in one way or another) that youth ministry is closely connected with practical theology, or that it is a specific kind of practical theology. Before I will turn my focus on contemporary discussions about the theological nature of youth ministry and different approaches to the theological reflection of youth, it is necessary to understand what it means for youth ministry to locate itself within practical theology. What does it imply for youth ministry? Is youth ministry really a form of practical theology?

Traditionally, practical theology was defined as a theological discipline focused on making theology (theological theories) applicable to praxis—to put theory into praxis. We still find such (or similar) definitions in many practical theology textbooks. Ray Anderson, for instance, writes about practical theology, "As a theological discipline, its primary purpose is to ensure that the church's public proclamations and praxis in the world faithfully reflect the nature and purpose of God's continuing mission to the world and in so doing authentically address the contemporary context into which the church seeks to minister. . . . The discipline of practical theology extends systematic theology into the life and praxis of the Christian community."[63]

And almost the same we encounter in *The Five Questions: An Academic Handbook in Youth Ministry Research* by de Kock and Norheim: "The study object of practical theology is religious praxis, and its strategic goal is the description, interpretation, and ultimately the enhancement of

60. Dean et al., *Starting*, 17.
61. Dean, *OMG*, xii.
62. Dean, *OMG*, 116.
63. Anderson, *Shape*, 22–23.

religious praxis. Taking on a practical theological perspective in the study of (theological) phenomena is then, more precisely, taking the empirical reality of the here and now as a main source for developing theological reflection."[64]

Contrary—though perhaps also complementary, since I acknowledge their value and relevance—to these more traditional definitions of practical theology, we find a somewhat different perspective in the work of the Australian practical theologian Terry Veling. Whereas Anderson conceives of practical theology merely as an extension of systematic theology, ensuring that the church's proclamations remain consonant with God's self-disclosure in Scripture and the doctrinal tradition, and de Kock together with Norheim highlight the empirical understanding of reality as a source for practical-theological reflection, Veling presents an alternative approach. When asking about the nature of practical theology, he adds, "we are asking about its theory."[65] Theory and praxis are for him (following Rahner) inseparable. They "indwell" in each other. Another influential practical theologian, Don S. Browning, suggests that all "our practices, even our religious practices, have theories behind and within them. We may not notice the theories in our practices. We are so embedded in our practices, take them so much for granted, and view them as so natural and self-evident, that we never take time to abstract the theory from the practice and look at it as something in itself."[66]

Contrary to Veling, who resists the technical division of theology into practical and theoretic, Browning (like Metz but with some nuanced differences) emphasizes the primacy of praxis over theory in opposition to the classical understanding of practice consisting of applied theories.[67]

Considering all three examples just mentioned, I am partial to the conception of Terry Veling, with whom I share a common aspiration for holistic theology. Following his vision of practicing theology, we may conclude that there is no practical theology separated from the theoretical. Instead, both attitudes are interwoven into a colorful pattern, a texture of doing theology or living our lives theologically (that is to say, reflecting on them considering Scripture, tradition, and revelatory experiences). Influenced by Heidegger's thought, Veling sees life as *venturing*. Without this venturing, the nature of human life loses its meaning, not only in

64. de Kock and Norheim, *Five Questions*, 245–46.
65. Veling, *Practical*, 4.
66. Browning, *Fundamental Practical*, 6.
67. Browning, *Fundamental Practical*, 67.

terms of speculative reasoning (theory) but also in terms of finding the purpose, value, orientation, or direction (practice) of one's own life.[68] "To venture a theological life is to live theologically. It is not so much to ask about the ways that theology can be made practical; rather, it is to ask how practices of my life can be made theological."[69]

Indeed, I think that practical and theoretical theology are inseparable. Biblical, fundamental, systematic, practical, moral, etc., are different disciplinary facets that form around the core of the genuine reflection on Christian life. This is always as theoretical as it is practical, happening in the scenes of people's lives at once. Like the bridge (above), the dynamic relationship between theory and praxis is not a one-way street but rather a bi-directional process instead. Theory and praxis are two sides of the same coin. They always operate together. According to Veling, practical theology is an attempt to heal the artificial division (characteristic to modern thought) between the theoretical and the practical, between thinking and acting, and, thus, an attempt to reconnect theology with real life. It is a conviction that thought and deed work inseparably together.[70] This approach appears to me as an explicit invitation to bring both fundamental and systematic theology into conversation on the nature of theology—because all these theological disciplines share the same concern about connections of theory with practice and action—in hopes to balance orthodoxy with orthopraxis, giving voices to theories by taking account of practices and actions seriously.

One might argue that this balanced relationship between theory and practice within theology has come about only recently. Throughout the history of theology, we can trace in each era ongoing dialectics between practical and theoretic emphasis in theology. While primitive Christian communities certainly tried to live their faith in practical ways (as prayer or spirituality, etc.), others emphasized the importance of theories in places where Christian practices may be grounded, especially against different adversaries and heretics. The early development of Christian doctrine and the formulation of the creed was marked by enormous intellectual efforts through which the theoretical bases for Christianity were established. Thus, from the very beginning, there were those who emphasized the practice of Christian life alongside others who instead emphasized theoretical reflections on it. But since the very

68. Veling, *Practical*, 139.
69. Veling, *Practical*, 141.
70. Veling, *Practical*, 5, 141.

beginning there was a common consensus on the fact that one cannot be without the other. For instance, in the medieval era, Aquinas and his successors emphasized the theoretical nature of theology. Bonaventure and his followers praised the merits of the maintaining that theology is predominantly practical. Without denying the merits of both theory and practice, unbalanced disputes of this kind continued throughout the history of theological development into contemporary theologians, where Wolfhart Pannenberg, for instance, endeavors to "return Christian theology to earlier, classical understandings that focus strictly on "talking of God" and "thinking of God."[71] Pannenberg proposes this in opposition to the *revisionist* theologies developed by various theologians like Bernard Lonergan, Hans Küng, or David Tracy;[72] (in a different style) by liberation theologians (e.g., Leonard Boff, Gustavo Gutiérrez); and also (with major reservations against the label "revisionist") by post-liberals (e.g., George Lindbeck) and existentialists (e.g., Karl Rahner, Paul Tillich, and Jürgen Moltmann). Whether we call them "revisionists" or not, these theologians recognize (some more than others, and all of them in different ways) the distinctive value of human experience for theological reflection and the practical nature of every theology (i.e., its social and political concerns for change or conversion and its orientation towards humanity perceived fundamentally in relation to God).

Following these developments, today it is suggested that theology is neither exclusively theoretical nor practical. Theology is rather both at once, and even though theologians may be concerned with (or specialized in) one of its disciplines, they must never forget the others. To put it simply, theories are born from praxis, and praxis comes out of theories. We need not decide which comes first but rather attempt to find a balance between them, in contemplation of their sources. Veling writes about the understanding of theology in early Christianity (commenting on and quoting Ellen Charry): "Theory was not opposed to practice. Rather, theology was an exercise of life."[73] This is that which is

---

71. Becker, *Fundamental Theology*, 93.

72. "David Tracy refers to the dichotomy between theory and practice as a 'fatal split.' When we divide theory and practice, we injure life, and it is the task of practical theology to heal this fatal wound." Veling, *Practical*, 141–42. I do not think it is only a task of practical theology. If Veling speaks of theology as a way of life, it suggests its totality, and so, it is the task of living as well as thinking. Theological life and theological thinking must merge to be able to reunite theory and practice in theology, which is a way of life and a task of thinking.

73. Veling, *Practical*, 140.

searched for by many contemporary theologians who want to overcome the theological dichotomies of the past to propose a holistic theology as a way and exercise of life. Yet we may still make use of the well-established categories and refer to ourselves as practical, fundamental, or systematic theologians. New ways of designing or practicing holistic theology are currently emerging.

Practical theology in terms of youth ministry is often understood as focusing more on the intentional interconnection between theology and praxis within ever-changing contexts, particular believers, and the communities in which they live. People design their identities, practices, and actions according to their shared experience of God's revelation (upon which fundamental and systematic theology reflects).

> Practical theology is essentially a theology of action and practice. And it is here that youth ministry scholarship should see itself. Youth ministry is a practical theology discipline that seeks to construct a theology of action/practice for younger generations of people. Therefore, the common identity of those in youth ministry scholarship (as well as with those in the broader fields of the ministry arts) is not an application (of theology), but in the fact that we are theologians of action/practice. We are those in the theological faculty that attend to reflection on God's action in concrete locations where young people are present, seeking to construct theories born from practice that led individuals and communities into faithful performative action in the world.[74]

We can see that claiming youth ministry to be a form of practical theology depends to a great extent on whether theologians, ministers, or any of those concerned with youth and youth ministry are willing to consider themselves practical theologians and youth ministry as practical theology and not just an "enriched" kind of social science, pedagogy, or psychology.[75] Kenda Creasy Dean identifies four characteristic points of youth ministry understood as practical theology. First, youth ministry matters to the church. It has both pastoral and theological significance and is thus truly a theological discipline focused on practices and actions. Second, just like practical theology in general, youth ministry too has an intrinsic interdisciplinary nature. Third, it is an orientation of action that makes possible a specific way of knowing—a practical knowledge

---

74. Root, "Practical Theology," 71.
75. Dean, *OMG*, 115.

or perhaps even "wisdom" (Aristotle's *phronēsis*)—which emphasizes Christianity as a distinctive way of life instead of a set of doctrines. Youth ministry tends to maintain the great Christian tradition of mystagogy based on reflective experiences with the revealing God.[76] Fourth, youth ministry as practical theology opts for singularity and human uniqueness. Each human story is relevant and correlates with the unique story of Jesus Christ.[77]

Within the traditional scheme dividing theology into theoretical and practical rubrics, we may agree that youth ministry is primarily a matter of practical theology or directly one of its forms, as argued by Dean, for instance. But from the perspective of an integral (holistic) approach (proposed above), we find that youth ministry matters for all theological disciplines. There is no doubt that youth is a theological question and youth ministry is a theological task (discovered or discoverable thanks to practical theology). But this must be accompanied and followed by a broader engagement and discussion with other theological disciplines. It is my conviction that this will be the future of youth ministry research. While it will remain embedded within practical theology, it will continue to become more engaged in dialogue with other theological disciplines as well. Youth ministry making its theological turn establishes itself as a new dialogue partner for other theological disciplines within academia by partnering itself with practical theology. Although its own terminology, rationale, and future directions remain a bit unclear, since youth ministry as such will "never fit neatly into existing criteria for academic research . . . The question we must ask . . . is whether youth ministry as practical theology can be researched and understood on its own terms."[78]

Currently this is believed possible. But criteria for evaluating youth ministry research often appears too postmodern and hardly accountable (e.g., in its commitments to theology, acknowledgement of interdisciplinarity, emphasizing experience, focusing on different practices and particularity). Moreover, it is still unclear which academic standards are to be used for assessing research and scholarship in youth ministry. "Systematic theology deeply informs our work but misses youth ministry's performative dimensions. The arts provide models for assessing performance, but youth ministry is far less subjective; relating to a teenager is

---

76. Some even see the role of youth minister (especially in worship practices) as the role of the mystagogue. de Kock and Norheim, *Five Questions*, 205.

77. Dean, *OMG*, 115–17.

78. Dean, *OMG*, 118.

not a matter of taste, but a matter of fidelity to the gospel. Social and hard sciences offer methods for empirical research—but insert God into the equation, and science suddenly gets skittish."[79]

It is tricky to predict the future directions of youth ministry research. But after all the possibilities are identified within its move away from the exclusively practical theology paradigm, it may find new ways to adopt a holistic paradigm of practicing theology (as proposed, for instance, by Terry Veling). Why must youth ministry insist on forcing itself into the traditional pigeonhole of practical theology? Should not youth ministry research (as an emerging discipline) enjoy the freedom to set off in its own direction—more postmodern, more ambiguous, dangerous, sometimes rocky and muddy yet still emphasizing a theological commitment, interdisciplinarity, practice, and particularity? Youth ministry might encounter like-minded seekers from other theological disciplines (and perhaps non-theological too) who also search for new ways to move their disciple forward, beyond being stuck or stalled in modern paradigms. In this way contemporary youth ministry represents a specific environment in which theology is not only accepted and transferred into practice but is, further, lived—"taught and written, danced and sung, sculpted and painted, even dreamed and cried."[80]

Youth ministry is going through the process of its own theological turn. As such, it recognizes itself as fundamentally theological. It is trying to listen to the authentic voices of young people and to their theologies. Youth ministry creates an environment that encourages and empowers young people to theologize. At the same time, it exercises a proper theological self-reflection in dialogue with other theological disciplines and contributes a significant deal to the establishment of youth theology (so-called) as a specific contextual theology, bringing young minds and souls to the fore, dwelling amidst the youth cultures and subcultures burgeoning in the contemporary world. Before I further explicate my understanding of emerging youth theology, it is necessary to discern who young people, and the youth, are from a theological perspective.

---

79. Dean, *OMG*, 117–18.
80. Sedmak, *Doing Local Theology*, 11.

3.2 WHO ARE YOUTH IN THEOLOGICAL PERSPECTIVE?

Traditionally understood, youth ministry addresses a specific age-related target group within a particular church community, like outreach ministries specifically tailored to the needs of the elderly. (Such similarities and entanglements between the two deserve their own patient and detailed analysis for research, beyond the scope of my present one). "It seems evident that youth ministry is about youth and is geared towards young people,"[81] as the Dutch sociologist of religion, Monique van Dijk-Groeneboer, argues. However, one finds almost the opposite or contrary perspective in Andrew Root and Kenda C. Dean: "Youth ministry is no longer only about youth."[82] Thus, the question becomes: Who are these young people addressed by youth ministry? Quite a long tradition has been established of addressing young people through the optics of diverse scientific disciplines, like sociology, psychology, cultural studies, etc. Dozens of empirical studies on youth and religion—or, more specifically, youth and Christianity—have been conducted by (practical or empirical) theologians using methods borrowed from the above-mentioned disciplines.

However, a theological discourse dominates the research on youth ministry today, after the theological turn in youth ministry as already discussed in section 3.1.2 above. Youth ministry is no longer defined or delimited to a simplistic and insulting form of babysitting provided by the church as part of the religious educational or church socialization processes (which, all too often, verge on proselytizing indoctrination). Rather, it must be understood as a matter of the whole believing Christian community. If youth ministry is to be understood as fundamentally theological, then it needs its own specific (theological) discourse on youth. In this, youth ministry seeks inspiration from other theological disciplines. Theology matters when we reflect on youth ministry, as well as when we engage in its practice. What is the specific theological understanding of "youth"? Who are young people from theological perspectives?[83] Pivotal questions such as these have been already asked (and responded to) from different points of view. Systematic and biblical theology were traditionally believed to give a broader context to youth ministry.[84] But at the same time, they were rather

---

81. Dijk-Groeneboer, "Youth," 25.

82. Root and Dean, *Theological Turn*, 31.

83. A comprehensive treatment of this question has been offered in de Kock and Norheim, *Five Questions*, 19–45.

84. Dean et al., *Starting*, 31–32.

absent (or, at best, invisible) in youth ministry research.[85] The following section endeavors to take up the challenge of these pivotal questions for various forms of theological engagement with youth.

3.2.1 Different Perspectives on Youth

What does "youth" mean? Is it possible or necessary to define youth in terms of age? Would we benefit, instead, from a different definition? If we take a quick look at some definitions of youth, we find that Plato understood youth as men and women between 17(18) and 30 years of age. The classical Latin term *iuventa* refers only to men between 30 and 45.[86] Van Dijk-Groeneboer defines young people as persons between 15 and 25 years of age.[87] The same age range is used also by practical theologian Pete Ward,[88] and the Czech sociologist Petr Sak places the period of youth between 15 and 30 years of age.[89] *The Vision of Catholic Youth Ministry: Fundamentals, Theory and Practice* textbook is more general when stating, "Youth ministry encompasses young people from early adolescence through to early young adulthood."[90] Sometimes it is assumed that youth as an age-related term is the product of the bourgeois thinking of eighteenth century. In any event, since the early twentieth century, the widely accepted concept of youth is an age-related category which is defined differently by various scientific disciplines such as sociology, psychology, cultural studies, and law.[91]

It seems unlikely (if not impossible) to frame youth into a precisely defined category of age. Contemporary researchers usually opt for less strict definitions to embrace reality in a more nuanced way. Some employ terms like "young persons" or "young people" instead of the vague term "youth." When two of the most prolific scholars on youth ministry today, Root and Dean, speak about young persons, they predominantly have in mind an adolescent person, a teenager. They see adolescence as a specific time of human development marked by advancement, preparation,

---

85. Becker, "Beyond," 10.
86. Kaplánek, *Pastorace*, 14.
87. Dijk-Groeneboer, "Youth," 27.
88. Ward, *Participation and Mediation*, 5.
89. Sak, *Proměny*, 13.
90. McCarty and Delgatto, *Vision*, 11.
91. Martínek, *Ztracená*, 23.

intellectual, spiritual, as well as biological growth.[92] A slightly different focus is provided by Bert Roebben, who identifies young people not only as teenagers but also as young adults.[93] According to his interpretation, there is further development in understanding young adulthood. While traditionally this "life-period" was framed between 16 and 25 years of age in the 1980s, it is also described as a "grey zone between childhood and adulthood."[94] In the 1990s, the young adult confronted globalization and postmodernity. It becomes almost impossible to define it anymore. For Roebben, such confrontation continues because relativity, individualization, flexibility, and multi-optionality remain characteristics of the contemporary young adult.[95] Being young today is certainly a different experience than it was a few decades ago.

All in all, being young today entails living in transition, from the perspective that this transitional state will continue throughout one's own whole life. Today's young people, through the postmodern experience of continuous uncertainty, put contemporary youth ministry in a position that must focus on "moral/religious self-clarification and the building of identity against the background of a blurred society."[96] Youth are still defined by a specific period in life. But at the same time, its specificity is blurred. Those who are labelled "youth" are young people, adolescents, or young adults. Their ages vary from early pubescence to late young adulthood. It accords well with the definition given by the Social and Human Sciences Sector of UNESCO, which is in favor of a broader exposition of youth: "'Youth' is best understood as a period of transition from the dependence of childhood to adulthood's independence and awareness of our interdependence as members of a community. Youth is a more fluid category than a fixed age-group."[97]

In summary, youth does not begin when people are 12 or 15, nor does it end when they are 25 or 30. Like the UNESCO definition, youth ministry applies to different youth definitions in different situations, as it carries out different activities. A precise definition always depends on a particular context (involving both interpretative frameworks, as well as a particular young personality). In general, when speaking of youth

92. Root and Dean, *Theological Turn*, 125.
93. Roebben, *Seeking Sense*, 216–17.
94. Roebben, *Seeking Sense*, 217.
95. Roebben, *Seeking Sense*, 217.
96. Roebben, *Seeking Sense*, 72.
97. United Nations, "Definition of Youth," para. 1.

in the context of youth ministry, it usually refers to young people (the broadest definition). But when it comes to a particular topic or activity, or to research (especially empirical research), the age is usually specified as optional. Thus, age still matters. But the characteristic features seem more important than actual numbers. Yet there is another way to "reveal" the content of the term "youth" in youth ministry (and beyond), and it is a theological one. No matter how important the social sciences, humanities, or other disciplines are and remain for understanding young people, a specifically Christian approach to youth must be theological. To this my discussion now turns.

3.2.2 Youth in Theological Perspective

From a theological perspective, youth is not a strictly age-related group but rather a special way human being relates to God. Therefore, we may see youth as inseparable from our whole humanity, or from the human condition. Youth is an integral part of each human being. It is an integral part of one's own identity. Ontologically, it belongs to our humanity. Once people are young, they will keep their youth, even though the time of their youth will diminish as they become adults or older, and vice versa. The potentiality of adulthood is embedded in every child and each young person. Therefore, childhood and youth remain during the whole duration of our lives. Despite this, youth is still *kairos*, a very opportune time, distinct from others. Youth remains distinctive due to its characteristics (e.g., longing for love and acceptance, searching for meaning, openness, excitement, activity, creativity, hope, development, expectation, etc.). These are inseparable from the totality of being human. Theology reflects upon the mutual relationship between people and their God, between human temporality and eternity. Such insights are found already in the Old Testament (e.g., Isaiah's prophecy). There, human life is seen as the process of aging in front of God, which is *not* so much age-related but, more importantly, "sin-related." The one who resists sin keeps one's youth, even if aged for a century. In Isaiah's words: "No more shall there be in it an infant that lives but a few days, or an old person who does not live out a lifetime; for one who dies at a hundred years will be considered a youth, and one who falls short of a hundred will be considered accursed" (Isa 65:20).

Sin takes us away from God. It sentences us to die and age older forever. Contrary to this, a Biblical perspective suggests youth as a symbol of hope in eternal life and an ontological transformation of the human being through salvation into a new creation (cf. Isa 65:17). This is further developed and freshly described in the New Testament. There, youth is not only a "sin-related" but also a "salvation-related" category. "Truly I tell you, unless you change and become like children, you will never enter the kingdom of heaven" (Matt 18:3). The context of this gospel narrative is of the disciples foolishly discussing their possible greatness. They go to their Master and ask him, "Who is the greatest in the kingdom of heaven?" (Matt 18:2). Jesus responds to their "foolish" question by pointing to the child from the street. Sin does not go away with advanced age, and a child should not be definitive of intellectual immaturity. The evaluation scale of the disciples is turned upside-down. Truly converted (and thus prepared to enter the kingdom of God) is the one who is humble and gives one's own life to the hands of God. It is not one who depends and relies exclusively on one's alleged individual achievements. True greatness is only in humility and through a close relationship to the Son and his Father.[98] "So, if anyone is in Christ, there is a new creation: everything old has passed away; see everything has become new!" (2 Cor 5:17). This Pauline expression connects with the passage from Isaiah (above) and reveals a transformation of the logic of sin that one may find in the Hebrew Bible into the "salvation" logic indicative of the gospels. Youth and childhood play important symbolic roles in both. Openness and devotion to the triune God are qualities attributed to a specifically youthful straightforwardness. Consciously or not, a strong scriptural case could be made that when Christians pray, "Thy kingdom come. . .," they always assume a youthful (or young-minded) standpoint in openness to salvation, hoping and longing for new creation (the new life given by God) and a strong orientation to the ultimate future in the kingdom of heaven. Christians are called to be "forever young" but not in terms of our consumer society seeking salvation. No earthly possessions can bring everlasting life. From a theological perspective, being young is a viewpoint. It is synonymous with the way to the kingdom of heaven, attempting to live its values already in this life by keeping a young mind and an open heart. Thus, the young person must be considered as a complete human being and not simply or dismissively as an underdeveloped one.

---

98. Wilkins, *Matthew*, 626–27.

This is discovered by Wesley W. Ellis,[99] who courageously critiques the colloquial ways in which churches, theologians, as well as the field of youth ministry, definitely approach "youth" with the sole intention of the formation and development of them, under the presumption that they, as and in being "young," are thereby only unformed and undeveloped and, as such, must be changed instead of appreciating what they really and already are. "What lies at the center, as ultimate concern, of this kind of youth ministry is not the youth as such but the Christian adulthood into which they are being developed. It is not that maturity, appropriately defined, is undesirable, but it cannot be normative for ministry if ministry intends to discover God's action in people's lives and not just in their futures."[100]

Even though he refers specifically to youth ministry, it would also apply to most of the theological or ecclesial interpretations of youth. According to Ellis, they have all accepted exclusively and uncritically the concept of young people presumed by developmental psychology (especially that of Erik Erikson).[101] Consequently, Ellis intends to find a new interpretative framework or ground for youth ministry, which "needs to be determined not developmentally but theologically."[102] For that purpose, he suggests a methodological preference for an ontological interpretation of reality (as opposed to an exclusively epistemological one). He aspires for a transversal methodology enabling theology and other sciences to intersect without losing their specific discourses and groundworks.[103] Youth, from Ellis's perspective, must be approached and interpreted on their own terms and lived experiences. Otherwise, there is a risk of what he calls (quoting Chris Jenks) "gerontocentrism." By this term Ellis understands (and critiques) the delimitation of young people from the exclusive perspective of what they shall become, or what they shall be made to develop into (by their superior adult masters). The aim of a gerontocentric orientation to youth ministry such as this is to develop or even produce (i.e., manufacture) a mature Christian adult. As such, any youth ministry (if it could even be called that, from this perspective) is not about youth at all. It is rather about adults as the desired product

---

99. Ellis, "Human Beings," 119–37.
100. Ellis, "Human Beings," 123.
101. Ellis, "Human Beings," 125.
102. Ellis, "Human Beings," 126.
103. Ellis, "Human Beings," 126–27.

THE STORY OF YOUTH MINISTRY AND EMERGING YOUTH THEOLOGY 157

of enforced and disciplined maturation.[104] In order to avoid this curse of gerontocentrism in youth ministry (and also in other frameworks for interpreting youth), we must instead emphasize the authentic humanity of young people: what (or who) they shall become.[105] Ellis thinks that there is an eschatological problem in the theological background of youth ministry. Thus, he applies the eschatology of Jürgen Moltmann to rule out development as a goal for human beings. Forfeiting the mantra of development, people should be allowed to focus more on youth as they are and not as adults (or church authorities) want them to be. However, it would not be wise to put completely aside the notion of development or "human becoming," as suggested by Ellis. Youth, as the mode of humanity, has not only an eschatological dimension but a soteriological dimension as well.

Christianity holds that salvation through Jesus Christ is the aim, goal, and fulfilment of humanity. Thus, a certain kind of development is necessary but naturally not the kind which sets up development itself as *the* goal or *the* end. Firstly, from a soteriological perspective, maturing is equal neither to advancement in age nor to development of skills. It is, rather, qualitative progress in discovering Jesus Christ and aligning one's own life path with his. Secondly, from a soteriological perspective, development is not simply achieved by human effort. It is also, and more importantly, the human openness and readiness to be qualitatively transformed and developed *by grace* (the gracious gifts of God). Consequently, what matters is not self-building or self-development but a confession of Jesus Christ: "If you confess with your lips that Jesus is Lord and believe in your heart that God raised him from the dead, you will be saved" (Rom 10:9). Thus again, for Christians, salvation comes only through Jesus Christ, and our humanity must be transformed and intensified into the fullness of being human (a saved human being). However, "not everyone who says to me, 'Lord, Lord,' will enter the kingdom of heaven, but only the one that does the will of my Father in heaven" (Matt 7:21). People can, but at the same time cannot, work out their salvation. They try to recognize and do the will of the Father in heaven, yet they cannot reach salvation through their own powers. That is only possible through Jesus Christ, for whom it is not enough to simply call Lord. A loving attitude towards life must be developed instead. It is a constant improvement of

---

104. Ellis, "Human Beings," 128–30.
105. Ellis, "Human Beings," 127, 130.

human love (*caritas*) that leads towards the ultimate, eternal Love: love that Christians await and hope for through practicing baptism.

> Practicing baptism is the process of being brought into the presence of the kingdom of Christ again and again. This kingdom comes to human beings through the gifts of the triune God: In this kingdom, the Holy Spirit calls and draws the baptized to Christ. When this happens, the lives of the baptized may be transformed—as they are gradually conformed to Christ, freed to practice the common order of Christian love, becoming Christ to the neighbor.[106]

A synonym for Norheim's "practicing baptism" might be a constant deciding for Jesus Christ, or a continuous or ongoing conversion of human religious ideas and practices. Becoming Christian means a fundamental option for Christ that starts an ongoing process of continuous discipleship and becoming—the carpenter's apprentice, a lifelong learner, who aspires and hopes to master the craft of being human and transform it (and oneself) into the art of humanity in the kingdom of heaven. It is the process Pierre Teilhard de Chardin called "Christification."[107] This is a gradual improvement of humanity (and the entire universe) into its fullness in Christ (Omega point), "the rebirth and ongoing transformation of all in Christ."[108]

In this horizon, the church may be seen as a learning community of theological virtues (faith, hope, and love) where young people can provide lenses through which believing communities may interpret reality in a young and salvific way. Consequently, it is right that youth ministry is developing its own (practical) theology as a reflection on religious experience, from the perspective of young people, for the sake of the whole church. Young people represent the future of the church and, at present, play a role in the "community's health barometer."[109] It is not a matter of a different theology as such. But it is a different way of doing theology. It is a different mode of living, a different way of expressing a relationship

---

106. Norheim, *Practicing Baptism*, 205.

107. "As a consequence of the Incarnation, the divine immensity has transformed itself for us into the omnipresence of Christification. All the good that I can do (opus et operatio) is physically gathered in, by something of itself, into the reality of consummated Christ. Everything I endure, with faith and love, by way of diminishment or death, makes me a little more closely an integral part of his mystical body." De Chardin, *Divine Milieu*, 123.

108. Imbelli, *Rekindling*, 6.

109. Root and Dean, *Theological Turn*, 16.

with God: maybe a new contextual theology where the youth are not only seen from a theological perspective but offer (and, indeed, already *are*) viable, crucial, and necessary theological perspectives themselves. Youth could become a kind of theological hermeneutical key and a way of interpreting reality theologically. Thus, the most important shift towards a theological vision of youth in Christianity appears when young people are recognized not merely as receivers of theology designed by ecclesial (theological as well as ministerial) gerontocentrism or the instrumental concerns of adults (Roebben) but rather as its active agents. Young people can produce their specific theology (e.g., Faix, Schweitzer, Schlag), and it can be relevant for the whole believing community, even for professional theologians or religious educators.[110] They must not simply seek what *they think* young people from a theological perspective should be. They must constantly attempt to hear young voices. They must seek what (or, better, who) young people are, who young people want to be. An emerging discipline called youth theology sets off this direction. It represents a new mode of contextual theology emphasizing the abilities of young people to theologize and get involved in the complex theological process of interpreting faith, Scripture and tradition within denominations and throughout Christianity. In this way youth theology, as a new kind of contextual theology, can be well resourced by the theological turn in youth ministry.

3.3 EMERGING YOUTH THEOLOGY

It is necessary to begin this section by noting that the concept of youth theology does not emerge only from the environment of theologically reflected youth ministry. A significant contribution to discovering and developing youth theology is also made by several experts in religious education (e.g., Schweitzer, Schlag, Roebben, and others will be addressed in this chapter below). My focus on the context of youth ministry was inspired from participating in the IASYM association. However, I do not dissociate religious education from youth ministry as strictly separated fields. Both intertwine and merge in their common quest for working together with young people and reflecting upon their practices in theological ways. Religious education and youth ministry both focus on being informative, as well as formative, within the lives of young people. It

---

110. Schlag, "Systematic Topics," 374.

should not be confined exclusively to providing information and formatting young lives into preset categories of adulthood. Ideally it would be about living in the presence of the other, reflecting together on experiences of revelation, faith, and community. Just as religious education must teach young people while also learning from them in return, youth ministry must minister young people while also ministered by them too.

Religious education and youth ministry are closely related fields in which those involved do theology together. While in the presence of the young, both disciplines have the potential to become a source of youth theology as a new contextual approach to theology, thought and lived in coordinates of complementarity of theology's many fields and branches, striving for holistic unity in inner diversity. In this respect, young people can serve by challenging adults, and other theological disciplines, to rediscover the principle of youth already present and at work in them; to rediscover their "young side." While focusing on the theoretical concept of youth, we must never forget that it is tightly bound to actual young people and their lives. In other words, it is necessary for anyone who approaches the notion of youth or interpreting young people from within the Christian faith to do it from theological perspective. Yet, young people are not merely objects of theological inquiry by academics, defining and deciding (by their scholarly authority) what "youth" means and who young people are. Young people are also, and predominantly, active agents of theology. This is clearly expressed by Tobias Faix: "Young people are independent theological protagonists of their own right."[111] Faix is not alone in this conviction. One reason (among many) by which we may perceive the emergence of youth theology being designed in different ways in the past two decades is a principle on which nearly all authors writing on youth and theology agree: that young people can produce their specific theology, and it can be relevant for the whole believing community, including adults, professional theologians, church authorities, youth ministers, and religious educators too.

Perhaps the best way how to understand youth theology would be as a kind of lay theology[112] helping to unveil new horizons within the complex research fields of youth and theology.[113] It is a way of doing theology instead of rational reflection on the Christian faith assigned only to academics or church leaders. Since theology was always an intellectual

---

111. Faix, "How Theology," 8.
112. Schweitzer, "Adolescents," 185.
113. Faix, "How Theology," 7.

and reflexive way of dealing with the reality of Christian faith, it cannot be reserved only to the theological elite. All believers (including youth) can be theologians and have a right capacity to theologize. In this sense, youth theology is an active participation in the process of theologizing. It should be young people themselves who search and create their own theological language and convictions for communicating Scripture, sharing theological insights, and understanding faith from their own perspective(s). Young people are not theologically impotent. Any attempt to bring (or deliver) them a theology that they, as youth, necessarily lack starts with the wrong assumption. The youth can think critically and reflectively about theological questions, but maybe not in the way that adults (and even they, the youth) would expect. Young people may do theology without even considering that what they are doing is theology. It is the task of professional theology to encourage and nurture these unsuspected abilities of young people and help them recognize or discern themselves as theologians. To frame these considerations about the theological abilities of young people into some kind of systematic framework, I would like to offer a brief overview of different perspectives on youth theology. It is most probably incomplete, but it at least tries to include the most important concepts I believe have emerged and are still emerging in the formulation of youth theology so far. (Later, I intend to present youth theology as an umbrella term able to accommodate differing conceptions, be they from the backgrounds of youth ministry or religious education.)

3.3.1 Different Shades of Youth Theology

Despite the common conviction about the crucial importance of a solid theological background for youth ministry (i.e., its own theological potential and theological understanding of youth as such), contemporary authors vary in their respective conceptual approaches. What do they mean when they speak about youth theology (Ger. *Jugendtheologie*) (Schlag, Schweitzer, Faix, and Roebben); theology of youth; theology of youth ministry (Noval, Roebben); theology for youth ministry (Borgman); or theology of, with, and for children, youth, and adolescents (Schlag, Schweitzer)? All these concepts wish to discover ways by which to engage theologically with youth/young people; suggest points of departure within theological discourse to theologize about young people, with them, and for them; and finally, to recognize and possibly understand the very theology that young people produce themselves.

1. **Theology of Youth and Theology of Youth Ministry (Noval).** The most popular labels or syntagms used today are probably "theology of youth" and "theology of youth ministry." The Danish Catholic theologian Christian Noval provides helpful distinctions between them, yet he maintains their close relationship. He asks, "Where does the discourse about young people belong within the theological landscape? What kind of theology is theology of youth?"[114] Noval has no difficulties with theology being designed for young people by professional theologians, especially if it comes from direct experiences of theologizing with them. But he points out certain problems that arise when it becomes a theology of youth/young people. Is it theology done by young people themselves? Or is it theology concerned about youth as such? To answer his questions, Noval distinguishes between theology of youth understood as a genitive objective and as a genitive subjective. The "of" could mean "either" or, more importantly, "both." As genitive objective, "of youth" means that young people are objects of theological investigation. As such, Noval thinks it would belong to systematic theology. "It is a theological reflection mainly based on revelation to explore the nature and significance of youth. It has youth and youthfulness as its topic and belongs to a certain extent within Systematic Theology and especially Theological Anthropology."[115] From this perspective, youth is researched as a special and theologically significant dimension of humanity.[116]

   Further, theology of youth, in terms of genitive subjective, considers young people as subjects of theologizing. Understood in this way, it is focused more on practical work with them instead of providing theories about them or about youth, in general. As such, it belongs, then, to the realm of practical theology. Appreciating young people as subjects of theologizing also encourages the possibility of their own theological capabilities. "When Theology of Youth takes the sense of a genitivus subjectivus it is the work with

---

114. Noval, "Youth and Creation," 35.
115. Noval, "Youth and Creation," 35.
116. Roebben, *Seeking Sense*, 131.

young people that stands at the center and as such it often belongs within the field of Practical Theology."[117]

With this distinction, Noval opts for theology of youth based on revelation and intends to discover who youth are with the help of theological anthropology. He identifies the period of youth (and childhood) as "part of God's relating to us,"[118] and, consequently, its constitutive potential for "who and how we ought to be as human beings."[119] According to Noval, contemporary theology of youth mostly has the form of a genitive subjective and thus, despite the scope implied by this name, takes the shape of what he calls theology of youth ministry.

Noval's key issue is growth as "an existential dimension of being human. And who are better than children and youth to express human continuous maturation?"[120] Theology of youth as genitive objective is, according to Noval "an important framework when we engage in often sociological based studies within Theology of Youth Ministry. It is important as it gives us a Christian understanding of youth."[121]

This is not to say that sociology (as well as other arts and humanities) does not have its own valuable perspectives on youth. But this does underline the importance of designing a specific theological framework for any kind of youth or youth ministry research done from a Christian perspective. In other words, the arts and humanities should not be omitted when designing a theological framework for any kind of youth or youth ministry research. However, theology must always remain its indispensable and crucial component.

Theology of youth, from the perspective of Noval, should be a necessary theological fundament for theology of youth ministry. But it must always carefully maintain its interdisciplinary nature. In fact, designing theology of youth for youth ministry research within a Christian religious background can become a great opportunity for (and platform of) dialogue between systematic and practical theology. Theology of youth in the genitive objective (as a matter of systematic theology and, namely, theological anthropology) from the perspective of Noval, provides "the theological lens through

117. Noval, "Youth and Creation," 35.
118. Noval, "Youth and Creation," 44.
119. Noval, "Youth and Creation," 44.
120. Noval, "Youth and Creation," 44.
121. Noval, "Youth and Creation," 36.

which Theology of Youth Ministry is formed in order to reform the practice of Youth Ministry. Christian Youth Ministry has to be constructed on a theological vision of youth and development. That is the task of Theology of Youth."[122]

2. **Theology for Youth Ministry (Borgman).** Another approach to theology and youth (quite like the conclusions drawn by Noval) is Dean Borgman's theology for youth ministry. Borgman holds that theology proceeds from Biblical scholarship (revealed, key, or master narrative), through historical theology (cumulative narrative), to systematic theology (selective narrative). But, for Borgman, all these theological disciplines culminate in practical theology.[123] He sees theology primarily as narrative (often paradoxical in nature). It is a story that touches upon all who consider themselves Christian and challenges those who do not. Nonetheless, not all Christians are professional theologians, according to Borgman. But they are theologians insofar as they think about God and search for relationship with him—and with other people too.[124] That means Christians are embedded in everyday life, in praxis, and in their multiple relationalities, where the personal triune God plays the central role. Each Christian interprets Scripture, community, and the self, says Borgman. Consequently, he calls theology a "threefold interpretative task."[125] Each academic theology should come out of practice and return to it as well. Theology does not start within our mind but in our hearts, states Borgman.[126] Building on James Loder, Borgman develops a theology of personhood on categories of growth and development that are characteristic of the period of youth.[127]

Here Borgman meets Noval, even though Noval sets off in the direction of systematic theology (theological anthropology) and Borgman keeps to practical theologian. The practical theology of persons (or personhood) proposed by Borgman leads naturally to culture, a space or landscape in which young people live as persons. He especially observes developments and changes within culture as

---

122. Noval, "Youth and Creation," 45.
123. Borgman, *Foundations*, 9–10.
124. Borgman, *Foundations*, 68.
125. Borgman, *Foundations*, 18–19.
126. Borgman, *Foundations*, 69.
127. Borgman, *Foundations*, 83–101.

it is lived by young people and witnessed (and reflected upon) by older ones. Investigating practical-theological principles (foundations), designing a theology of persons, and immersing himself and his thoughts into the melting pot of contemporary cultures leads Borgman towards a Christ-centered, holistic youth ministry, which flows out of a Christ-centered, holistic (even though sill practical) theology.[128] In summation, Borgman attempts to design practical theology *for* youth ministry, not theology *of* youth ministry, even though it would most probably fit into Noval's theology *of* youth ministry (in the genitive subjective).

3. **Theology of Embrace (Roebben).** Independently of Miroslav Volf,[129] Roebben introduces the metaphor of embrace into the context of religious education and youth ministry. According to Volf, the metaphor of embrace expresses most essentially "the will to give ourselves to others and 'welcome' them, to readjust our identities to make space for them . . . prior to any judgment about others, except that of identifying them in their humanity. The will to embrace precedes any 'truth' about others and any construction of their 'justice.' This will, is absolutely indiscriminate and strictly immutable; it transcends the moral mapping of the social world into 'good' and 'evil.'"[130]

This could serve as a résumé for Roebben's overall understanding of youth theology, which strives to embrace young people as they are, without any instrumental preoccupations, prejudices, or fast judgments of what is good and bad. In his youth theology of embrace, Roebben wants to see young people as they truly are because only such an approach does justice to their humanity. Young people are not to become human, for they already are human in a particular stage of their development.[131]

Further, Roebben construes his youth theology of embrace (as do many practical theologians from Europe) according to the structural-hermeneutical tradition of Western Roman Catholic pastoral theology, consisting of three hermeneutical stages: perceiving

---

128. Borgman, *Foundations*, 280.

129. Volf, *Exclusion*; Volf, "Vision," 195–205. Even though Roebben did not have Volf's theological reflection on embrace in mind when formulating his own "theology of embrace" in the context of RE, an encounter of Roebben's reflection with that of Volf may become very interesting theological adventure.

130. Volf, *Exclusion*, 29.

131. Štěch, "Who Are Youth," 131.

(seeing), judging, and acting.[132] Theology of embrace involves young people (young adults), their ministers, and the context of the particular ministry alike. Those who minister with youth should let young people define and express themselves (the voices of young people shall speak and shall be heard), even though the opposite is often true, observes Roebben critically. Instead of inserting their views, youth ministers and religious educators should develop the spiritual capacity to see God, who manifests himself amongst and through the lives and stories of young people, who are perceived individually as unique personalities.[133] This can lead to a practice of the empowerment of young people in a spiritual and social way too. Youth ministry and religious education perceived and done in this way is "about maieutic, about the vocation of the pastor to give birth to new life, who reveals unexpected capacities and opportunities in the life of the adolescent, who supports a broadening of perspective and who sometimes challenges the other to change or radically adjust his perspective."[134]

In the perspective of Roebben, it is central to any kind of youth theology to embrace young people in their specificity and uniqueness. Youth theology is a form of living theology in the presence of the (young) other; it is doing theology with open arms ready to embrace our fellow human beings, the realities of this world, as well as God who is the (Triune) One searching for each of us with open arms.

> Many times I have been given the opportunity to experience that this view on God in the hands of human beings really can appeal to adolescents. They have an aversion to immense theological projects in which God can be found somewhere out there. For them the fountain of life is immanent, hidden in daily acts of brother- and sisterhood, in the desire for a more humane world and in the surprising ingenuity of human minds and souls to bring this into realization. God is in here, within the whirling undercurrent of a life that asks for animated storytellers."[135]

All in all, Roebben's theology of embrace reminds me strongly of the philosophy of Gabriel Marcel, who in his metaphysics of hope emphasized an open attitude of spiritual availability to others as the

132. Roebben, *Seeking Sense*, 237.
133. Roebben, *Seeking Sense*, 239.
134. Roebben, *Seeking Sense*, 240–41.
135. Roebben, *Seeking Sense*, 242.

most authentic way of human life.[136] An authentic theological life in the presence of the (young) other and in the presence of (the Triune) God, whom we can meet everywhere in this world, constitutes the baseline of Roebben's theology of embrace. Roebben's theology of embrace represents a distinct model of youth theology for religious education and youth ministry. In one of his books,[137] Roebben left behind his metaphor of embrace, but in fact he develops his theology of embrace a little further. I think "Theology of Embrace" could be an alternative subtitle of that book because Roebben still pursues the same values of the embrace style of theology as he proposed in his earlier work—inclusiveness, attention for difference and the other, openness, a welcoming attitude towards the other, etc. Roebben invites all people, including children and youth, to one round table, and as Aaron Ghiloni expresses in his review of Roebben's book *Theology Made in Dignity*: "Roebben's table is big; its round space accommodates a wide range of diners—children, atheists, poets, pragmatists, rock musicians, true believers, Ivy Leaguers. *Theology Made in Dignity* listens to all their voices."[138]

And, I would add, Roebben embraces all whom he invites to his big roundtable, including young people, whom he accepts not as objects of his educational efforts but rather as partners in a common adventure of doing theology together. In his understanding of youth theology, Roebben is very close to the so-called German religious education school of children and youth theology,[139] which is the last conception of youth theology to be presented here.

4. **Young People as Theologians and Explicit Youth Theology (German RE School).** The contours of an explicit youth theology appear more clearly in another concept of European origin emerging from the context of religious education. During the last decade of the twentieth century, children's theology appeared on the theological agenda.[140] One of the most outstanding authors promoting this idea

---

136. Marcel, *Homo Viator*, 17.

137. Roebben, *Theology Made in Dignity*.

138. Ghiloni, Review of *Theology Made in Dignity*, 238.

139. "In 2011 a network for youth theology was established with its accompanying yearbook for youth theology . . . since 2012." Roebben, *Theology Made in Dignity*, 81. We can hence speak not only of a school but also of a theological or religious pedagogical movement. Roebben, *Theology Made in Dignity*, 90.

140. Schweitzer, "Children as Theologians," 179–90.

was certainly Friedrich Schweitzer. He offered children's theology[141] as an extension of the already established concept of children as philosophers. His assumption is that if children can ask philosophical questions and show philosophical abilities, then this would extend also to religion and theology. In due time, children's theology became an established concept, especially within the field of religious education in Europe. It has continued to spread worldwide.[142] In addition to Friedrich Schweitzer and Anton A. Bucher, scholars like Gerhard Büttner, Friedhelm Kraft, Petra Freudenberger-Lötz, Hartmut Rupp, Elisabeth Schwarz, and Mirjam Zimmermann count among the pioneers of children's theology. Those who are touched with their writings, reflect on them, and are engaged with the topic today are numerous and cannot be all named, here. Principles and methods of the children's theology concept also extend to adolescents and young people and naturally grew beyond the field of religious education and became a "hot topic" for research fields in youth ministry and practical theology as well.

However, Schweitzer does not stop by proclaiming children as theologians. He continues to extend his concept, and quite recently (based on a joint project with Thomas Schlag),[143] suggests that adolescents or young people are to be viewed as theologians too.[144] It may seem easy to proclaim young people as theologians. It is, of course, more difficult to argumentatively support such a claim. Some of the major objections against this way of seeing young people as theologians are simple questions, such as: Who is theologian? Is a youngster a theologian? Schweitzer anticipates this: "Whoever tries to view children or adolescents as theologians is likely to encounter critical comments, especially concerning the ambiguous meaning of 'theology' or 'theologian' in this case. Does it

---

141. Friedrich Schweitzer used the term "*Children theology*" (Ger. *Kindertheologie*) for the first time, when he wrote a preface to the German translation of the book *God Talk with Young Children* by John M. Hull. Schweitzer, "Children as Theologians," 179. The concept of "children as theologians" (*Kinder als Theologen*) appeared earlier in 1992 (in the inquisitive, with a question mark) in an article Bucher, "Kinder als Theologen," 19–22, who in the same year also published an article using the term "*Kindertheologie*" (*children theology*) in the journal, *Schweitzer schule*. Bucher, "Kinder und die Rechtfertigung Gottes," 7–12.

142. Zimmermann, "What Is Children's Theology," 1.

143. Schlag and Schweitzer, *Brauchen*; Schlag and Schweitzer, *Jugendtheologie*.

144. Schweitzer, "Adolescents as Theologians," 184. Adolescent theology is sometimes used as an alternative to the term "youth theology."

make sense to apply the same term to children or adolescents on the one hand and to academic researchers on the other?"[145]

According to Schweitzer it does. But this is not to be reduced to an equivocation between them. Theology of young people is certainly different from the one produced by professional specialists, yet their theologies are (and shall be) related. It is about a different way of doing theology, a way which tries to overcome the isolating or alienating boundaries between academic and ordinary theology.

As already mentioned in the previous discussion of the "scientific" character of theology in chapter 1.2, ordinary theology identifies theology as an integral part of everyday life. Its conception came from practical theology but touches closely upon both systematic and fundamental theology too. One of the major proponents of ordinary theology, who also coined the term, is Jeff Astley,[146] who is also an editor and contributor to another volume on ordinary theology,[147] in which he writes, "I have defined ordinary theology as 'the theological beliefs and processes of believing that finds expression in the God-talk of those believers who have received no scholarly theological education.' As not all such discourse can count as theology, I restrict the designation to 'reflective' God-talk. We should not automatically deny reflective status to theology of these believers, although the reflections of ordinary theologians are frequently less precise than the academy expects."[148]

Quoting Farley and Barth, he continues to describe what he means by "ordinary theology" in relation to academic theology.

> I hold that the difference between ordinary and academic theology is only a matter of degree—no pun intended. Even academics normally begin by doing theology in an ordinary way, and this ordinary theology often continues to underlie their more academic theological expressions. And, historically speaking, the academic mode of theology owes much of its origin—and develops alongside—this less conceptual, technical or systematic form of theology, which begins as "cognitive disposition and orientation of the soul" that represents the "wisdom proper to the life of a believer" and becomes a personal, autobiographical and aphoristic "irregular dogmatics."[149]

145. Schweitzer, "Adolescents as Theologians," 185.
146. Astley, *Ordinary Theology*.
147. Astley and Francis, *Exploring*.
148. Astley, "Analysis," 1.
149. Astley, "Analysis," 1.

Even though many like Jeff Astley have tried to overcome the barriers dividing academic theology and ordinary, lived, or everyday theology, there remains a tension between them. Perhaps it is unwise (and most likely impossible) to completely remove this tension. Barriers and clearly delimited frontiers are sometimes useful (if, though, also oppressive), and tension can become an inspiring force in the process of theologizing. As Roebben remarks, the tension between academic and ordinary theology "should be productive and creative, rather than destructive."[150] If such a creative tension between "hard" (academic and church) and "soft" (lay, ordinary, everyday) theology occurs, it yet has the potential to further dialogue between systematic and practical theologians. It is at hand that practical theologians tend to enjoy more ordinary theologies, and systematic theologians are more at home within the church official structures and the world of academia. Both seem to be prejudiced against one another in different ways. But the development of youth theology may perhaps bring them closer together. Roebben believes "that practical and systematic theologians can encounter each other on a deeper level in their public presence, when they engage together in a globalizing society and try to read the signs of the times in the light of the gospel."[151]

The environment of youth ministry and religious education can become a great platform for such a desired encounter. This, however, requires a conversion of theologians. They must recognize that they do not have a monopoly on interpreting Christian narrative, neither from the systematic nor the practical side of the spectrum. Expert opinion always matters. But the voices of ordinary people, especially of those who are marginalized, matter just as much. Roebben summarizes it in these words: "The essential characteristic of children's theology and youth theology is the assumption that there is no substantial but only gradual difference in theologizing. The difference between young people and adults is about the same level of magnitude as between ordinary believers and professional theologians: gradual and not substantial. Both raise the same (substantial) questions, but the complexity of their answers is (gradually) different."[152]

According to Schweitzer, youth theology is a particular kind of ordinary or a "special type of lay" theology,[153] because the right to theology

---

150. Roebben, *Seeking Sense*, 272.
151. Roebben, *Seeking Sense*, 272.
152. Roebben, *Theology Made in Dignity*, 81–82.
153. Schweitzer, "Adolescents as Theologians," 185.

(if there is such a thing) would be not only granted to adults alone. Such conviction is rather rare and thus truly innovative, since young people are usually excluded from the scope of theology. Theologians, unfortunately, are often convinced that theology cannot be of any interest to those who are young. They "seldom include young people with their intended audience," and "most of them are writing in a language that is not understandable or attractive to young people."[154]

Despite this diagnosis, Schweitzer believes that theology is useful for young people and vice versa; those insights and (ordinary) theological reflections and considerations of young people may be useful for professional theologians too. Young people are not theologically incapable. Thus, the attitude of bringing theology to them as something they definitively do not yet have seems to be a dangerous assumption. Academic theology must start the dialogue with young people because they are not only able to formulate such questions. They are also more capable of offering answers.[155] They can think critically and reflectively about theological questions, and thus, a fundamental task for professional theology might be to open new horizons to young people, encourage their theological abilities (often indiscernible to them themselves), and thus help young people think of themselves as theologians. "If theology in the broadest sense means reflective engagement with religious ideas, images, and convictions, the transition to the personal faith of adolescents necessarily entails theology. More specifically, it entails adolescents practicing the activity of theological scrutiny, even if they do not call it theology."[156]

Thus, realizing young people as theologians, or as having a theology of their own, is crucial, especially for new (and innovative) perspectives in youth ministry and religious education, says Schweitzer.[157] I think it is helpful to extend this claim to the whole of theology. The expressions of faith by young people can provide a distinctive hermeneutical key or perspective for all theological disciplines. Consequently, any theology which receives inspiration from interactions with young people may be called youth theology—the theology preferring a biographical-exploratory style over the dogmatic-affirmative.[158]

---

154. Schweitzer, "Adolescents as Theologians," 186.
155. Schweitzer, "Adolescents as Theologians," 187.
156. Schweitzer, "Adolescents as Theologians," 188.
157. Schweitzer, "Adolescents as Theologians," 190.
158. Roebben, *Theology Made in Dignity*, 90.

3.3.2 Systemizing Youth Theology

It is now beyond doubt that among the differing conceptions of youth theology, the explication of it by the German RE school abounds with the best conceptual clarity. The reason for this is most probably its grounding in the broader history of children's theology (*Kindertheologie*) research. This is where Schweitzer coined a threefold scheme for describing the complexity of the process of theologizing in the presence of children.[159] There is (1) *theology of children* emphasizing their own theological abilities, (2) *theology with children* involving adult partners (parents, educators, ministers, professional theologians, clergy, etc.), and (3) *theology for children* done by adults whose primary audience or target group is children. Later, Schweitzer (together with Thomas Schlag) proposed the same scheme for *Jugendtheologie*—theology of young people,[160] and more recently, for adolescent theology,[161] replacing "children" with alternate categories of youth or adolescents. Schweitzer's systemization of these different facets of theological engagement with children, youth, and adolescents, as well as emphasizing their own theological abilities, provides helpful models for understanding the nature of children, youth, and adolescent theology, and basic coordinates for the relations between academic theology and ordinary (lay, lived, every day, children, youth, adolescent . . .) theology. Using these models in youth theology also opens theological reflections and engagements different from practical theology, youth ministry, or religious education. For following presentation, I am using terminology focused on the category of "youth" from Schlag and Schweitzer's publications on Jugentheologie.

The first perspective, labelled as (1) *theology of young people* (Ger. *Theologie der Jugendlichen*, or *Theologie von Jugendlichen*), refers to young people *as* theologians. This perspective is a presupposition for any kind of theological engagement with (Ger. *mit*) or for (Ger. *für*) young people. The way Schlag and Schweitzer present their theology of young people (*Theologie von Jugendlichen*) corresponds with Noval's theology of young people in the sense of the genitive subjective.[162] Thus, translation of their term *Theologie von Jugendlichen* as "theology of youth" (and consequently also

---

159. Schweitzer, "Was ist und wozu," 18; Schweitzer, "Children as Theologians," 179–90.

160. Schlag and Schweitzer, *Brauchen*; Schlag and Schweitzer, *Jugendtheologie*.

161. Schweitzer, "Adolescents as Theologians," 190–96.

162. Noval, "Youth and Creation," 36.

Theologie mit Jugendlichen and *Theologie für Jugendliche* as "theology with youth" and "theology for youth"), which is used for instance by Roebben,[163] can be a bit misleading since it does not take into account theology of youth in terms of the genitive objective and, as such, is not an ordinary theology produced by young people but rather theology which takes youth and youthfulness as its topic.[164] If we would use "theology of, with, and for youth," it shall be in German—"Theologie von, mit und für Jugend"—but when Schlag and Schweitzer use the word *Jugendlichen*, I believe and suggest that it should be translated into English as "young people"; i.e., those who are young. Otherwise, we are ever confined to the *exclusive disjunction* of speaking about youth either in the genitive subjective or objective. We should always endeavor instead for an *inclusive conjunction* of both the genitive and subjective roles of young people.

It is for these reasons that I prefer to translate and think these German terms as theology *of, with, and for young people*, because they connote a more practical theology or religious pedagogy. If we take the perspectives of systematic or fundamental theology, we shall perhaps speak about theology *of, with, and for youth*, because by the term "youth," we understand the objective principle (a theological interpretation of youth, possibilities of theological engagement with youth, and designing theology for youth) instead of a subjective particularity (theology or theologies of young people, theologizing with young people in practice, designing theology for particular young people).

Moving beyond these interminable terminological difficulties, let us return to the theology of young people as the first perspective of the threefold scheme of Schlag and Schweitzer. Tobias Faix sees it as "providing insights into ways of thinking, feeling and acting common to the faith of adolescents."[165] This is not wrong. But it sounds too functional (perhaps prone to instrumentalization, critiqued above). The theology of young people does not only inform us about the ways of thinking, feeling, and acting of contemporary youth! Young people do not only have their own religious thoughts, feelings, and practices, but they also reflect on them,[166] insofar as they too are theologians. Thus, a theology of young people can disclose and discover a whole dimension of theological reflection that is often utterly unknown to or underappreciated by adults,

163. Roebben, *Seeking Sense*, 270; Roebben, *Theology Made in Dignity*, 90.
164. Noval, "Youth and Creation," 35.
165. Faix, "How Theology," 9.
166. Schweitzer, "Adolescents as Theologians," 190.

church officials, youth ministers, teachers of religion, or professional theologians (or, at worst, completely forgotten, dismissed, or ignored by them). It is about gaining access to this dimension. Only insiders can provide keys for those left on the outside. Only young people themselves can decide who can enter and to whom the access is denied. But maybe this is too reductive and not the case. Maybe access to the theological dimension of young people is already wide open and waiting for those who show themselves in possession of young minds and open hearts. Maybe only these kinds of hearts and minds may find the door open and perceive theology not far removed from everyday life.[167]

If we consider young people as theologians, we can see them also as partners for theological discussion. Therefore, there is a space for the second perspective of Schlag and Schweitzer called (2) *theology with young people* (Ger. *Theologie mit Jugendlichen*). This primarily takes the form of dialogue, which for Schlag and Schweitzer occurs chiefly within the realm of religious education and youth ministry. Many youth ministers, as well as religious pedagogues, find dialogue with young people to have an impact on the budding theological formation of young people on the one hand and nurturing their own theology (as religious educators, youth ministers, and adults) on the other. For instance, Bert Roebben claims his own work to be rooted in such dialogue: "My personal stance as a religious education scholar is situated in the 'theology with children.'"[168]

Theology with young people challenges seemingly solid and certain concepts of those who already have them (teachers of religion, church officials, theologians, and adults in general, too). It is very dynamic and, indeed, often provocative.[169] Theology with young people is never only an intellectual exercise. It is not a scientific debate. Rather, it has a relational base. Theologizing with young people is by no means an easy task. To theologize with them means to enter relationship with them. This demands that the relationship entail a mutual connection between those who want to enter such a relationship. Any relationship should be optional rather than enforced or paternalistic. It must always endeavor to be an act or effect of freedom. Theology with young people holds that young people should be free to decide if they want to become partners for theological discussions with others (young or adult). If a theology of youth is performed in youth ministry or religious education, it must be

---

167. Schweitzer, "Adolescents as Theologians," 189.
168. Roebben, *Theology Made in Dignity*, 91.
169. Schweitzer, "Adolescents as Theologians," 193.

clear that all those who participate are welcomed into the relationship with the teacher or youth minister. Theology with youth helps those who are involved (both young and adult) to rethink their faith, to recognize and interpret their experience from religious perspectives. Bert Roebben offers a helpful model for theology with young people from the perspective of religious education:

> Within the complexity of late modern (de-traditionalized and multi-religious) societies, religious education teachers are not allowed to leave students alone with their own moral and religious identity formation, but should help them didactically into exciting "narthical playgrounds," . . . into enriching "green pastures" of (1) performance, (2) thick description, and (3) meta-reflection, where their imaginations are stirred up by Bible and other sacred stories, classical texts, meaningful others, sacred spaces and practices, to name only a few.[170]

Theology with young people includes young people into the process of the ongoing ancient Christian practices of theological discernment, mystagogy, and missionary witness (participating in *missio Dei*). It is about inviting young people as partners to the inner theological reflection about the fundamentals of Christian faith practiced within believing communities, along with any witnessing outside those communities, as well as to others, about the faith, hope, and love that Christians find and continue to discover in their relationships with God. It is like the systole and diastole of the cardiac rhythm, a vital theological circulatory system. A theology of youth welcomes young new partners into the beating hearts of the Christian life.

The third perspective proposed by Schlag and Schweitzer is (3) *theology for young people*. It is simply all theology, including young people in its scope. It is theology designed with special attention to and for the young or adolescent developmental stage.[171] The two previous perspectives recognized the theological abilities of young people and emphasized their own theological expressions. This last perspective represents another crucial element. "If the intention is to support them (young people) in their own doing theology and to enhance their abilities of theological

---

170. Roebben, *Theology Made in Dignity*, 91–92.
171. Faix, "How Theology," 9.

thinking, it will be quite useful to let them participate in what ideas and insights theology has to offer."[172]

Without theology for young people, the whole theological spectrum would be incomplete and would easily run aground and stall in theologically shallow waters. Theology for young people cannot be without theology of and with young people. It should not be limited to the style and language of catechisms handing down "divine" truth to passive or neutralized recipients to be blindly accepted by them. Instead, theology for youth is a passionate challenge for theologians (practical, systematic, biblical, fundamental . . .) to discover the inclusive, supportive, useful, attractive, helpful, understandable, and interdisciplinary potential (and language) in their own theological disciplines and share them with young people in a way that they do not manufacture them as inheritors of readymade truths. There must be true dialogue partners (theology with young people) whose own theological constructions or convictions are truly respected and taken seriously (theology of young people), even when adults, youth ministers, religious educators, theologians, or church officials disagree with them for various reasons.[173] According to Roebben, Schlag and Schweitzer "are convinced that the implicit and personal 'theologies of youth' [young people] should be the starting point for educational [read: explicit and reflected] processes of 'theology with youth' [young people] and 'theology for youth' [young people]."[174]

At this point it is possible to conclude that all three aspects of youth theology proposed and systemized by Schlag and Schweitzer (and widely discussed and accepted by other scholars) should be held in a balanced relationship. Youth theology can benefit the most from the equal presence of theology of, with, and for youth, because only in this case may the desired aim of doing theology together be fulfilled. If we overemphasize one aspect over others, we run the risk of distorting youth theology into (1) pointless affirmation of the theological capacities of young people, (2) theologically shallow chatting with young people, or (3) delivering them something we may think is theology but in fact could be something that falls short.[175] Youth theology, from the perspective of the German RE school, is about relationships where those who reflect upon their religious experiences meet, speak, and listen to each other. It is collaborative

---

172. Schweitzer, "Adolescents as Theologians," 195.
173. Schweitzer, "Adolescents as Theologians," 196.
174. Roebben, *Seeking Sense*, 270.
175. Root and Dean, *Theological Turn*, 80.

learning in which everyone involved can teach lessons and learn from others, including teachers or ministers. Youth theology is, however, not just about words and study. It is a living process of doing theology together in public space. It is about performative practices and collaborative actions too.

3.3.3 Summarizing Youth Theology

An overview of the different approaches to youth theology now brings us to a place where we can reiterate the story of youth ministry and emergent youth theology from the perspective of a fundamental theologian. While reflecting on youth ministry, we have been brought to the shore of an uncharted and unmapped sea. Pioneers of that sea have already started exploring it from their rafts. The task now is to build proper ships to cruise through and discover what can be discovered there. Some are already working on that task. In this section I would like to summarize the main findings of the explorers of the sea of youth theology from reports of their adventurous expeditions towards new horizons.

Under the rubric of youth theology (Ger. *Jugendtheologie*), we may subsume the actual theological expressions of young people, as well as theological reflections about them. Youth theology includes *theology of, with, and for young people* (1) as it is presented by theologians with more practical concerns and (2) as a concern of the more theoretical approaches of systematic theologians. This helps us to distinguish between practical and theoretical starting points, motivations, and emphases. Both, as pointed out earlier, have influences on terminology too. Youth theology encompasses the theology of youth/young people (*about*—genitive objective and *by*—genitive subjective); theology with and for youth/young people. While in the German language the concept of youth theology (*Jugendtheologie*) has quite clear contours, in its English translation (*Youth theology*) it appears less well defined. In terms of terminological clarification and with respect to the content of particular terms, I suggest reserving the term "theology of youth" for reflections about youth, as such, about the phenomena of youth (in genitive objective), exploring "the nature and significance of youth,"[176] and to label theology produced by young people as "theology of young people" (in the genitive subjective). Youth in this sense is an abstract theoretical concept, and young

---

176. Noval, "Youth and Creation," 36.

people are real persons, together with whom we live in our communities. Clearly, both attitudes are different in principle. But in reality, they are inseparable. There always must be concrete people behind each abstract concept or theory (and vice versa). There always must be a space for theoretical reflection on the practices of particular people. Youth theology springs out of good practice of comprehensive religious education and youth ministry. At the same time, it represents their resource as well. Therefore, youth theology is a true practice of theology created within an ongoing process of living a theological life. As such, youth theology "is a strong reminder to academic theologies to remain life-related and rooted in actual religious practices"[177] because, after all, each theology should always maintain a "focus on grassroots experiences and lived faith, in order to become a real living theology."[178]

Youth theology is predominantly about emphasizing the abilities of young people to theologize and questioning how to involve them into the complex theological process of interpreting faith, Scripture, tradition, and signs of the time. In connection, Tobias Faix considers youth theology to unveil new horizons in the research fields of youth and theology and mentions three characteristics delimiting its areas of operation.[179] For him, youth theology is (1) a way of lay theology. Since theology was always an intellectual and reflexive way of dealing with the reality of Christian faith, it cannot be reserved only to a theological elite. All believers (including young people) deserve to be considered as (lay, ordinary) theologians and enjoy the right to theologize. In this sense, youth theology is also (2) an expression of active participation in the process of theologizing and the life of the church. Finally, youth theology is (3) communicating the gospel in a distinctive way. Young people can create their own specific, theological language and modes of expression for grasping their unique religious experiences.

When Schlag and Schweitzer systemized youth theology by distinguishing its three perspectives (theology of, with, and for youth), they also discerned five dimensions which make youth theology properly theological.[180] The first of them is (1) *implicit*, and it encompasses the life experiences of young people. They are not supposed to be explicitly religious or theological. Yet, they can be grasped and interpreted theologically. These

---

177. Roebben, *Seeking Sense*, 21.
178. Roebben, *Seeking Sense*, 241–42.
179. Faix, "How Theology," 7.
180. Schlag and Schweitzer, *Brauchen*, 59–62.

THE STORY OF YOUTH MINISTRY AND EMERGING YOUTH THEOLOGY   179

are, for instance, experiences of beauty, goodness, and meaning in their lives. I believe these three could be key values, unlocking experiences of the divine in young people's lives.[181] The second dimension is (2) *personal* and suggests that theology is not primarily an abstract system surpassing individual personality. It starts, rather, with the individual person and a personal conception of God, the practice of faith, and a sense of community. Theology is personal because the Christian God is (tri)personal, and Christian theology is always done within a community of persons. It is a common (social) quest of faith seeking understanding, where any gender, race, or age differences should not be reasons for exclusion. The third theological dimension of youth theology is (3) *explicit* and includes an overt expression of the theological concerns of young people formulated in their specific usage of theological, as well as ordinary (common), language. The fourth theological dimension is especially important because one's own personal, implicit, and explicit theology (4) *encounters dogmatic or magisterial pronouncements*. Here, personal faith and theology meet their social and institutional counterparts. Decisions of the inclusion or exclusion of people in accordance with a particular church tradition are taking shape here. Finally, the fifth dimension suggests that young people are (5) *able to use distinct theological argumentation in debates* (among themselves and with adults) on different grounds, e.g., in youth ministry groups, religious education classes, etc.

For their three perspectives on the relationship between theology and youth/young people, along with these five dimensions of youth theology, Schlag and Schweitzer provide a cross-tabulation to clarify the relations in their proposed scheme. The following is the tabulation taken from Faix,[182] in accordance with the proposals of Schlag and Schweitzer,[183] that I have adapted (slightly) to emphasize youth theology as an umbrella concept for all perspectives and dimensions involved.

---

181. Štěch and Muchová, "Sustainable Youth Ministry," 65–66.
182. Faix, "How Theology," 9.
183. Schlag and Schweitzer, *Brauchen*, 179.

	Youth Theology (*Jugendtheologie*)		
	Theology *of* Young People (*Theologie der/von Jugendlichen*)	Theology *with* Young People (*Theologie mit Jugendlichen*)	Theology *for* Young People (*Theologie für Jugendliche*)
Implicit Theology	X	x	–
Personal Theology	X	x	–
Explicit Theology	–	x	x
Theological Interpretation	–	x	x
Young People Debate Using Distinctly Theological Arguments	X	x	–

As we can see, youth theology as a form of theology *of* young people (implicit, personal, yet able to debate using theological arguments) meets with theology *for* young people (explicit, ecclesial, doctrinal) at the platform of theology *with* young people, where young people are enabled to express themselves in theological debates with adults, teachers, ministers, theologians, or church officials. Theology with young people involves openness from both sides. Predominantly, it is a particular form of intra-religious and intergenerational dialogue in which the transmission of the Christian religious tradition is at stake.[184] Adult church folk (parents, teachers, theologians, church officials) desire to deliver and share what they themselves received (cf. 1 Cor 15, 3–5): the place in the world they found for themselves. They want to advise directions for those who follow them. On the other hand, there are young people seeking to find their own place in the world, interested in who they are and how others accept them. They seek a future on their own terms. They search for direction as they encounter the Christian/church tradition interpreted and offered by adults. These two "worlds" must meet, interact, and dialogue, if any creative reception of that tradition shall occur, if the gift of faith shall be passed on to the next generation. But it must not be carried out *by necessity*. Rather, it can only come about by the spirit of welcoming participation in the process of active acquisition.[185] Young people encounter revelation in their own way. They can meet Jesus Christ in their contextual situation both as a question and an answer for their lives.

184. Zimmermann, "What Is Children's Theology," 1.
185. Bucher, "Kindertheologie," 23.

Young people develop their faith as a matter of their own creativity in consonance with the gift of God's grace. They socialize with those outside and inside the (local) believing community. They deal with existential questions and questions of identity, but they engage with all these in their own (creative) ways, appropriate to their age. It is a way of low threshold, a lay or ordinary theology open to everyone and committed to active participation in church life that creates a specific theological language, communicating Scripture and theological insights, understanding faith from young or youthful perspectives. Hopefully, that does not mean it is shallow theology in any way.

However, the main problem with youth theology is the ambiguous meaning of "theology" and "theologian."[186] My initial question (What is theology?) in this text returns forcefully in this context. Can we use the term "theology" for young-minded fantasies about God (as some tend to call children's and young people's theological expressions) and, at the same time, for publications or lectures by respected university professors? Is it possible to "apply the same term to children or adolescents on the one hand and to academic researchers on the other?"[187] If we perceive theology in terms of ordinary (or lay) theology as faith seeking understanding, it is still yet possible to conceive of young people as theologians, because everyone who meditates God's revelation, even without any theological education, could be called—and certainly is—a theologian. But if we perceive theology in terms of an academic discipline, it is difficult, if not impossible, to call young people theologians simply because they lack any kind of theological training. There is certainly a difference between the youth and academic ways of doing theology. But in principle, they are interrelated. Perhaps it could be said that youth theology has the potential to drive young people closer to theology as an academic endeavor.

Another problem we are most likely to encounter when engaging with youth theology is about a discrepancy between the espoused and operant theology mentioned in Dean Borgman's *Foundations for Youth Ministry*. He quotes his personal conversation with Pete Ward, who "has made an interesting observation . . . that youth (and all of us) have both an 'espoused theology' and an 'operant theology.'"[188] Espoused theology is one related to official church doctrine, in which believers claim to believe. (But reality is sometimes different.) Real theology is the one Ward

186. Schweitzer, "Adolescents as Theologians," 185.
187. Schweitzer, "Adolescents as Theologians," 185.
188. Borgman, *Foundations*, 7.

(quoted by Borgman) calls operant theology. It operates within the lives of concrete believers. Operant theology is closer to the concept of lived theology—a theology of everyday life. For the sake of living theology, I think that the difference between espoused and operant theology should be as little as possible. It is the sign of institutional failure when the gap between them seems insurmountable. Preserving doctrine (or, perhaps better, preserving certain formulations of doctrine) which does not engage real life is, after all, quite hopeless. The desired ideal is to live what is believed and believe what is lived. But, of course, an ideal is not to be fulfilled once and for all but to be ever pursued, because the ideal ceases to be ideal when it is easy to fulfill (or believed to be already fulfilled).

To sum up, youth theology appears today to be a widely accepted framework for each theological engagement with those who can be considered the "youth." But it is not only about youth or young Christians whose theologies we can listen to, whom we can theologize with, and for whom we can design theology. The term "theology" suggests that it is happening between God and human beings who seek to find him and discover his work in their lives. In that searching, age does not really matter. Encountering divine revelation, people receive and establish (both at once) their faith, which is to be shared with others. Theology is not about handing over readymade doctrines and formulating propositions to conserve great truths conquered by human reason alone. It is about sharing our religious experiences, sharing our faith, and no one shall be excluded from this continuous process described as faith seeking understanding.

But, at the same time, theology is not only a frivolous or adventitious sharing of experiences. It is always also about the rational reflection of faith—personal as well as communal. It is about understanding our relationships with God, fellow human beings, and, finally, the church, the Lamb's bride (Rev 19:7). Like all sorts of theology, youth theology is a mode of life and a form of study. If we are committed to live in the presence of young people and to study youth, it involves 1) careful listening to what young people are saying (a credible option for youth on their own terms); 2) giving them space to express themselves (attentiveness to the theology of young people); and 3) readiness to theologize with them (doing theology with young people). Doing youth theology means doing hospitable theology[189]—a constant effort to welcome young people into

---

189. Perhaps I should have been using the term "hospitable theology," instead of the terminology of "invitation" or "inviting," from the very beginning, because it now appears to me as more suitable for what I am trying to argue.

our communal discussions/faith sharing, because as human individuals and unique personalities they have (or shall have, should they not yet have it) their indispensable place within our faith-seeking-understanding communities (an inclusive and dialogical theology for young people). According to Roebben, children's theology "is anchored in a positive anthropology. The human being (including the child) has the necessary resources and tools to think critically (to philosophize) and to articulate a personal relationship with the transcendence (to theologize)."[190]

I think the same is true for youth theology as well, if for no other reason than this anthropological one. The right to theologize must be granted to young people and protected by those who hold power in families, churches, or theologizing communities (e.g., academic theology). However, young people's abilities to theologize must sometimes be discovered, assisted, supported, or helped. That places high demands on academic theology, which must be done with respect for young people and take them seriously into account as partners, not only as those who are to be formed and informed. If the believing community loses young people, it loses important prophetic voices, and, more importantly, it forfeits its future.

---

190. Roebben, *Seeking Sense*, 132.

4

Who Do You Say I Am?
The Way of Theologian

"Simply having a religion or a theology, however well balanced and well informed, is after all pointless if it does not speak directly to the human condition in all and any of its circumstances. If Christ is not effectively recognizable to faith as the center of human life and the search for ultimate meaning, the theological enterprise is simply irrelevant. If Christ is not perceived as the icon of unconditional love, the Christian contribution to the human dialogue is ineffective."[1]

I DECIDED TO BORROW the title of this entire work, and also this chapter, from a small but outstanding book by Jacques Dupuis.[2] He uses the question that Jesus asked his disciples in Caesarea Philippi (cf. Matt 16:15; Mark 8:29; Luke 9:20) as an entrance point for his ecumenical explication of the central theological concern of the identity and meaning of Jesus Christ. Disciples were most probably quite surprised by that question. Jesus first wanted to know what people are saying about him. He wanted to know who he was from the perspective of the crowd following his

---

1. Newlands, *Transformative Imagination*, 162.
2. Dupuis, *Who Do You Say*.

public teachings. So, they told him that some say he is John the Baptist, and others consider him the incarnation of some of the big prophets of Israel. But then he demanded his disciples to say how they themselves see him. Who is he for them? And they remained silent, just Simon Peter stood up and courageously said, "You are the Christ of God" (Luke 9:20); "You are the Christ" (Mark 8:29); or "You are the Christ, the Son of the living God" (Matt 16:16). "Whatever the wording, the difference is probably less then it appears at first sight. Peter's answer might be seen as the first-ever Christological statement, yet it was but an anticipation, a prefiguration of the Christological faith that would be born with Easter."[3]

This is perhaps why Jesus commented on this possibly inaugural Christological confession as to God's revelation to Simon Peter (cf. Matt 16:17) and continued with foretelling his own death and resurrection, but at the same time he still maintained his desire to be referred to as "Christos." It is hard to guess what the disciples thought at that time. They must have been confused and asked themselves, Who is this Jesus we follow? This situation got even more complicated and might appear even more confusing for contemporary readers of the Synoptic Gospels than it was to disciples of Jesus on that day. The one who just confessed Jesus as Christ, the Son of the living God, is called "Satan" by Jesus when he tries to convince Jesus that nothing that he said about suffering in Jerusalem and about his own death and resurrection is going to happen (cf. Matt 16:21–23) because the disciples led by Peter can surely work out some plan. No. Jesus refuses any human plans, because they do not count with the divine plan for humanity. People must give up their life for Jesus to find it again. "For those who want to save their life will lose it, and those who lose their life for my sake will find it" (cf. Matt 16:25). That must have sound completely ridiculous to the disciples of Jesus at that time in Caesarea Philippi. It sounds ridiculous to me today, as I write these lines at home in the early morning, while my family is still asleep.

Who do you say I am? This question appears easier to answer in the light of Easter as testified by Peter's preaching on the day of the Pentecost in Judea (cf. Acts 2:14–36). After denying accusations of the disciples of being drunk, he preached Jesus as Messiah (the Christ), the Lord, and the Son of God. These three titles stand at the center of the earliest Christological faith up to our present time. Yet it is still way too hard, even today, having more than two thousand years of Christian history behind it to

---

3. Dupuis, *Who Do You Say*, 1.

confess Jesus as Christ. It is still hard to answer the question as it was asked at Caesarea Philippi, because it is not just a confession of who Jesus is for me but a confession of my own identity as well. The answer to the question of Jesus is the answer to the basic question of human identity. To say who Jesus is for me is always already answering the question of who I am. I think that from a Christian perspective, the question of human identity is never simply answerable in human terms. Such a Christological confession was nothing that Peter could work out by the powers of his own reason (theology in the classical way of understanding the word) at Caesarea Philippi. Yet, it is said to have become possible, as revealed to him by God the Father (cf. Matt 16:17). This revelation, however, seems to resonate with Peter's reason and experiences of being a disciple of Jesus. Later, in Jerusalem, it was the help of the Holy Spirit which allowed him to confess and preach Christ to people of Judea and to all those who lived in the cosmopolitan city of Jerusalem. For Christian faith is never simply the result of purely human reasoning. It is received as a gift of God. Disciples of Jesus soon learned that responding to the question of their master's identity is not a one-time task. It is rather a lifelong process of building their own personal identities as Christians. Trying to understand who Jesus the Logos of God is (cf. John 1:1) becomes a continuous process of doing theology—a process of re-actualizing, rethinking, and reimagining the identity of the One who is and could become (if people receive him into their hearts), the source of human identity. If that happens and Christians discover and accept by faith that Jesus Christ is the way, the truth, and the life (cf. John 14:6), they set off in the direction(s) of becoming theologians.

> Jesus revealed God by revealing himself as Son; that is, by living his sonship of the Father under the astonished eyes of the disciples. In him and through him the mystery of the unknowable Father was unveiled to them. The same law applies to disciples today: Christology leads us to theology, that is, to God revealed in the most decisive manner in Jesus Christ while at the same time remaining shrouded in mystery. . . . Theological reflection ascends from the Christ of God to the God of Jesus; from Christology to theology.[4]

Becoming a theo-logian means understanding that people are the words in which God tells his story, as we have seen earlier with John Shea

---

4. Dupuis, *Who Do You Say*, 4.

and Edward Schillebeeckx. Doing theology (being a theologian) is a process of growing into Christ. People, as words of God's story, are directed and are heading towards the Word of God, which is God alone (cf. John 1:1). "Christianity is Christ,"[5] says Dupuis. I would add that Christianity is also becoming Christ in the terms of 1 Cor 15:28: "When all things are subjected to him, then the Son himself will also be subjected to the one who put all things in subjection under him, so that God may be all in all." From a Christian perspective, being is becoming, and therefore, being Christian is becoming Christian at the same time, just like being human is becoming human as well.[6] Analogously, doing theology is living a theological life when (in a specific time) and where (in a specific place). Being a theologian is participation in a soteriological and eschatological process of becoming a theologian—growing into Christ. In the words of Teilhard de Chardin, Christ is "the alpha and omega, the principle and the end, the foundation stone and the keystone, the Plenitude and the Plenifier. He is the one who consummates all things and gives them their consistence. . . . He is the single center, precious and consistent, who glitters at the summit that is to crown the world."[7]

The picture of Jesus Christ as unifier and re-capitulator of all things is the invitation to reframe the whole interaction of fundamental theology and youth ministry, from which youth theology partly originates and springs, from a Trinitarian perspective (i.e., through Jesus Christ we have and access to the Father through the Spirit). Therefore, I would like this chapter to be a kind of Trinitarian concluding doxology focusing on (1) what it means to be Christian, (2) what it means to do theology, and (3) how to understand the process of becoming a theo-logian. I perceive these three areas of common concern for both fundamental theology (in its more theoretical and academic modes) and for youth ministry continuing to pursue its theological turn (in more practical and ordinary theological ways)—and possibly for youth theology as well. In the introduction I summarized the three perpetual questions arising from my work as a professional theologian. But when encountering the environment of youth ministry, I realized that no matter how I answer young people's questions, the answers must always remain incomplete and never definitive.

---

5. Dupuis, *Who Do You Say*, 2, 142.
6. Ellis, "Human Beings," 127.
7. Teilhard de Chardin, *Science and Christ*, 34–35.

What is theology? How can we communicate theology? And what is substantial or fundamental to theology? We must ask these questions repeatedly during the life journey of a Christian. Being Christian, doing theology, and becoming a theologian is the lifelong journey. It is a pilgrimage towards Christ, who is the cornerstone of Christian identity, the exemplar for each practice of theology, and the challenge to make our theological lives better on our way to his kingdom, which is already present in the public spaces of this earth and yet to come in its eschatological fullness (cf. Mark 1:14–15).

Encountering youth ministry and teaching fundamental theology for several years, I have become increasingly aware that I will not be able to answer these perpetual questions by myself. If the answers shall be never comprehensive but continually searched for, it must be endeavored through and together with others. In the mutual asking of "who do you say I am?," we must ask this question to one another. One must be open to giving answers to those who ask that question as well. It is not simply individuals who shall be asking and answering these questions of identity. The same must happen on a disciplinal level too. "Who do you say I am?" asks theology as such—and fundamental theology, youth ministry, and youth theology, too—when seeking each one's own identity. All these disciplines (fundamental theology, youth ministry, and youth theology) also provide answers to anyone who asks. In previous chapters I attempted to give a short (and surely imperfect) account of how I perceive theology: what my understanding of fundamental theology is, how I see youth ministry, and, consequently, youth theology as well. Now when I look back, I can express the conviction that each Christian auto/Theo-biography is a kind of Christological narrative. Christ is central to Christian identity. Christ is central to each way of doing theology. Christ is central to our lifelong pursuit to become theo-logians, even though it is necessary to see that the whole Trinity is at work there. Theo-logians are not only people who speak words of/about God (or words we think are of God). Through Jesus Christ and the Spirit, they become the unique words of God—historically and geographically, they become specific parts of God's story: his own Auto/Theo-Biography (Theosis).

Therefore, youth ministry and fundamental theology meet in their respective searches for Christian identity. They both try to do theology and ever strive to become theologians. Each, from their perspective and through their own specific skills, try to track the carpenter from Nazareth and seek to answer the question he addressed to everyone: Who do you say I am? The answer reveals one's personal self to others, to those who ask. We should not fear asking nor answering this question to anyone who asks. Only through exchanging questions and genuine attempts to answer may we reveal to each other ourselves as persons and personalities. It is perhaps also what Jesus Christ wants us, his disciples, to learn—to be able to reveal ourselves to others as we truly are and being able to receive revelation from others. The same is true for any possible dialogue partners. If fundamental theology and youth ministry should engage in mutual, creative dialogue, they should start with asking each other: Who do you say I am? As in a jam session, we need to show what we play and play it in a way that invites others to join. That is only possible if we ourselves perform in a hospitable way. Yet performing ourselves in a hospitable way would not be enough if we are not ready to patiently listen to what others play. Only from out of genuine mutual interest and loving acceptance of otherness can opportunities for common action, true collaboration, and communal living together (convivence) be born.

In what follows I proceed from discerning briefly the question of Christian identity, which is central to fundamental theology as well as to any theological reflection happening within and from the context of youth ministry. While fundamental theology, through intellectual (academic), reflections helps to set up one's life perspective and seeks to define human identity in Christian terms, youth ministry is an environment through which participation in the lives of the young people of the church can design and develop their Christian identities. And if Christianity is Christ, there is no other way to ground Christian identity than in Jesus Christ. Further, I proceed in this chapter with revisiting the question of doing theology, which is, above all, a re-actualization of an ancient concept of mystagogy and thus another area of possible common interest for both youth ministry and fundamental theology alike. It is essential for any Christian to do theology (be they young or adult, professional theologian, or layperson), because the first one who does theology is God alone: God (Theos) who pronounced his Word (Logos) that became flash and lived among us (cf. John 1:14) and taught us how to do theology because he was, is, and will be the theology himself. Through following the path of the Lord Jesus Christ, through narrating our life story as auto/Theo-biography, people do or practice theology and continuously becoming theo-logians—words of God's own narrative. Doing theology means living in relationship with God through Jesus Christ and in the Holy Spirit. Precisely because of this, Christians ought to undertake the journey of becoming theo-logians—a journey of Theosis (deification)—as they are people "on the way towards the mystery of life . . . people dwelling in Christ on the way to Christ and into Christ."[8] Christians are people on their way towards the fullness of their humanity in union with God, through Christ and in the Spirit. Being Christian means doing theology, and doing theology is a process of becoming a theo-logian—aligning one's own life with the life of Jesus Christ, the One who is the Word of God (*Logos tou Theou*) himself. This will be the concern of the last part of this chapter.

4.1 BEING CHRISTIAN (ON CHRISTIAN IDENTITY)

"For no one can lay any foundation other than the one that has been laid; that foundation is Jesus Christ."—1 Cor 3:11

It is very hard, if not impossible, to define *identity* in the broad field of the humanities. Different definitions are provided from the various perspectives of psychology, sociology, social anthropology, ethnography, pedagogy, science of religion, and theology too. Whereas psychology generally regards identity as a matter of an utterly intimate core of the human being, sociology often thinks the opposite.[9] In general, we may find together three different identity types: *personal identity*, *social identity*, and *collective identity*.[10] People accept or reject various identities from these types during their lives, but they are involved in the process of making all of them. On top of that, combinations and other alternatives are suggested as well. For instance, some authors consider personal identity as a conjunction of social and psychological identity (Smékal), and others even consider personal identity as the spiritual identity of a human being (Jones).[11]

Loosely understood, identity is the specific uniqueness of each person defined at the very core of the self and narrated as self-understanding and the understanding to others, as well. This interpretation is suggested by the social anthropologist Dorothy Holland and her coauthors in their seminal book, *Identity and Agency in Cultural Worlds*:[12] "People tell oth-

---

8. Štěch, *Tu se jim otevřely oči*, 350.
9. Giddens, *Sociologie*, 550.
10. Snow et al., "Identity," 390–93.
11. Muchová, *Budete mými svědky*, 13.
12. Holland et al., *Identity*.

ers who they are, but even more important, they tell themselves and then try to act as though they are who they say they are. These self-understandings, especially those with strong emotional resonance for the teller, are what we refer to as identities."[13]

From this perspective, human identity appears not as a static, stable, or readymade thing to be accepted once and for all but rather as a dynamic and continual process of constructing, deconstructing, and reconstructing our own complex identities in relation to (1) the self, (2) to others, and (3) to particular social, historical, cultural, and geographic context—to the complex landscapes people live in. Alternatively, the social-anthropological definition of human identity suggests that we may interpret identity, together with Erik Erikson, in more psychological terms. It is the condition in which a human person understands the quality of his or her own existence (within a given cultural environment) as a consequence of social interaction[14] in which he or she as a human subject participates and through which he or she receives impulses for perceiving his or her continuity[15] and stability throughout the time.[16] Even though Erikson's understanding of identity admits the crucial importance of social interactions in the process of shaping or constructing personal identity, the main emphasis is still on the person as a subjective individual. In ancient times people constructed identity chiefly through communal relations (e.g., family, tribe, geographical area—city, castle, etc.). In the contemporary era, people tend to identify themselves by their individual function and value for society, which has become an abstract term rather than a concrete web of social relations where each can find its home. Contemporary society is fragmented into individualities, and in such a context, identity building "is a multi-vocal construct: it means to reconsider oneself as wholesome within fragmentation. To be oneself means to become of 'one piece.'"[17] But becoming of one piece is still endangered by functional individualism because today our identity is often not defined

---

13. Holland, et al. *Identity*, 3.

14. "Identity is a concept that figuratively combines the intimate or personal world with the collective space of cultural forms and social relations. . . . Identities are lived in and through activity and so must be conceptualized as they develop in social practice." Holland et al., *Identity*, 5.

15. Identity can be also referred to as a *"temporal continuity of the self."* Frei, *Identity*, 96.

16. Erikson, *Identität*, 17–18.

17. Roebben, *Seeking Sense*, 217.

by answering the question "Who am I?" or "Who am I related to?" but rather by "what I do" instead.[18]

According to Simon Chan, this shift to the individualistic understanding of human identity was characteristic of modernity and can be traced back to Descartes, who emphasized the thinking self in his famous "*Cogito, ergo sum.*" There were, however, thinkers who emphasized the self even more then Descartes did. Just think of Johann Gottlieb Fichte, Arthur Schopenhauer, or the extreme example of Max Stirner. This modern move towards the self was, however. challenged by dialogical personalism in the twentieth century (e.g., Buber, Marcel), which rediscovered "communal roots of personal identity."[19] Understanding identity in terms of unique human qualities like rationality, freedom of choice, or conscience is for Chan substantially different from the relational understanding of identity, which is "ultimately determined not by the qualities I independently possess but by my relationship with another person. . . . rationality, freedom, etc. are the conditions for personhood but the development of personhood is in the events of interpersonal relationships; that is to say, personal identity has to do with one's history or story involving a web of personal relations."[20]

Considering these two horizons of defining human identity (individual and relational), I would opt for their complementarity rather than keeping them in opposition. Human identity that claims to be Christian identity as well could be, from my perspective, defined by who we are (Christians) as well as by what we do (Theology). It is an identity of what we proclaim in words as our faith and what we do in deeds mirroring our faith. It is an ancient ideal of the identity of orthodoxy with orthopraxis, praised for instance in Jas 2:14–16: "Faith by itself, if it has no works, is dead." Faith should be shown by human good works (cf. Jas 2:18) because people are not justified in front of God by their faith alone (cf. Jas 2:24).

Questions of identity are often regarded as anthropological questions. They relate to who we are as human beings but also to what we do. But when we get closer to the notion of religious, or more explicitly Christian religious identity, we immediately see that anthropologically oriented questions of human identity become Theo-anthropic questions of human relating not only to other people but also to God. In relation to that, we may perceive the human and divine as limit coordinates for

18. Chan, "Christian Identity," 123.
19. Chan, "Christian Identity," 124.
20. Chan, "Christian Identity," 124.

searching for religious identity. In other words, if the person's unique story involves faith, human identity becomes religious identity as well, and that opens the way to specifically Christian identity if the divine is understood in terms of Christian revelation. "If personal identity has to do with each person's unique story, then the Christian identity has to do with how our own life-stories are intersected and reshaped by the Christian Story; the story of God's eternal plan, creation, the fall, the coming of Jesus Christ as the center of the Christian story, and finally, the new creation."[21]

All in all, Christian religious identity is intrinsically connected to Jesus Christ and his personal identity of being fully God and fully human being, both inseparably and at the same time. Jesus is the divine-human person where both natures are hypostatically united in a way that they are theoretically distinguishable but practically inseparable. There is no Christian identity without Christ. There is no Christianity without Christ. Yet each Christian identity is closely related and inseparably linked to the identity of humankind in general. We may demonstrate this with the phenomena of human expectation of the future, which is a phenomenon characteristic to all human beings. It is worth considering that this is even more characteristic for youth. "To be young is to look with expectation to the future,"[22] writes Bert Roebben. Young people expect the future in hope. They want to advance and progress. They plan. They want to do better than their predecessors. They want to define their identity. They want to form their lives and fill them with meaning. But deep down, there is a shadow of knowing that human existence is not a bottomless jug. Each human life ends sooner or later, thwarted by death. Expecting belongs to humanity, and it is particularly intensified in youth. But what is there to expect, if there is nothing to be expected? Where there is nothing more to come? Expecting the future—while awaiting one's own death—seems to be one of the most intrinsic paradoxes of human life. This paradox does not ask only for explanation; it asks for a solution. It may be argued that young people are not interested much in dying, but as Josef Zvěřina, one of the icons of twentieth-century Czech theology, notes, "In unmapped depths of the young soul, where psychology and sociology cannot reach, there is a zone of fundamental questions no one answers."[23]

21. Chan, "Christian Identity," 124.
22. Roebben, *Seeking Sense*, 235.
23. Zvěřina, *Pět cest*, 77.

People in general, and especially young people, live an experience of freedom for the future. This freedom expects the limitless future, exceeding all that can be imagined. At the same time, it experiences its own insufficiency in terms of constructing the future. From this perspective, each human identity is a fragile one, threatened by fear from the future. Freedom for the future is ruined by fear from future. Yet, people continue to expect future, but their expectation is marked by uncertainties.

At this place, I would like to return to Vladimír Boublík, whom I named above as one of my theological sources. Despite his fundamental Christological concern, his theology is strongly shaped also by reflections on the phenomena of expectation related to the exercise of human freedom. Boublík offers a theological solution based on the experience of Christianity. His solution is not applicable to Christians only but is generally open to everyone who expects the future. He writes, "Wishes of freedom are limitless; abilities of freedom are limited, weak, controlled by finality, and often also by sin."[24] Such limited freedom desires its own extension behind the scenes of its contemporariness, given by the coordinates of time and space. It wants to reach limitless horizons and the fullness of life in love. Such expectation of human freedom, according to Vladimír Boublík, awaits Christ. Perfect realization of human being does not reside in the death of God, as was suggested by Nietzsche or Sartre. It rather comes from patient expectation in openness, awaiting God to come into the places where people live to sanctify them and into human history to reveal its meaning and plan of fulfillment. Nietzsche and Sartre did not want to expect and wait. Contrary to that, Christian theology claims that expecting the future and awaiting Christ is the same. Expectation may become awaiting Christ explicitly through conversion or even implicitly, through a genuine expectation of future in freedom desiring its perfection. Who do you say I am? The same question Jesus asked to his disciples in Caesarea Philippi is asked to everyone who expects the future today and depends on the answer if expectation of the future will become awaiting Christ. Christian religious identity is open to anyone, and each human identity can become Christian through conversion. Christianity as such is a celebration of true humanity, and therefore, Christians are utterly connected to the whole of humanity, in whom "nothing genuinely human fails to raise an echo in their hearts" (GS 1). In this respect we

---

24. Boublík, *Člověk*, 19.

may understand Christian religious identity as a mode of human identity. Nothing human should be strange to Christians.

Searching for human identity can become searching for religious identity if people perceive the divine as present in their contextual environment or as directly working in their lives. Searching for religious identity may become a quest for Christian religious identity if we resonate positively with the "Who do you say I am?" question of Jesus and consider ourselves as those who are asked to reply. What would be our response to Jesus' question from Caesarea Philippi? If we seize our search for religious identity in Christian terms, we enter the arena of different Christian traditions, where we may define our Christian religious identity more precisely, according to a specific Christian denomination. Therefore, I think that complex Christian religious identity comprises three interconnected components (general, particular, and specific).[25]

The first component of Christian religious identity is (1) based on the relation of human being to transcendence, or to the general idea of the sacred. At this stage of discovering religious identity, a person recognizes the world not as Godless but as full of God instead. But this God is, however, the unknown God (cf. Acts 17:23), the God uncertain in shape and face, the God liquid and fluid, marked with a significant evanescence upon the pattern of the world. This God is the God of people who perceive the divine in their life, but for some reason they cannot ascertain who (or what) that God is—nor are they able to name that God[26] or discern implications of the belief they affirm for their own lives.

The Christian religious identity is born within its own second component, (2) which results from the affirmation of the central Christian kerygma about the origin, life, death, and resurrection of Jesus Christ. People are usually not happy with general or indeterminate (vague) feelings of the divine. They want more. They search for more certain and definite expressions of feelings they have towards the mystery experienced. In the process of Christian conversion, an ambiguous conception of the sacred receives firmer contours. The uncertain feeling of the sacred through the resonance between human and divine becomes the certainty of faith through experiences of Christian revelation. The character and intensity of such an experience frankly require sharing. This leads those who have that experience towards searching for a community of faith in

---

25. Štěch and Muchová, "Sustainable Youth Ministry," 11; Štěch, "Fundamental Theology," 82–84; Štěch, "Fundamentální teologie a křesťanská identita," 34–35.

26. Halík, *Vzýván*, 88.

which they can share and exchange their experiences. Here the process of religious socialization starts, and also, consequently, the consolidation and strengthening of Christian faith newly born. It is beyond doubt that individual Christian identity must have its communal expressions. The church is essential to Christian identity. "We cannot even conceive of a Christian simply as an individual. As the ancient Church Fathers put it, *unus Christianus nullus Christianus* (one Christian is no Christian). Each person is a Christian by virtue of his or her being a member of the church. Together they are constituted the people of God, the body of Christ and the temple of the Spirit."[27]

This brings us to the third and final component of Christian religious identity, (3) which could be called denominational. A good community or church environment enables Christians to feel at home within their Christianity and motivates them to participate in church identity-building. True Christianity cannot live only from its individual dimension—quite the other way around. It always requires its collective dimension as well.

> In Christ we are no longer to see ourselves as self-determining individuals but as members of his body, that is, members of his church. In Christ we have a new identity that transcends even family ties. Family, ethnic, racial bonds are still there as they are part of being human. The book of Revelation gives us a picture of the church made up of 'a great multitude' from 'every nation, tribe, people and language' (Revelation 7:9; cf. 5:9). Cultural diversity adds to the richness of the church, but culture is no longer the most determinative. What is most determinative is that we now belong to the household of faith through baptism where we are enabled by the Spirit to address God as our Father (Romans 8:16; Galatians 4:6) and Christ as our Brother (cf. Hebrews 2:11–12).[28]

Through baptism, Christians are baptized by one Spirit into one body (cf. 1 Cor 12:13), and therefore, Christianity is above all a social issue[29] meant to form community. Individualization and privatization of religion stand in clear contraposition to the Christian understanding of revelation, faith, and the church, because all these three fundamental categories of Christianity are primarily relational. Within this kind

---

27. Chan, "Christian Identity," 125.
28. Chan, "Christian Identity," 125.
29. Kasper, *Theologie*, 62.

of relationality, the individual does not vanish—on the contrary, it is strengthened and intensified. From a Christian perspective, this relationality includes the world, others, and the (tri)personal divine, through which the individual can grow and thrive.

It is necessary to note that even when Christian religious identity is established and confirmed, the first component of generic religiosity is not simply surmounted. It is still present within a personality as a building stone for a more specific discernment of religious identity in Christian terms. I have experienced, firsthand, that this general relationship of the individual towards the sacred or divine is usually especially downplayed in Christian youth ministry or religious education, since the other two are usually emphasized. I am convinced that a balanced Christian identity must pay equal attention to the cultivation and development of (1) generic religiosity, (2) the fundaments of Christian faith, and (3) the foundations specific to different denominations. If we manage to hold these three aspects together in equal proportion (in our lives, theologies, youth ministries, and religious educations), then we have a chance to build firm yet dialogically open religious identities which are able to cope with the immense plurality of the contemporary world and, at the same time, offer safe refuge and certainty of faith to believers anchored in one of the many Christian denominations. If we fail in this task, we are risking turning our faith and religion into some kind of unhealthy religious practice to which religious fundamentalism is one of the primary expressions.[30]

Of course, the catastrophic scenario is an extreme case. From my own experiences of working as religious educator and youth minister within the Roman Catholic Church in the Czech Republic, I find a profound emphasis on the denominational component of Christian religious identity. I believe very little attention is given to the other two components. Young people involved in religious education and/or youth ministry are often able to say precisely why they are Catholics or why it is important to receive the sacraments. But when asked why they are Christians (what is their relationship with Jesus Christ?), or why they believe in God (what is their concept of transcendence?), their answers are rather vague, or silence simply settles over the group.

---

30. Štěch and Muchová, "Sustainable Youth Ministry," 71–72.

But the same may be said about those whom we can consider advocates of an implicit religion.[31] In the context of Christianity, implicit believers are those who affirm their Christianity but for some reason do not want or are not able to identify with any of the Christian churches. This is accurately expressed by Leslie J. Francis in an article summarizing his empirical research considering implicit religion, explicit religion, and purpose in life among young people between 13 and 15 years of age: "Those who express this implicit religiosity through belief in Christianity are likely to take the view that 'You don't have to go to church to be a Christian.'"[32]

As far as I can see, implicit Christianity is often the result of different prejudices, misunderstandings, and even indolence, rather than of personal experience or critical study.[33] In any event, I am convinced that fundamental theology may contribute towards the process of building a balanced Christian religious identity because it strives to define the sacred in general, and its aim is to explicate essentials of Christianity. That also helps shed light on the true nature of the church, which is an open, dialogical, and relational community of disciples doing theology and becoming theologians as they pursue always a more perfect realization of their Christian identity. In fact, we may perhaps speak about the triune Christian religious identity, because its first component (1) emphasizes the human relationship with God the Father, its second component (2) highlights the human relationship with God the Son (Jesus Christ), and its third component (3) points out the role of God the Spirit in the process of being and becoming the church of Jesus Christ. Right within the church, the human relationship with the Spirit can be found and lived, because it is the community of disciples and not a single individual to which the Spirit was sent during the Pentecost (cf. Acts 2). Pneumatology also sheds some light on the diversity of churches within the Christian religion and points out the necessity to struggle for unity in diversity.

At this place I would like to offer one last association to support my claim about the triune nature of complex Christian religious identity. When Cardinal Dulles discusses the relevance of fundamental theology for Christian conversion, he writes, "Conversion is a dynamic process

---

31. Bailey, *Implicit Religion*, 67.
32. Francis, "Implicit Religion," 911–12.
33. Hamplová, "Religiozita dospělých," 23.

demanded at every stage of the Christian life, and that fundamental theology is therefore of existential import to all believers."[34]

Fundamental theology, according to Dulles, helps Christians during the process of ongoing conversion. Being Christian is about an everyday discernment and readiness to affirm the essentials of Christianity again and anew. No one can say that he or she will for sure still be Christian tomorrow. No one knows what can happen in life or how one's own faith might be threatened or shipwreck during the storms of life. Therefore, continuous conversion is principal to Christianity. It is a *modus operandi* in the process of searching for and building Christian religious identity, which is not set up (or gained) once and for all (e.g., by primary conversion or baptism). Rather, it is a lifelong process of practicing theology (being Christian, doing theology, and becoming a theologian) or living the dynamic of the Christian life, oscillating between three poles of revelation, faith, and the church. The inner dynamics of Christian life is synonymous with the process of building Christian religious identity in relation to God, to others (Christians and non-Christians alike), and to the complex environment of the world in which people live. This drama of life itself happens between human and divine, in which case the essential attributes of the Christian God, the unconditional and eternal Love per se, are his revealedness and hiddenness. Therefore, each attempt to get closer to a potential defining of the Christian religious identity must account for its own inner plurality and even with its kind of paradoxical nature, because Christian religious identity is something always still in the making. It is a gift people cannot possess or claim but only receive with gratitude and take care of with a loving attitude.

Karel Skalický is also aware of the fact that it is impossible to give a single, comprehensive definition of Christian religious identity (at least not in contemporary times). In the past, when denominational struggles (especially those between Catholics and Protestants) dominated Christianity, it was possible to define Christian identity in clear terms. Back then, only the one who was baptized in the true church of Christ, confessed the true creed, and subordinated oneself to the only true church authority had Christian identity.[35] Skalický understandably refuses this way of defining religious identity and offers an alternative. He thinks that Christian religious identity may be defined by three interrelated paradigms:

---

34. Dulles, *Craft*, 54–55.
35. Skalický, "Kdo je křesťan," para. 4.

(1) the paradigm of God's self-communication (Karl Rahner); (2) the paradigm of the first and the second creation (Karel Skalický, Vladimír Boublík); and (3) the practically oriented paradigm of following Christ (Hans Küng).[36] I think a combination of these three approaches allows for a relatively complex discernment of the Christian religious identity.

Skalický's first paradigm conceives Christians as able to accept God who freely communicates (reveals) himself to humanity (1a) in the historical event of Jesus Christ, continues to communicate with people through (1b) being encountered in the life of individuals and communities, and finally (1c) promises to pronounce the concluding word towards this world in the eschatological future of the definitive implementation of God's kingdom announced by Jesus Christ. However, Skalický favors the second approach (because it is his own), which defines Christian identity within the bipolarity of the first and second creation.

> Such bipolarity is significant even within the nature of Christian identity. The Christian is a human being like anyone else, but still the new and last Adam, the Risen one, who anoints each person with his Spirit, lives in him or her. By the power of this anointing each Christian is born twice: bodily from his or her parents and spiritually from the resurrected humanity of Christ, through the anointing of the Holy Spirit. From a theological point of view, such an identity is not homogeneous but heterogeneous, in the sense that the whole humanity of the first creation is oriented towards the risen Christ, who is the tree of life, the perfect kingdom of God, the heavenly Jerusalem.[37]

Such a gradual transformation of the first creation into the second is possible according to Skalický only through the praxis of following Christ. This aspect is emphasized in the third of the abovementioned paradigms. However, true Christian identity cannot be established exclusively by following the crucified Jesus but also by following the risen Christ. As it is not possible to separate Jesus from Christ, it is not possible to separate his death from resurrection and the other way around. Both moments of his life must be considered and meditated in close unity; otherwise our Christian religious identity suffers again from a (theological) imbalance having effects on the practice of Christian life.

It is now possible to see that questions of Christian religious identity are individual as well as communal, actual as well as perennial, relevant

36. Skalický, "Kdo je křesťan," para. 11.
37. Skalický, "Kdo je křesťan," para. 37.

for a particular person as well as for whole communities. But I think that they can be perceived also as truly public questions relevant for non-Christians too. It has been argued that searching for Christian religious identity is in fact searching for human identity in the light of (or as an experience of) Christian revelation. This could be a particular perspective which Christians could bring to the society-wide, public process of discernment and realization of the ideals of humanity and contribute towards forming basic human identity. Everyone who wants to realize fully their own humanity naturally searches for the absolute horizon of humanity. If this is true, the Christian endeavor to find and get closer to such a horizon (perceived in Christianity and experienced through revelation) represents a challenge open to everyone. Christians are not following Jesus Christ for the sake of their own salvation but for the sake of the welfare of all humanity.

It was in 1982, during his political imprisonment, when Václav Havel, the famous Czech intellectual, playwriter, dissident, and later also president of Czechoslovakia (1989–92) and, eventually, the Czech Republic (1993–2003), wrote:

> People seized the world in a way that they de facto lost it; they subjugated it in a way that they destroyed it. . . . The deepest causes of this tragic development are obvious, I think: continually deepened crisis of experience of the absolute horizon growing out of the very spiritual structure of our civilization leads towards losing sense of the integrity of existence, of the mutual interconnection of beings, and of their independence. From phenomena of the world, their mysterious meaningfulness drains out (they are neither mysterious nor meaningful anymore), and everything turns into "conciseness"—and what is most important: crisis of experience of the absolute horizon leads naturally towards crisis of substantial responsibility of human beings towards the world and for the world—that means towards themselves and for themselves. And where there is no such responsibility—as meaningful basis of the relationship between people and their environment—human identity, as the unmistakable place of human being in the world set by such a relationship, vanishes inevitably.[38]

Havel's essay "On Human Identity" depicts very well the nature of human identity from a general perspective. Human identity finds its place

---

38. Havel, *O lidskou identitu*, 349.

not only in the coherence of the person with his or her own personality, nor does it lie solely in the relationship of human beings with the world they create and live in. Rather, it is also in relation to experiences of the absolute horizon of humanity. Havel sees the absence of such an absolute horizon as a deep source of societal crisis, which is, after all, a spiritual crisis. Much has changed in the world since Havel wrote his essay on human identity, but I think the message of his text is as urgent today as it was then. Dehumanizing tendencies in the contemporary world are even stronger than they were at the end of the twentieth century. People still suffer through a crisis of their identities now as much (or more) than they did before. Havel's diagnosis of the problem is simply perfect. He suggests that people should try to behave responsibly, that is, in a way they think is right to behave and that they think (according to their most honest conviction) that all people should actually behave.[39] Who would not perceive in this kind of thinking the age-old wisdom of the "golden rule": "What you hate, do not do to anyone" (Tob 4:15). But is it all right if we ground our identity (and our morals) in these personal convictions about what is right or wrong?

As a humanist, Havel is hesitant in all his writings to name the transcendence perceived, and therefore, here and elsewhere he sticks rather to the general term "experience of the absolute horizon" because he takes seriously practically all ancient religious traditions: "Christian, Jewish, 'Pagan,' Hermetic, Asian."[40] Martin C. Putna, author of a book on the spirituality of Václav Havel, perceives Havel's first presidential address (January 1, 1990) where he expressed the intention to invite the Pope and the Dalai Lama to Prague, as a symbolic act of claiming allegiance to old spiritual traditions of the world in front of the mostly secular Czech society. Havel's willingness to listen to the experiences of different religious traditions is perhaps the most important spiritual heritage he left to us. He reminds us that the most important thing is to free ourselves from prejudices and keep the public space open to different voices of different traditions of ancient wisdom, which may help humanity grow.[41]

Havel's experience of the absolute horizon is, from a Christian perspective, an experience of Jesus Christ and of God's divine revelation. It is an experience with transcendence which has a name "above every name that is named" (Eph 1:21). It is a transcendental experience of faith

39. Havel, *O lidskou identitu*, 351.
40. Putna, *Spiritualita*, 79.
41. Putna, *Spiritualita*, 79.

manifested as courage to the fullness of life's meaning.[42] Contrary (but also complementary) to Havel, Christianity offers a clear and concrete vision of the absolute horizon which is not only to be experienced or perceived but which we may find ourselves having a relationship to after all. In Christianity, the absolute horizon of humanity is not merely a vision but a particular person. It is the person of Jesus Christ, who asks everyone searching for meaning to respond to the question "Who do you say I am?"

Searching for Christian identity is, therefore, not a mission impossible but rather a mission responsible. It is so in two ways: (1) It is about responsibility (response-ability) towards the self, the other, and the world, in the sense of Havel's thought where responsibility seems to be about transforming values to action. (2) It is about the ability to respond (response-ability) to the call of God to do his will (cf. Matt 7:21) and also about the ability to respond to the question Jesus posed at Caesarea Philippi. Christians are not Christians just to be Christians. They are Christians for others. Consequently, Christian life is about being on mission responsible. It is about participation in the mission of God (*missio Dei*) in the world, which means, above all, to do theology in the style of the anointed One sent from God to "bring good news to the oppressed, to bind up the broken-hearted, to proclaim liberty to the captives, and release to the prisoners; to proclaim the year of the Lord's favor, and the day of vengeance of our God; to comfort all who mourn" (Isa 61:1–2).

Much later, during his synagogue preaching, Jesus identified himself with this "Yahweh's anointed," from the prophet Isaiah (Luke 4:16–30). It was precisely in this sense that he spoke to his disciples when sending them out into the entire world (cf. Mark 16:15) into "the midst of wolves" (Matt 10:16; Luke 10:3), and where "he himself intended to go" (Luke 10:1). It is now at hand that Jesus' mission in the world is the basis for the mission of the apostles (and for all disciples throughout the ages) into the world (John 17:18). It is the mission responsible, a mission of searching the ability to respond to the most disturbing, and at the same time most important, questions by which human beings are challenged. It is the mission of searching for Christian religious identity which is shared by fundamental theology (as academic discipline) and youth ministry (as practice of faith and the environment for typical and theological reflections, i.e., youth theology). In searching for Christian religious identity,

---

42. Říha, "Fundamentální teologie," 139.

both theological environments find their common ground and are inspired to cooperate on their common mission of doing (responsible) theology in the sense described above.

To seek one's Christian religious identity is already to engage in theology, since Christian life and theology—understood as a multilayered interpretation of the mystery—form a pair of communicating vessels through which this identity emerges and is endlessly renewed through pulsating questions of human identity in relation to myself, others, the world, and to God, who reveals in Jesus Christ and invites individuals into relationship with himself. From the perspective of Clemens Sedmak, the question of identity is "one of the basic questions of theology. In this sense we do theology all the time, because we constantly try to find our place in our community, in society, in the world. Questions of identity are theological questions."[43]

There is no Christian religious identity without human identity, without being human in the first place. Searching for Christian religious identity helps us to discern what it is really like to be a human and personal being in return. If we search for Christian religious identity, we may start to perceive "Christ's face in the faces of the others. If we are at peace with God, if we are in God's love, we carry the image of Christ in our soul. It comes out in each good deed, in each encounter with the other. Through the veil of the human face, we see something of the divine beauty of the Holy face, which fades in unseen light."[44]

4.2 DOING THEOLOGY (ON MYSTAGOGY)

"Theology is something constructed with others, not something we give."[45]

It has now become clear that if we start pondering about our Christian religious identity, if the question of Jesus Christ from Caesarea Philippi appears challenging to us, we realize we've already started to do theology. Even without reading much of the Bible yet, even without studying theology at all, we are doing already theology. Theology is a process of re-actualizing Christian identity, and it is as much about reading and

---

43. Sedmak, *Doing Local Theology*, 74.
44. Říha, *Hledání*, 74.
45. Root and Dean, *Theological Turn*, 86.

study as about the practice of everyday life. Theology is done through all of what Christians do. There was a time, says theologian Laurie Green, a bishop in the Church of England, "when students would go to the college or university to 'read' theology rather than 'do' theology,"[46] but nowadays it is widely agreed (especially due to the influence of different engaged theologies like liberation, feminist, political, etc.) that theology is an activity not only within but also beyond the shelter of academic ground. Theology is to be done in religious communities as well as in all public spaces of wider culture, ranging from "farm fields to corporate offices."[47] From this perspective, doing theology is an exercise of Christian life which is theological after all. Theologians Howard Stone and James Duke express this convincingly at the very start of their groundbreaking book, *How to Think Theologically*.

> If you practice your religion, live according to your Christian faith, or even take seriously the spiritual dimension of life, inescapably you think theologically. It is a simple fact of life for Christians: their faith makes them theologians. Deliberately or not, they think—and act—out of a theological understanding of existence, and their faith calls them to become the best theologians they can be. Not me, you may say. I believe what I've been taught, but I am not equipped for theological thinking. Maybe I'm not even very interested in it—to me theology is a subject for academics, philosophers, professors, Ph.D.s. Such a response is understandable. Theology is widely taken to be a field for experts alone, too arcane for the day-to-day concerns of ordinary parishioners and their ministers. This impression is due in part to their off-putting encounters with the writings and speeches of theologians. "If this is theology," they say, "it's not for me."[48]

When Stone and Duke speak of thinking theologically, they have in mind not only interior reasoning over a preset or chosen topic but also outer acts of life. Academic theology is only one of the styles of doing theology. There are certainly more styles, including those of very basic, or even only implicit theological expressions. An option for doing theology is, after all, an option for inspiring theology. It does not intend, however, to replace the classical style of academic theology because it is necessary to have expert theologians who are deeply committed to their task of

---

46. Green, *Let's Do Theology*, 4.
47. Roach and Dominguez, *Expressing Theology*, 26.
48. Stone and Duke, *How to Think Theologically*, 1.

researching deep through the mines of sacred doctrine or discovering far-away, abandoned islands on the edge of our theological maps. Yet there is often a difficulty with their writings. They do not necessarily inspire or enable readers to go and do likewise.[49] Sometimes this is simply because people do not understand the point they are making, or sometimes just because they do not understand the language of the academic terms they speak. It is important that all Christians realize (1) their own ability to do theology, even without any special theological training; (2) the value of professional theologians for Christian community; and (3) the dialogical and communal nature of theology. These three aspects are needed so that healthy theology may circulate as blood through the veins of the church. In such an ideal case, believers (including children and youth) are not going to be scared off by theology, because they will find out that it is what they do anyway. Work of professional theologians will be recognized and will receive its proper place within a believing community. Boundaries between academic theology and ordinary, everyday theology will become permeable from both sides without any special visa required for crossing. Finally, doing theology will not be a lonely process of the individual anymore but a communal issue instead. Theology is never yours or mine. It is never private theology only. Of course, to a certain extent, it is always "private" because theology is part of human stories. But despite this (and maybe above all), it is always Christian theology which makes theology a matter of the whole community of faith. Sometimes particularized within denominations (Catholic, Protestant, Evangelical, Pentecostal, etc.), sometimes fragmented into specific fields, sometimes ecumenically open and weaving different voices from different churches into Christian theology in general, but it is always a matter of personal as well as communal (social) auto/Theo-biographies.

Above I considered the process of searching for Christian religious identity as common to youth ministry and fundamental theology. The same is true for the process of doing theology. Doing theology is a common task of all believers, including young people and professional theologians alike. Doing theology "must be a shared community affair, open to all and not in the hands of any elite group."[50] That speaks clearly for including young people into the complex process of doing theology, because theology is nothing to be given to them but rather something we

---

49. Stone and Duke, *How to Think Theologically*, 3.
50. Green, *Let's Do Theology*, 12.

must create together with them.[51] No limits should be installed between potential partners for theological conversations. Doing theology together could be considered a mantra of this work. I am even convinced that it is for the benefit of theology to include, in our everyday practice of it, even those who believe differently or not at all. Theology is inclusive by its very nature because God, as the source of all theology, wants to include everyone without preference.

It has been already suggested that doing theology is a mode of existence. Through theologizing (doing theology), we grow as theologians (both intellectually and in our humanity). Doing theology is also an ongoing transformative process. It is continuous conversion (as argued earlier in dialogue with Cardinal Dulles). When I tried to find the most helpful models to explain doing theology as a common task for all Christians in general and as a common ground where youth ministry can meet with fundamental theology, I rediscovered for myself the ancient concept of *mystagogy*.

The original meaning (if there is such a thing) of this Greek word is *initiation into the myster*ies (or to *lead through* them). Mystagogy can be traced back to times and cultures prior to Christianity. David Regan,[52] one of the most prolific apostles of the revival of mystagogy in Roman Catholic theology during last three decades of twentieth century, says, "Mystagogy was not a Christian invention but a borrowing from the worldwide, human practice of initiation."[53] This, however, emerges only in the fourth century, as Christianity became officially recognized in the Roman empire first as equal to other religious cults (313) and, later, even as the official state religion (380 or 391). The Christian church at that time faced a massive influx of new members, and mystagogy was discovered as a good tool to welcome them. At the same time, it prevented faith

---

51. Root and Dean, *Theological Turn*, 86.

52. It should be noted that already in 1940s, Romano Guardini called for reinvention of mystagogy and emphasized its pastoral relevance. He was followed by Karl Rahner, who approached the idea of mystagogy in relation to the nature of fundamental human experience. Bennett, "Mystagogy," 857. Subsequently the "official" revival of mystagogy (at least within the Roman Catholic church) is dated back to the year 1972 and is linked with the promulgation of the Rite of Christian Initiation of Adults (RCIA), which explicitly recommends mystagogy as suitable way for post-baptismal catechesis or formation. Regan, *Experience the Mystery*, 29–32. This idea was taken up and is propagated by some of the new ecclesial movements, like the Neocatechumenal way for instance.

53. Regan, *Experience the Mystery*, 7.

from dilution through post-baptismal *catechesis* (mystagogy).[54] Fathers of the church (e.g., Cyril of Jerusalem, Ambrose of Milan, John Chrysostom, Maximus Confessor, and Theodore of Mopsuestia), are known for promoting mystagogy in their homilies.[55] In the time of church fathers, mystagogy was perceived as an integral holistic approach to faith transmission—an initiation "into a mystery of God's love in Christ, . . . and into a community."[56] Patristic mystagogy was clearly distinguished (or at least, such distinction seems to have been endeavored and intended) from the esoteric mystery cults of the pre-Christian era. Yet it remained accessible only to those who were baptized. It had, for the most part, a Trinitarian structure. (Also, the Trinity—the concept and the very word itself—was just being developed at this time too, just a generation prior, by Tertullian.) It also found its indispensable place in the liturgical practice of the church. Mystagogy could be perceived as kind of theological practice (practicing theology, doing theology), initiating believers into the Christian way of understanding life in relation to the mystery of God and to the mystery of humanity within a context of community (the church) and the world. Therefore, mystagogy is often referred to as, primarily, a pastoral approach[57] or as a "pastoral tool."[58]

As such, mystagogy was present in the church even before theology as an intellectual effort or rational reflection upon complex (doctrinal) teachings of the church was invented in the Middle Ages with the rise of Scholasticism. When Christianity entered the age of Christendom, there were technically no adult candidates for baptism anymore because infant baptism had become the norm. Christianity started to count the numbers of souls (which included only the baptized). Church life became more a matter of the clerical elite or monks, and scholastic theology reserved "theology" for intellectuals. Most Christians in the age of Christendom (i.e., since the early medieval period) were degraded into a mass of religion consumers and the initial model of the church as a community of disciples was slowly transformed into hierarchical communion and started to be perceived in terms of political society or institution. This was, for instance, famously affirmed by the Jesuit theologian and cardinal Robert Bellarmine (1542–1621), who conceived a societal church

---

54. Elshof, "Mystagogy," 145.
55. Regan, *Experience the Mystery*, 14–24.
56. Regan, *Experience the Mystery*, 22.
57. Gallagher, *What Are They Saying*, 38–39.
58. Regan, *Experience the Mystery*, 2.

"as visible and palpable as the community of the Roman people, or the Kingdom of France, or the Republic of Venice."[59] In such a setting, there was no longer a place for mystagogy, as has been preached by the church fathers. Mystagogy was regarded as useless[60] and was forgotten for many centuries. Regan continues to acquaint us with this: "At the beginning of the modern era, the word 'mystagogy' was debased, sometimes to the level of being placed alongside superstition and sorcery, as signifying a practice alien to true religion."[61]

This may not necessarily have been the case for the Reformed or Protestant churches, but within the Roman Catholic church, the perception of mystagogy is only dramatically addressed, salvaged, and reconceived with the Second Vatican Council, when

> the Catholic church began, perilously late in the day, to face up to the theological problems raised by the Reformers, by the advent of modern science and by the end of the colonial era. During the centuries since the Council of Trent, the problems of the modern world had been swept under the convenient carpet of condemnation. New ways of doing theology were needed and experimentation began. The shelving of the thousand-year-old Scholasticism left perplexity in the minds of many clerics, religious educators and thoughtful laity. The rise of new theologies . . . has offered pluralism where before a monolithic system prevailed.[62]

It is beyond doubt that the Second Vatican Council opened the possibility for a revival of mystagogy because it rediscovered the importance of experience (namely in GS) for Christian life and theological reflection. Regan concludes, "Religious experience was no longer outlawed; it was even accepted, together with study and episcopal preaching, as a way in which tradition grows."[63] That was a useful corrective towards "excessively intellectual"[64] theology and catechesis as it was done and practiced before the council, where praxis of mystagogy was generally missing.

When it comes to the relationship of mystagogy to theology, it could be said that because Christian mystagogy seeks to lead to God through

---

59. Dulles, *Models of the Church*, 26.
60. Hughes, *Saying Amen*, 12–13.
61. Regan, *Experience the Mystery*, 11.
62. Regan, *Experience the Mystery*, 4.
63. Regan, *Experience the Mystery*, 28.
64. Regan, *Experience the Mystery*, 27.

experiences it endeavors to unite all of theology. Today, mystagogy "points theology once more in the direction of its center, correcting the centrifugal tendency of the intellectual analyzing typical of Scholasticism,"[65] says Regan. In other words, we can remember that once, theology was much more than intellectual reasoning and contributed to changing our perspectives on theology. We may begin to see it again as way of Christian life. Precisely in this way, mystagogy is intrinsically linked to the notion of Christian identity. There would be no mystagogy without an initial decision to accept Christian identity (in baptism) and set off in the direction of its constant re-actualizing of itself. From this perspective, instead of learning truths and assenting to doctrinal prepositions, people are instead invited to consider their practical experiences when introduced to the practice of faith within a faithful community (the church). This is what Tomáš Halík calls "learning to live with mystery."[66]

Mystagogy as practicing faith and doing theology together, indissociably, all at once, is, after all, a continuous process of learning to live with mystery. People repeatedly try to understand God, to whom they call together (as in Ps 4), "Answer me when I call, O God of my right! You gave me room when I was in distress. Be gracious to me and hear my prayer" (Ps 4:1). People always experience God working in mysterious ways. God does not always (perhaps ever) adhere to human logic, as the book of Job bears the best witness. God is, instead, Mystery itself, the One who reveals all "deep and hidden things" (Dan 2:22). God is Mystery above all, the source of all mysteries. Therefore, the way to live with the Mystery found in the Old Testament was that of faithful and prayerful (yet fully subordinate) affection towards the "wholly different" (Otto) mysterious One—the God of Israel. Despite this, people never gave up their attempts to understand the mystery of God by their own powers of their reason, as for instance testified in the book of Wisdom. "Wisdom is radiant and unfading, and she is easily discerned by those who love her and is found by those who seek her" (Wis 6:12). Seeking wisdom, which has an origin in God, alone unifies faith with reason. Through faith we may love wisdom and discern her; through reason we may seek and find her. And isn't discerning and seeking wisdom a matter of doing theology?

Further, the New Testament teaches that God has made his own mysteriousness known to us in Christian revelation (cf. 1 Tim 3:16). After

---

65. Regan, *Experience the Mystery*, 7.
66. Halík, *Patience*, x–xi.

Paul, people may call God their "Father" (Rom 8:14–16). Both relations, (1) the relation of God to the chosen nation (from above) and (2) the relation of the people of Israel to God (from below), were transformed by the paschal event of Jesus Christ into humanity's new relationship with God, to whom—through his Son, our Lord Jesus Christ, and in the Holy Spirit—every human being has access. In such a relationship, God appears to us paradoxically. He remains fully transcendent and mysterious. He does not lose any of his mysteriousness, yet he bends down to people and makes them friends—children of God. "See what love the Father has given us, that we should be called children of God; and that is what we are" (1 John 3:1). Through this relationship, people are brought into God's school, as Ps 71 says: "O God, from my youth you have taught me, and I still proclaim your wondrous deeds" (Ps 71:17). That school is the school of faith, hope, and love. In that school people may learn to live in relationship with Mystery because they have a personal experience of the transcendental dimension of human life, as Karl Rahner convincingly argued in his *Foundations of Christian Faith* and elsewhere.

Though there is much to say regarding Rahner's understanding of mystagogy, for the limited purposes of this chapter, it is important enough to note five key points:

1. "To Rahner, theology is more than faith seeking understanding; it is as well a mystagogy that gives the people of God experiential union with the faith by leading them into their own deepest mystery."[67]

2. Rahner speaks of mystagogy as essential to fundamental theology because it takes human experience as its starting point.[68]

3. Rahner's experiential starting point connects mystagogy to practical (in his words, "pastoral") theology, because it focuses on communicating the mystery experienced not only within a community of faith but even beyond. It is this shift in Rahner's concept of mystagogy that distinguishes it from that of church fathers: "Unlike Church Fathers, who focused their mystagogical praxis on the baptized, Rahner's mystagogy connects to the presumed innate openness of every human being for God's mystery."[69]

---

67. Egan, "Translation's," xi.
68. Gallagher, *What Are They Saying*, 38.
69. Elshof, "Mystagogy," 145.

4. Rahner's primary concern when it comes to mystagogy is to make it relevant for contemporaries. In this respect he anchors mystagogy more in the ancient practice of discernment of spirits, which inspired the style of his own Ignatian spirituality (spiritual exercises of Ignatius of Loyola), rather than in the sacramental rites of initiation evoked by the church fathers.[70]

5. Mystagogy, from the perspective of Rahner, involves a new hermeneutical rereading of tradition, which includes not only church fathers but also Scripture. When I say "rereading," I mean not only written texts but also practices. The ancient texts and practices of the church may help people today understand their life experiences. But for this to be the case, they must be reinterpreted to become meaningful anew. Reinterpretation of mystagogy, as encouraged by Rahner, may serve as a concrete example of such an attempt for constant hermeneutical renewal of tradition. David Regan considers Rahner's interpretation of mystagogy to be one of the elements that makes possible "the fresh alliance between speculative and pastoral thinking which is one of his [Rahner's] contributions to Catholic theology renewal. Mystagogy, as a pastoral/spiritual factor, helped him bridge the centuries-wide gap between abstract theology and untheological spirituality."[71]

Based on Rahner's reflections, mystagogy could be seen clearly as a common ground to youth ministry, as a way of doing practical (youth) theology (or even performing theology) and fundamental theology, perceived as merely an academic reflection of theological foundations. Both of these disciplines are concerned with religious experience, from which Rahner's understanding of mystagogy grows.

Even though mystagogy is not a strange thing to youth ministry, I was unable to find any scholarly treatment of this subject specifically, as it would relate to youth ministry. A cursory search on the internet finds that mystagogy is practiced (and reflected) in many of the youth ministry groups throughout Christian denominations across the globe. It is as easy as typing "mystagogy" and "youth ministry" into your browser search. Yet in some of the most outstanding books reflecting on the theory and practice of youth ministry, we find implicit hints pointing towards something akin to what I am here referring to as "mystagogy." One example

70. Regan, *Experience the Mystery*, 33.
71. Regan, *Experience the Mystery*, 34.

is Kenda Creasy Dean, whose book *Practicing Passion*[72] might remind us of the mystagogical theology of Karl Rahner.[73] This is especially the case when she explains her understanding of a "passionate curriculum" for youth ministry[74] and, also, when she addresses mystery in its singular relation to young people. "Postmodern young people do not view mystery as a problem to be solved as much as a truth to be revealed in the course of human experience."[75] She continues: "God is the divine mystery who ecstatically reaches towards them (young people) in passion, and the human mystery in whom joy and suffering, life and death cohere. The postmodern inclination to conceptualize truth in terms of paradox—'both/and' rather than 'either/or'—embraces the three persons of the Trinity as both the source of ecstatic unity and the source of differentiated identity, as both tremendous mystery and an intimate friend.[76]

In another book, Dean evokes a kind of mystagogy even more specifically yet without explicitly mentioning the term. On that matter she writes, "Ancient church leaders believed that only by participating in the mysteries of Christ's presence in the bread and wine was it possible to truly recognize Christ's presence in them. In many ways, youth ministry intuitively continues this tradition, immersing young people in the 'way' of Christian life, making connections between these practices and the stories of the teaching of Jesus as we go."[77]

In fact, mystagogical aspects can be found in most major books reflecting upon the theory and practice of youth ministry. I would suggest the same is also true for fundamental theology. As far as I can find, there is no specific fundamental theological treatment of mystagogy, except perhaps that offered by Rahner (mentioned above). But it is worth considering that mystagogy is precisely the theme on which both disciplines might unite. It is certainly relevant to ever remember what the church fathers said about mystagogy. But we must, together with David Regan, also keep in mind that "its significance for young people with no experience of God in their lives, as in the third millennium"[78] unfolds.

---

72. Dean, *Practicing*.
73. Roebben, "International," 203.
74. Dean, *Practicing*, 161–72.
75. Dean, *Practicing*, 103.
76. Dean, *Practicing*, 105.
77. Dean, *OMG*, 116.
78. Regan, *Experience the Mystery*, 145.

Further, two additional inputs or sources of inspiration for fundamental theology and youth ministry to come together and rethink mystagogy as a model for doing theology today might be mentioned. First is the recent development within the field of religious education (e.g., Roebben, Schambeck) that is closely related to the field of youth ministry and youth theology. Second is the concept of the fundamental theology of ministry as developed, for instance, by Thomas O'Meara. Regarding the first, some scholars of religious education have started to call for engaging the mystagogical element by focusing upon the religious experiences that stimulate students' sensibilities to the mystery that is experienced in their lives.[79] Toke Elshof further considers Bert Roebben and Mirjam Schambeck[80] to be important advocates of this mystagogical approach to religious education. Even though certain aspects of these authors vary, both share a conviction that students in religious education "should be able to gain experiences with religion, not aiming at their initiation into church life, but at their personal and social development."[81] They also both give special attention to the contexts in which young people live today. Schambeck speaks of the post-secular context. Roebben calls it post-Christian. Elshof identifies, quite lucidly, several features characteristic to the mystagogical learning process common to both. It is important to focus upon (1) experiencing religious expressions within the contexts of religious diversity; (2) mysterious experiences that students may discover in their own lives, about which they are thereby empowered to discuss; (3) the relevance of religious perspectives for student's own lives; (4) the critical correlative relationship between the world of young people and the world of religion, including the possibility of further developing one's life perspective upon experiencing love and relation; (5) emphasizing the balanced relationship between both the constructive and receptive aspects of identity construction; (6) an important opposition to instrumental treatments of religion; and (7) promotion of the transformative potential of religious education.[82]

At the end of her evaluation, Elshof levels important critiques of both Roebben and Schambeck. She suggests that they (1) reject initiation and mission as indispensable parts of Christian mystagogy and, further, (2) neglect the pneumatological dimension of mystagogy. These critiques

---

79. Elshof, "Mystagogy," 143.
80. Schambeck, "Mystagogisches Lernen," 400–15.
81. Elshof, "Mystagogy," 144.
82. Elshof, "Mystagogy," 147–48.

appear to me partially legitimate. But if we consider the declared contexts from which Roebben and Schambeck are thinking, their works may yet possibly prepare the field for evangelization. This may, in turn, eventually result in conversion, initiation, and mission. I perceive their focus to be pre-evangelizational, which I believe is justifiable in the context of inclusive religious education. Secondly, though the concepts of Schambeck and Roebben may not overtly address pneumatology, they yet seem to include the Spirit, since they focus on young people's transcendental or religious experiences, which are places where the Spirit is perceived to be at work (pneumatologically speaking). Yet it is true that their writings would benefit from closer contact with pneumatology.

Regarding the second source of inspiration we come to Thomas O'Meara, who works out a solid fundamental theology of ministry. He defines ministry as "doing something, for the advent and presence of the Kingdom of God, in public, on behalf of a Christian community, as a gift received in faith, baptism, ordination, and as an activity with its own limits and identity existing within a diversity of ministerial actions."[83] According to O'Meara, ministry is predominantly a matter of action. It is dynamic. I would say it is even a mystagogical process of doing theology for the sake of a Christian's fellow beings and the world. Christians are not simply servants to the world and its things. They are, rather, ministering to the world. Thus, there is nothing else needed by a Christian to become a minister to the world than this initial calling rooted in baptism. Further vocations, identities, and roles come later, as one's own Christianity deepens through participation in the life of the church. For to be an ordained or appointed youth minister, one must be baptized first. But not everything that Christians do need be regarded as ministry. Ministry must be explicit and public speech enacted on behalf of the church, pointing towards God's kingdom.[84] Moreover, ministry is open to all Christians, be they ordained or simply lay persons.

For O'Meara, the most important aspect for living Christian ministry is the Holy Spirit that mysteriously ensures continuity of any contemporary Christian ministry with the ministry of Jesus Christ and his disciples. What is changing over time are the cultural-historical contexts in which ministry is practiced. However, O'Meara's fundamental theology of ministry focuses predominantly on the question of who a minister

---

83. O'Meara, *Theology*, 141.
84. O'Meara, *Theology*, 145.

is. He is less concerned with what it means to do ministry. This lacuna has been filled by Kathleen Cahalan in her inspired article relating O'Meara's fundamental theology of ministry to the idea of Christian discipleship.[85] She perceives discipleship as an absolutely fundamental component of each Christian ministry, and thus she is surprised to find this concept missing in O'Meara's theology of ministry, as well as in other referential works on that matter.[86] Discipleship, from her perspective, means a constant process of learning what it means to be disciple. It is living in "permanent state of mystery or mystagogy."[87] Discipleship is therefore not an achievement; it is an identity—Christian identity—which is constantly under construction in the process of doing theology while trying to live an honest Christian life. In other words, discipleship is a positive response to Jesus' call to "come, and follow me" (Matt 4:19) and a constant attempt to answer his "provocative" question, "Who do you say I am?"

It is possible now to conclude that doing theology today is about living a theological life. It is about discernment of spirits in a continuous process of mystagogy, not necessarily bound to sacraments and liturgy (as it was for church fathers) but intrinsically bound to human experience, which may at certain point become religious experience as well. This links fundamental theology to youth ministry as it links mystagogy to pneumatology, because it is the Spirit that unites all that seems initially different. Regan underlines it in this way:

> The experiential, holistic and Mystery-centered characteristics of mystagogy remind us of its dependence on the Spirit. The Spirit is behind genuine religious experience, inspires unity and makes the Mystery operative—in Christ and in his Church. Mystagogy, like the Spirit, belongs to the practical order, eludes categorizing and is capable of pervading many aspects of Christian life. If such a discreet, yet all-pervading role makes mystagogy resemble the Spirit, perhaps that is why mystagogy has been invisible to the Church during so many centuries—so was the Spirit.[88]

It is also the Spirit who is at work in religious experience as, for instance, charismatic experiences in groups at prayer bear witness.[89]

---

85. Cahalan, "Toward a Fundamental Theology of Ministry," 104.
86. Cahalan, "Toward a Fundamental Theology of Ministry," 110–11.
87. Cahalan, "Toward a Fundamental Theology of Ministry," 112.
88. Regan, *Experience the Mystery*, 7.
89. Regan, *Experience the Mystery*, 137.

However, charismatic experience is not limited to prayer gatherings. Rather, it is any experience of the Spirit at work in our lives. Charismata are gifts of the Spirt and they are countless. Important is the fact that each charism (gift of the Spirit) serves to build up the community first. Only secondarily is it for the good of the person who receives it. I also hold that charismata are not exclusively given for the sake of the church—the community of faith—but for the sake of everyone that lives in relation to the gifted person (including the natural environment).

In my rather short, certainly imperfect, and perhaps also a bit chaotic exposition of mystagogy, I forgot to mention the role of the mystagogue. In pre-Christian Greek mysteries, as well as in Christian antiquity, the mystagogue was the one who takes the lead, the one who initiates others into m(M)ystery. Who would be a mystagogue today? It could, for sure, be a priest, a minister, a respected elder. Further, I believe that anybody can become a mystagogue in a certain sense to anyone, as far as he/she makes him- or herself available to the Spirit, available to be used for leading others into the mysteries of human life in which they find (from a Christian perspective) their resemblance to the Mystery of the Triune One. Spiritual availability (Fr. *disponibilité*), the most authentic way of human life according to Gabriel Marcel (as I mentioned earlier) makes a Christian not only available to other human beings but also open to and available for the works of the Spirit.

Let me give an example. My good friends lost their only son (who was also my friend) in a motorcycle accident. That ruined their life. They never fully recovered from that tragic experience. But as we continue to be friends, I am sometimes exposed to long talks with them about their grief and enormous loss—loss of life's meaning. They are not explicitly religious, but they somehow adhere to the local Christian tradition more culturally than spiritually. I regard talking with them and being with them in times they are feeling hopeless as kind of reciprocal mystagogy. It is perhaps not explicitly Christian but certainly mystagogy nonetheless. I function as one who helps them understand the mystery of life that they faced deeply in their tragedy by trying to counsel them whenever they need it. In turn, they make me part of their story while they also play the role of mystagogues to me and my life. They truly lead me deep into the Mystery of life, which I perceive in Christian terms. My openness and availability to the Spirit helps me be available and open to them as well. Moreover, having listened and spoken to them gives me strength in hard times. At those moments, I always silently and desperately pray, *Veni Sancte Spiritus*!

This kind of experience may serve as an initial inspiration for a possible response to the question of how we can keep mystagogy Christian while also hospitable to non-Christian others and, indeed, everyone. My suggestion is to emphasize mystagogy as doing theology which, as has been argued, is a way of Christian life after all. I strongly hold that for Christians, there should be no difference (so typical for modernity) between Christian and ordinary life. If we are truly Christian, we consider our whole life as Christian. This may not necessarily be the case in days to come. But if today I am searching for my Christian religious identity and trying to respond to who and where Jesus Christ is in my life, then I do theology—I participate in the mystagogy of life. Through all of this I am becoming a theologian. It is to this process of becoming that I now turn in the last part of this chapter, in which the two previous parts (Christian identity and doing theology) may find their purpose.

4.3 BECOMING THEO-LOGIAN (ON THEOSIS)

"To be Christian at all is to be a theologian. There are no exceptions."[90]

I think it has been sufficiently argued that if we consider ourselves Christians (if we enter the dynamic of searching Christian identity), we do theology in all that we do. Of course, this need not be done necessarily in an academic or intellectual way. But, certainly, done in an ordinary or everyday mode. In this sense we may be perceived as theologians. At this point, the question of who a theologian is inevitably arises. There are many possibilities of characterizing theologians, ranging from scholar to prophet and storyteller. As Roach and Dominguez propose, theology needs them all. Theology needs scholars, teachers, poets, translators, preachers, prophets, pastors, storytellers, musicians, artists, social critics, and, sometimes, just friends of the soul as well.[91] Therefore, for the purpose of this chapter, I will limit myself to an understanding of a theologian in the most general sense of the term. To put it simply, every Christian is a theologian because every Christian does theology by living his/her life. However, being a theologian is not a fixed label or entitlement. It is not

---

90. Stone and Duke, *How to Think Theologically*, 2.
91. Roach and Dominguez, *Expressing Theology*, 30–34.

a once-and-forever category. Being a theologian means always becoming a theologian at the same time because theology is "an ongoing conversation that will never come to a definitive end, at least in this existence."[92] Stone and Duke explain:

> To engage in theological reflection is to join in an ongoing conversation with others that began long before we ever came along and will continue long after we have passed away. . . . It is not up to you or me or anyone else to invent Christian theology, to control it, or even to perfect it. We are called only to do the best we can, given who and where we are. This is actually the best that theologians ever manage, not only because as humans they are limited and fallible and because times change, but because the final word is God's alone. Until that final word is spoken, each and every Christian has a contribution to make to the conversation—a duty to listen, and a question to ask.[93]

Theology from this perspective is a history-wide process, to which God alone will pronounce the last Word (*Logos tou Theou*) as he also pronounced the first one. In the course of history, his Word even became flesh and lived among us (John 1:14). This has a deep consequence for Christians because they believe through relationship to the incarnated, crucified, and resurrected Word of God—through Jesus Christ—they are. Yet they are only insofar as they are also becoming theo-logians—words through which God tells his story (as argued, above, with Edward Schillebeeckx). When Christians do theology, they are. While they are, they are becoming theologians. They walk their ways toward the final word of God (*Logos tou Theou*), which they believe will be pronounced at the end of the world as a conclusion and fulfilment to all theology done since the world came into existence. What (or better, who) that word would be, Christians already know because it is revealed to them in the event of Jesus Christ, who himself is the Word incarnate, the word which was at the beginning (cf. John 1:1), lived among us (cf. John 1:14), and will come at the end of all days (cf. Rev 1:8). Becoming theologian means participating in this perennial task of doing (thinking and living) theology, expecting the future and awaiting Christ to come in eschatological glory. "See what love the Father has given us, that we should be called children of God; and that is what we are. The reason the world does not know us is that it did not know him. Beloved, we are God's children now; what we

---

92. Roach and Dominguez, *Expressing Theology*, 27.
93. Stone and Duke, *How to Think Theologically*, 4.

will be, has not yet been revealed. What we do know is this: when he is revealed, we will be like him, for we will see him as he is" (1 John 3:1–2).

In this sense, we may perceive the process of becoming a theologian as a way of *Theosis*. This term, domestic to the Orthodox theology, is equivalent to the term deification (sometimes also divinization). Ivana Noble suggests that "theosis," or "deification," "offers a better possibility for speaking about unity and communion with God,"[94] than the classical term "sanctification," which is more typical of Western Christian thought. Deification (Theosis) means union of human beings with God and *not* their equivalence or equality. It is not homogenizing. Human being cannot participate in the essence or nature of God. It is only through salvation that our genuine human nature is deified in a sense that it is enabled to share with God his eternal life. In other words, to be united with God does not mean we are united with God *in essence*. Unfortunately, precisely this was widely misunderstood in much of Western theology. As such, the doctrine of deification was usually treated with suspicion. For a long time, it was forgotten (sharing a similar fate with mystagogy). This was most probably due to the conviction that it might bring confusion into precise definitions of nature and grace or to the strict differentiation between the natural and supernatural orders (typical to scholasticism). On this point, we may remember Maurice Blondel, who was accused of messing up the clear boundaries set between the natural and supernatural orders with his apologetics of immanence. Perhaps we may even say (with a necessary simplification) that, in principal, Blondel's thought was a kind of Western philosophical interpretation of Theosis because he wanted to reach fullness of being (deification) through Jesus Christ, to whom humans are lead *not* by speculative proofs of transcendence but rather by the way of immanence (thinking and acting in the world).

Rediscovering the concept of deification in the West occurs only in the second half of the twentieth century, when Western theologians started to seek inspiration in forgotten concepts and ideas—when they went back *ad fontes*. Often, they discovered them preserved and well developed within the writings of Orthodox theologians. Like mystagogy, the doctrine of deification (Theosis) was not only rediscovered but became again theologically acceptable. I can provide an easy example from my own Christian tradition: the Catechism of the Catholic church (further abbreviated as CCC).

---

94. Noble, *Theological Interpretation*, 10.

The Word became flesh to make us "partakers of the divine nature": "For this is why the Word became man, and the Son of God became the Son of man: so that man, by entering into communion with the Word and thus receiving divine sonship, might become a son of God." "For the Son of God became man so that we might become God." "The only begotten Son of God, wanting to make us sharers in his divinity, assumed our nature, so that he, made man, might make men gods." (CCC 460)

Further, the Catechism of the Catholic Church speaks of the grace of Christ received in baptism as "sanctifying or deifying" (CCC 1999). These two examples demonstrate well a return of the doctrine of deification into Western theological discourse. But, at the same time, there is a lot of work still left ahead for theologians, who should first study developments of the doctrine of deification in the East. Only then might they eventually become able to further develop their own perspectives.

In Orthodox theology, the idea of Theosis is closely linked to soteriology in a way that while salvation is perceived as a gift, deification is a task. Both are needed for a "full spiritual growth towards the fullness of life in God."[95] Our life is a gift, and at the same time, it is given to us. As given, it represents the task for humanity: the task of living. The same is valid also for the world, because the task of living can be carried out and eventually accomplished only within the scene of the world, which was created by God as an environment or medium for life. From a Christian perspective, people are part of the whole of creation, and therefore they are intrinsically linked to the entire world (creation). People are living on both an abstract plane of time and a concrete plane of physical places within the world. Noble states this succinctly:

> The world as a given place has two meanings. First, . . . it is a gift, a good gift given out of love by the creator. Second, as we were reminded by Martin Heidegger, it is a given. We are thrown into a world that we did not choose, in which we have to find direction, to understand ourselves and our possibilities, make our life projects. Both the world as gift and the world as given need to be understood dynamically. The first employs a utopic imagination; the second interprets the journey of deification in such a manner that the world participated in the ascent towards God.[96]

---

95. Noble, *Theological Interpretation*, 61–62.
96. Noble, *Theological Interpretation*, 65.

Therefore, we may see that the process of deification is not just a matter of humanity but includes the whole world, which is to be transformed together with humanity and elevated into the state of divinity so that it may partake in the eternal life of God. This idea is very similar (if not completely identical) with what Pierre Teilhard de Chardin thought of as the historical process of the world evolving into the fullness of Christ—his famous Omega Point. What Teilhard presents as Christification[97] seems to me to be another iteration of what I understand here by deification or Theosis.

As far as I can see, there are principally three sources for the doctrine of deification (Theosis): (1) creation after an image and likeness of God (cf. Gen 1:26); (2) incarnation of the Word of God (cf. John 1:1, 14); and (3) the possibility of participation in the life of God through Christ (cf. 1 Cor 12:27) and in the Holy Spirit (cf. Rom 8). The idea of deification further oscillates between both the apophatic and cataphatic ways of doing theology. While the first one is rooted in the theology of God's absolute differentness from humanity and its principal unattainability, the other is anchored in the teachings about spiritual adherence of humanity to God through Jesus Christ in the Holy Spirit. The cataphatic and apophatic theological traditions contrast as well as complement each other. While the first emphasizes God as being accessible to the human intellect through metaphor and image, the second attempts to refrain from images entirely. The apophatic tradition does not deny the natural world but tries to empty the mind. It is convinced that no kind of human analogy can grasp God, who is never properly available to us at any place or in any kind of image.

This spectrum of theology marked by the movement from cataphatic to apophatic theology and back again (oscillation) is mirrored in the descent-ascend structure of the Nicene Creed. It "tells a compact drama, one whose confessants are thoroughly self-implicated as subjects of and respondents to God's triune activity."[98] The triune activity of God is, in the Nicene Creed, presented as threefold: creation, redemption, and deification (Theosis, sanctification, salvation), as common work of the Father, the Son, and the Holy Spirit. The central role of Jesus Christ is maintained because the convergence of the self-giving of God to humanity and the self-giving of humanity to God in the person of Jesus Christ "makes

---

97. Teilhard de Chardin, *Divine Milieu*, 123.
98. Mueller, *Theological Foundations*, 43.

possible redemptive 'participation' in divine life, namely theosis."[99] Through Jesus Christ and in his Spirit, the interpersonal relationship between the personal God and human persons is made possible. Through Jesus Christ and in his Spirit deification (Theosis), the union of creatures with their Creator is made possible. Consequently, we may see that becoming a theo-logian is no more and no less than a way of Theosis—a way of becoming a word of God, as Jesus Christ is from the beginning—is now and ever shall be—the Word of God.

If in previous sub-chapters (4.1 and 4.2) I considered Christian religious identity and the process of doing theology as common themes for fundamental theology and youth ministry, then it is for the same I propose that I do so here, with the concluding concept of becoming a theologian. It was argued earlier that from a theological perspective, young people are not just human beings, as suggested by Wesley Ellis, who used eschatology to rule out development as a goal for human being, but also human becoming. It is not enough to claim oneself to be a theologian. Being a true theologian means also becoming a theo-logian—being on the way of searching to discover who am I as Christian, living my life theologically, and, after all, being on the way towards full communion with God . . . living towards Theosis. The eschatological perspective must be always accompanied by a soteriological perspective when trying to propose a balanced theological anthropology (in general and of youth in particular). From a Christian theological perspective, *human beings* are always also *human becomings* because their true eschatological meaning is to be found in salvation—that is, to be found in the plan God has for human beings, which reveals what people are invited to become. But the decision is theirs. It is a matter of their freedom.

It is not just about human beings searching for Christian identity and doing theology but also human becomings heading towards unity with Christ. It is through him and in the Spirit heading towards the kingdom of God, which will consist of temples of the Holy Spirit (cf. 1 Cor 6:19), which shall be identified with the heavenly Jerusalem descending from skies at the end of the times (cf. Rev 21:2). Those who search for Christ and have lived their lives in a theological way will first enter that city and become its citizens. They would become identified with Christ in salvation if they identified with him in his life, suffering, and death (in one way or another) during their earthly pilgrimage. Having the same Spirit,

---

99. Mueller, *Theological Foundations*, 43.

they will become identical with the donator or sender of that Spirit. Yet in this same Spirit they will remain recognizable in their true "singularity," because they will be recognized by the One who is the source of all unity: the One who will finally accomplish their Theosis. "When all things are subjected to him, then the Son himself will also be subjected to the one who put all things in subjection under him, so that God may be all in all" (1 Cor 15:28).

In this sense people who searched for Christian religious identity, who were doing theology in, by, and through the practices of their life, and who set off on the path of becoming theo-logians will, as such, become theo-logians forever. They shall be revealed as words of God within the Word of God, partakers of an eternal union of God with his creation. We may perceive *prayer* as a model for the process of becoming a theo-logian. The American fundamental theologian, Jerry D. Korsmeyer, describes prayer as way of life and even as a mode of being in the world.[100] Living payer means praying with one's whole life, opening up to God's gracious initiative, learning to listen in order to be able to pick up the frequency of God's broadcasting (revelation of Jesus Christ) in the air of the world. Such prayer results in the presence of the Spirit (cf. Luke 11:13). In the Spirit, human prayer intertwines with God's word, which starts to sound out on the same frequency and resonates in association of human being with God.[101] This harmony or consonance then springs into the world through loving human action. Authentic prayer connecting creativity with love brings people to the real presence of God, in which God reveals Godself not simply as a term or concept about which it is possible to speculate but rather as a loving person with whom human persons can have a relationship. This kind of practice—the practice or life of prayer—which is always necessarily accompanied by action, might then serve as an example of the process of becoming a theo-logian. Living the relationship to God in terms of prayer unites persons with God in such a way that he/she is distinguishable from God but remains inseparable in the ongoing resonance. Korsmeyer refers to this process as "tuning in to the divine."[102]

Deification or Theosis, understood as tuning in to the divine—becoming a theo-logian—represents purpose and meaning for Christianity, as well as for all kinds of doing theology. This is the basic fact which

---

100. Korsmeyer, *God*, 177.
101. Korsmeyer, *God*, 171–75.
102. Korsmeyer, *God*, 181.

relates it clearly to the environment of fundamental theology and youth ministry (including youth theology as a part of its context). I propose it as a third platform for their mutual encounter. Both environments share a common interest in searching for meaning and in the processes making meaning. It suggests (as discussed above) doing theology together. The idea of deification has also an environmental connotation which resonates with contemporary youth and in theology alike. Hans-Georg Geiser even pleads for ecology to become a central topic for fundamental theology in the future.[103]

The reason why I think it is useful to engage the notion of deification when attempting to do theology together (between fundamental theology and youth ministry) is simply the fact well emphasized by Hans Küng. He says that a patristic theology of deification is completely unintelligible to contemporaries. Our problem today is not that people would like to become God but, more importantly, would like to understand what it means to be human.[104] What value does our humanity have in times of prevailing emphasis on the "deified" idea of the conscious self, individuality, and personal achievements? The question of humanization seems to be more pressing to Küng than the one of deification. But, as was already mentioned, the idea of Theosis is about becoming *like* God (not God), and therefore, it discerns a road towards the fullness of humanity and emphasizes the ultimate value of being human. It is a process of "growing in shared humanity,"[105] in relation to God, others, and the world.

When we embrace Theosis as a theological interpretation of an ultimate meaning of humanness (or simply of humanization), we find ourselves returning to the notion of Christian religious identity inseparable from human identity. The circle closes. We may now perceive that all that was presented above has an intrinsically Trinitarian structure. Recall what Karl Rahner said about the Trinity: "When entering upon the doctrine of the Trinity, we need not hesitate to appeal to our own experience of Jesus and his Spirit in us as given in the history of salvation and faith. For here the immanent Trinity itself is already present. The Trinity is not merely a reality to be expressed in purely doctrinal terms: it takes place within us and does not first reach us is the form of statements communicated by revelation."[106]

103. Geiser, *Community of the Weak*, 444–49.
104. Küng, *On Being*, 442.
105. Roebben, *Theology Made in Dignity*, 43–61.
106. Rahner, *Theological*, 98.

Before we can formulate anything on the Trinity, we already have experience of it. This is because we have an experience of searching for Christian religious identity. We encountered Jesus asking us, "Who do you say I am?" We also have an experience of doing theology—encountering Mystery in our lives and being initiated into its depths. Finally, we attempt to grow in our humanity and realize that we already participate in the process of our own deification—growing into Christ and becoming ourselves more clearly a particular word of God, becoming theo-logians. While searching for Christian religious identity, we predominantly encounter Jesus Christ as our cooperation partner. In doing theology, we experience the work of the Spirit in our lives, and we let him lead our way deep to the Mystery of God, where the ultimate meaning of being ourselves—being humans—is revealed to us.

To put it simply, I proceeded in this chapter through the Son in the Holy Spirit to the Father. Contemplating the Father, at the end, we returned to ourselves, to our very humanness. Therefore, I consider the three topics of this chapter to have special potentials by which to bridge the gap between the academic and ordinary ways of doing theology, the gap between theory and practice, between fundamental theology and youth ministry, from which youth theology originates and springs. Questions of Christian religious identity and of theological action (which are intrinsically connected to the spiritual life and prayer), and of meaning and purpose of our humanity, all call for doing theology together. It invites former strangers to do theology together. When I say *doing theology together*, I mean, after all, *living together*. Even those who are not able (or cannot, for some reason) do theology are our neighbors and companions with whom we pursue our theological lives. We are all pilgrims, people on the road hoping to quench our thirst for the fullness of life and realizing that, from the well of life, nobody drinks alone.

Conclusion
Doing Theology Together

DOING THEOLOGY TOGETHER IS by no means an easy task. It involves entering relationships with others who do not necessarily view everything exactly as we do. In fact, it demands that we relate precisely with such folk. It involves entering the community, which is not always comfortable for our own individuality. But, at the same time, it is necessary when we want to understand better our humanity. From the well of life nobody can drink alone. It is an irony of our time that we emphasize individuality while yet longing for relationships and searching for community. I realized that the idea of doing theology together is central to all its parts. Several times I mentioned, above, the metaphor of playing jazz, borrowed from Ann Pederson and Hans-Georg Geiser. It is an apt metaphor as far as I am concerned. But it is perhaps more than a mere metaphor. Doing theology together requires both our own performances as well as moments of our own passivity and reception of others' performances when listening to what others perform, when we must pause to reflect on what we have been performing while exposed to the tunes (ideas, actions, etc.) that are strange and different from our own. Attentive listening (and, indeed, attentiveness, in general) to others inspires us and pushes our own performance on to a higher level. It enables us to perform together. Does not this sound like a method? A method of an "open mic," a generous and welcoming space, where we may do music, sport, study, fun, meditation, grieving, suffering, and theology together? The French fundamental theologian Marcel Neusch puts it this way: "Theology only assumes its task fully if it is able to show that the Christian fact has a universal significance, and that this universality is justified by the common destiny of humankind. To give up its task would mean to enclose oneself in a sentiment and to take its share in making the Christian experience incommunicable. However, the claim of the Christian experience is to open up a space of meaning and life accessible to all."[1]

Doing theology together is an option (perhaps *the* "preferential option") for a theological method starting from ordinary, everyday, human experience, and from there, creating generous spaces where anyone can join the process of doing theology from any background and perspective. This method has also been suggested as suitable to the specific needs of youth ministry. Bert Roebben's concept of a "playground for transcendence"[2] could serve as an example. Doing theology together is an inclusive method in the welcoming sense of the inclusiveness. Here, inclusivity does not mean simply that we comprehend everything and everyone automatically (as the term is sometimes interpreted). Instead, it becomes a principal, welcoming inclusiveness, emphasizing and granting everyone freedom to join and leave. Doing theology together is messy and colorful. To put it simply, doing theology together is about life, because theology, as such, is about life[3]—it comes from life, and it returns to it.

"The neighboring community, life experiences, stories and memories, newspaper articles and local histories, city spots, world events and art galleries, movie theatres and concert halls, peace demonstrations and community projects . . ."[4] are to be part of our theologies. As such, theologies simply cannot be done individually but in the presence of and in community with others. That is true not only in the case of individuals grouping into communities of doing theology together but also in the various cases of whole (theological) disciplines. It is suggested in this text that youth ministry (seen as a kind of doing practical theology), accompanied by youth theology, may do theology together with fundamental theology that is too often considered purely theoretical or only an academic theological performance.

In chapter 2.3, I used another metaphor, that of the *bridge*, to suggest that fundamental theology and youth ministry/youth theology are not separate but connected disciplines within one, holistic theology understood and shared as auto/Theo-biography (or a shared plenitude of auto/Theo-biographies). Perhaps a more apt metaphor would be that of a complex frontier landscape. Fundamental theology and youth ministry/

1. Neusch quoted in Geiser, *Community of the Weak*, 231.
2. Roebben, "Shaping," 332–47.
3. Sedmak, *Doing Local Theology*, 1.
4. Geiser, *Community of the Weak*, 225.

youth theology need to remain distinguishable. But their boundaries should not be closed, devoid of any Iron Curtain, Berlin or Trump wall, or closed borders, with guards or "experts" selecting who is or is not allowed to cross the borderline. The frontiers between youth ministry/ youth theology and fundamental theology (as between all other theological disciplines) must be open and free, like those in the Schengen Area. Yet they are not without natural barriers. There are moors with swamps, dark woods, and even wild animals between their actual territories. There are several dangers which need to be avoided, surpassed, and bridged so that people can travel safely to and fro and visit each other. We should constantly search for roads and paths to keep the connection open and passable from both sides. It will help all those who are out there on these roads to keep their theology alive, relational, spiritual (prayerful), biblical, committed, action-oriented, and public.

To achieve this goal, theology in general must adopt a new a holistic mind. It is high time to start understanding theology again. For instance, an argument for such a shift could be found in Regan's masterful treatment of mystagogy:

> Much of the lack of interest in "religion," as a subject, whether in secondary school or university, is bound up with the fragmentation of the content of the teaching. The division of the intellectual "content of faith" into so many truths to be learned and believed, or so many rules to be kept, soon dries up the innate curiosity or good will students may bring to the subject. The powerful and unified center provided by focusing on the one Mystery of Christ overcomes much of this atomization. When this center is not a truth to be learned, but a burning core to be experienced, the whole exercise changes character.[5]

From Regan's perspective, we need to think of theology holistically (i.e., as a whole) to try to overcome the divisions between different doctrines. They were separated and fragmented in the past for good reason: to find a system in the complex teachings of Christianity. But while we arguably lost a sense for theology over the centuries of detailed clarifications, the system prevailed. Now, we often have only such a system and, by consequence, must dig deep if we want to find the meaning of theology, again. While a rationalist way of understanding theology as a systematic science was strong *in analysis*, a holistic approach to theology

---

5. Regan, *Experience the Mystery*, 146.

might yet become even stronger *in synthesis*. Endeavoring a holistic theology makes theology a more organic, welcoming, and hospitable place. This could become an argument for including the theological voices of young people in serious consideration. Moreover, professional theologians and youth ministers, as well as religious educators and church representatives, may perhaps also find that it is not enough to take young people's (or children's) theologies seriously. A better way is perhaps to welcome them to do theology together. (Refusing to welcome them as such is already a failure to take them seriously in the first place.) This requires a large capacity for humility that many academics, ministers, education council presidents, and church officials are not often trained in and too often lack. If we take academics as an example, they are usually trained for (and forced to excel by) the institutional standards of publishing a lot of "good science." But, as far as I am concerned, far too few academics really take care or *attend to* the vocation of humility (and fallibility). There's a well-known rule in today's academia, worldwide: publish or perish! Perhaps this is true. But perhaps it is preferable for academic theologians to perish than publish: to perish from universities (at least for a while) and get in touch, re-acquaint, or re-attune themselves with real life.[6] Especially, when engaged in theology and youth ministry, or theology and pedagogy, we must be aware of the fact that "yesterday's message in yesterday's language, is not an adequate answer to the problems the young face today."[7]

Doing theology together in the contexts of encounters with contemporary young people requires us not to be shy or scared to tell them our stories and, also, to be ready to listen to theirs. These must be received not in a paternalistic way or from a presumption of already "knowing it all." We must be prepared, ready, and willing to be surprised by them. Though the course of writing this text, I also opted for more narrative language, especially in the foreword and introduction. I tried to anchor my theology in my personal auto/Theo-biography. I also attempted to narrate the story of fundamental theology, youth ministry, and emerging youth theology from a more personal point of view. It may be that precisely because of this, there are a lot of inconsistencies and weaknesses in my text. But nothing human is perfect, especially in the fields of theologies. I do not consider this text to be an all-encompassing manual

---

6. Geiser, *Community of the Weak*, 228.
7. Regan, *Experience the Mystery*, 147.

for fundamental theologians, nor for youth ministers or practical theologians. It is simply written to challenge them to ask about the principles, essentials, and fundamentals of their own disciplines and theologies. It perhaps also endeavors to empower those who are not professional theologians to narrate or even write their theologies. I am convinced that all of them matter. David Regan finished his book on mystagogy with a quotation ascribed to G. K. Chesterton: "Anything worth doing is worth doing badly."[8] I think theology, especially, is a thing worth doing (if it is a thing at all). Nothing is perfect. But my experience is that if we want to do theology, we must not do it by ourselves or for our own sake. We must do it together with others and for the sake of others.

The overall aim of this text is to welcome readers to join me in my quest for searching the abandoned and hidden trails which may interconnect academic theology with daily life; theoretic or systematic theology with practical theology; fundamental theology with youth ministry; youth theology with theology done by adults. I hope this aspiration will persuade any future devastating critiques to be at least merciful. I am very much aware that all concepts and theories I use and engage might well be more clarified. There are several weaknesses and inconsistencies to be found in the text. Overall, it is merely offered in humility as a personal contribution to (and perhaps also a stimulation of) theological debate (and maybe, also, to common theological action) on the themes with which it is concerned. It welcomes reactions, critiques, supplements, corrections, and further developments of anything presented above. It welcomes doing theology together.

With reference to Christianity, I perceive human being as living in relation to other human beings, the world, and God. Consequently, human being might be called *Homo Theologicus*—the theological human—because, in the depths of one's heart, soul, eyes, body, and face, Homo Theologicus mirrors God and his face (Jesus Christ). Such reflection is enabled by the Spirit, who dwells everywhere. To describe such a reflection in academic theological terms is not easy. It is perhaps more a task for a poet than a scientist. Despite this (and perhaps because of it), theology seems to be an appropriate discipline for such a task since it unites poetics together with efforts of reason and faith to search for understanding. Such an understanding is always somehow provisional and suffers great evanescence. Homo Theologicus is, therefore, intrinsically

---

8. Regan, *Experience the Mystery*, 148.

also *Homo Viator* (as Gabriel Marcel would put it): the human pilgrim throughout inner and outer landscapes of this world. The human pilgrim becomes a seeker of the sense and fulfilment, always opting for hope over despair and hopelessness.

Nothing human is perfect. Yet, as human beings, we still desire perfection. As a theologian, I am convinced that Christianity offers a road to perfection for our humanness, especially when considering the notion of Theosis. Yet anything that could be confused with perfection is still uncertain, since it is only the convictions of our faiths which inform us of all that is possible. We must believe.

When I used to teach Introduction to Christian Theology, I always told my students that I really believe in Jesus Christ and the Christian interpretation of his teaching, life, death, and resurrection. I always intimated to them that I consider it to be an absolute and unsurpassable truth. But in the same breath, I would add that it is an absolute, unsurpassable truth of faith, which does not mean it is necessarily an objective truth and that, in principle (even though I don't believe it and I don't think so at the same time), it is possible, perhaps, that everything might be completely different. Who is not fallible? Perhaps when I die, the Buddha will welcome me and say, "Haha! Another Christian! Welcome, brother, and enjoy eternity in the company of other enlightened ones." Perhaps not. Perhaps nothing of it will happen, and there will be just an eternal silence and emptiness completely irrelevant to what we think. Who knows? My students usually laughed when I performed this confession. I found it useful for welcoming everyone in the class to discuss issues of faith. Usually it worked. They felt more at ease talking about their personal beliefs and convictions and were able to connect many theories we discussed into their actual lives. Most of the time, we really experienced doing theology together.

I hope to achieve the same through this text, to offer my ideas and beliefs beyond the lecture hall and the inescapable restrictions of my mother tongue. Don't just read it. Please feel welcome to react. In this way we might do theology together, no matter where or when are you right now. And who knows? Perhaps somewhere out there, we will meet a stranger or pilgrim like the one encountered by Jesus' disciples on the road to Emmaus (cf. Luke 24:13–35), whom we will invite for a meal. And that will change everything.

Bibliography

Anderson, Ray S. *The Shape of Practical Theology: Empowering Ministry with Theological Praxis*. Downers Grove, IL: IVP Academic, 2001.
Astley, Jeff. *Ordinary Theology: Looking, Listening, and Learning in Theology*. Burlington, VT: Ashgate, 2002.
———. "The Analysis, Investigation and Application of Ordinary Theology." In *Exploring Ordinary Theology: Everyday Christian Believing and the Church*, edited by Jeff Astley and Leslie J. Francis, 1–9. Burlington, VT: Ashgate, 2013.
———., and Leslie J. Francis, eds. *Exploring Ordinary Theology: Everyday Christian Believing and the Church*. Burlington, VT: Ashgate, 2013.
Bailey, David. "Enacted Faith, Youth Ministry and Theological Shorthand." *Journal of Youth and Theology* 2 (2014) 25–39.
Bailey, Edward I. *Implicit Religion: An Introduction*. London: Middlesex University Press, 1998.
Bauman, Zygmunt. *Liquid Modernity*. Cambridge, UK: Polity, 2000.
Beck, Ulrich. *Risk Society: Towards a New Modernity*. London: Sage, 1992.
Becker, Matthew L. *Fundamental Theology: A Protestant Perspective*. New York: Bloomsbury, T&T Clark, 2015.
Becker, Ron. "Beyond a Godless Understanding of Youth: Why Exegesis Matters to Youth Ministry." *Journal of Youth and Theology* 1 (2006) 10–30.
———. *Reading the Young Testament*. Rotterdam: Ron Becker, 2025.
Bennett, Byard. "Mystagogy." In *Encyclopedia of Christian Education, Vol. 3*, edited by George Kurian at al., 856–57. Lanham, MD: Rowman & Littlefield, 2015.
Bergmann, Sigurd. *God in Context: A Survey of Contextual Theology*. New York: Routledge, 2017.
———. *Religion, Space and the Environment*. New Brunswick, NJ: Transaction, 2014.
Berman, Rivka C. "Sukkot: The Lulav and the Etrog." Mazornet, Mar. 7, 2017. http://www.mazornet.com/holidays/Sukkot/lulav.htm.
Bevans, Stephen B. *An Introduction to Theology in Global Perspective*. New York: Orbis, 2009.
Boeve, Lieven. *Theology at the Crossroads of University, Church and Society: Dialogue, Difference and Catholic Identity*. Oxford: Bloomsbury, T&T Clark, 2016.
Borgman, Dean. *Foundations for Youth Ministry: Theological Engagement with Teen Life and Culture*. 2nd ed. Grand Rapids: Baker Academic, 2013.

Boublík, Vladimír. *Člověk očekává Krista*. Kostelní Vydří: Karmelitánské Nakladatelství, 1997.
———. *Duchovní deník*. Edited by Jiří Žůrek and Karel Skalický. Olomouc: Refugium, 2010.
———. *La predestinazione: S. Paolo e S. Agostino*. Rome: Libreria Editrice della Pontificia Università Lateranense, 1961.
———. *Setkání s Ježíšem*. Kostelní Vydří: Karmelitánské Nakladatelství, 2002.
———. *Teologická antropologie*. Kostelní Vydří: Karmelitánské Nakladatelství, 2006.
Brofsky, David. *Hilkhot Mo'adim: Understanding the Laws of the Festivals*. Jerusalem: Koren, 2013.
Browning, Don S. *A Fundamental Practical Theology: Descriptive and Strategic Proposals*. Minneapolis: Fortress, 1996.
Bucher, Anton A. "Kinder als Theologen?" RL: *Zeitschrift für Religionsunterricht und Lebenskunde* 1 (1992) 19–22.
———. "Kinder und die Rechtfertigung Gottes? Ein Stück Kindertheologie." *Schweizer Schule* 10 (1992) 7–12.
———. "Kindertheologie: Provokation? Romantizismus? Neues Paradigma?" In *Jahrbuch für Kindertheologie / "Mittendrin ist Gott": Kinder denken nach über Gott, Leben und Tod*, edited by Anton A. Bucher et al., 9–27. Stuttgart: Calwer, 2002.
Budden, Chris. "The Necessity of the Second Peoples' Theology in Australia." In *Contextual Theology for the Twenty-First Century*, edited by Stephen B. Bevans and Katalina Tahaafe-Williams, 55–68. Eugene, OR: Wipf & Stock, 2011.
Bulst, Werner. *Revelation*. New York: Sheed & Ward, 1965.
Burrell, David B. *Towards a Jewish-Christian-Muslim Theology*. Malden, MA: Wiley-Blackwell, 2011.
Cahalan, Kathleen A. "Toward a Fundamental Theology of Ministry." *Worship* 2 (2006) 102–20.
Carey Patrick W. *Avery Cardinal Dulles, SJ: A Model Theologian*. New York; Mahwah, NJ: Paulist, 2010.
Chan, Simon. "The Christian Identity: A Theological Perspective." *Church & Society in Asia Today* 3 (2010) 123–31.
Coe, Shoki. "A Preliminary Word from the TEF Directors: In Search of Renewal in Theological Education." *Theological Education* 9 (1973) 233–43.
Comstock, Gary L. "Two Types of Narrative Theology." *Journal of the American Academy of Religion* 4 (1987) 687–717.
Cullmann, Oscar. *Christ and Time: The Primitive Christian Conception of Time and History*. Philadelphia: Westminster, 1964.
Davidsen, Markus A. "Fiction and Religion: How Narratives About the Supernatural Inspire Religious Belief—Introducing the Thematic Issue." *Religion* 4 (2016) 489–99.
Dean, Kenda C. *Practicing Passion: Youth and the Quest for a Passionate Church*. Grand Rapids: Eerdmans, 2004.
———., et al. *Starting Right: Thinking Theologically About Youth Ministry*. Grand Rapids: Zondervan, 2001.
———., ed. *OMG: A Youth Ministry Handbook*. Nashville: Abingdon, 2010.
de Kock, Jos, and Bård Norheim. *The Five Questions: An Academic Handbook in Youth Ministry Research*. Eugene, OR: Pickwick, 2022.

de Lubac, Henri. *Catholicism: A Study of Dogma in Relation to Corporate Destiny of Mankind*. New York: Mentor-Omega, 1964.
Doehring, Carrie. *The Practice of Pastoral Care: A Postmodern Approach*. Revised and expanded ed. Louisville: Westminster John Knox, 2015.
Dreyer, Yolanda. "A Public Practical Theological Theory for Religious Education of Secularized Youth." *HTS Theological Studies* 3 (2004) 919–45.
Driscoll, Jeremy. *Theology at the Eucharistic Table: Master Themes in the Theological Tradition*. Leominster, UK: Gracewing, 2003.
Dulles, Avery. *The Craft of Theology: From Symbol to System*. New York: Crossroad, 1995.
———. *A History of Apologetics*. 2nd ed. New York: Ignatius, 2005.
———. *Models of the Church*. Expanded ed. New York: Doubleday, 2002.
———. *Models of Revelation*. New York: Orbis, 1992.
———. *Revelation Theology: A History*. New York: Herder & Herder, 1969.
———. *The Splendor of Faith: The Theological Vision of Pope John Paul II*. Revised and updated ed. New York: Crossroad, 2003.
———. "The Symbolic Structure of Revelation." *Theological Studies* 1 (1980) 51–73.
———. *A Testimonial to Grace: Reflections on a Theological Journey*. Kansas City: Sheed & Ward, 1996.
———. "Vatican II: The Myth and the Reality." *America* 188:6 (2003) 7–11.
Dupuis, Jacques. *Who Do You Say I Am?: Introduction to Christology*. New York: Orbis, 1994.
Durkheim, Emile. *The Elementary Forms of Religious Life*. Translated by Karen E. Fields. New York: Free, 1995.
Egan, Harvey D. "Translation's Editor Preface." In *The Content of Faith: The Best of Karl Rahner's Theological Writings*, xi–xiii, edited by Karl Lehmann and Albert Raffelt. New York: Crossroad, 1993.
Ellis, Wesley W. "Human Beings and Human Becomings: Departing from the Developmental Model of Youth Ministry." *Journal of Youth and Theology* 2 (2015) 119–37.
Elshof, Toke A. J. M. "Mystagogy, Religious Education and Lived Catholic Faith." *Journal of Religious Education* 3 (2017) 143–55.
Erikson, Erik H. *Identität und Lebenszyklus*. Frankfurt am Main: Suhrkamp Verlag, 1995.
Faix, Tobias. "How Theology Takes Shape in the Faith of Young People: An Introduction to Youth Theology Based on the Example of an Empirical-Theological Study Among Young People." *Journal of Youth and Theology* 2 (2014) 6–24.
Feldman, Daniel. "Sukkot: Pri Etz Hadar." *Mazornet*, Mar. 7, 2017. http://www.mazornet.com/holidays/Sukkot/pri-hadar.htm.
Fischer, Kathleen R. *The Inner Rainbow: The Imagination in Christian Life*. New York; Mahwah, NJ: Paulist, 1983.
Francis, Leslie J. "Implicit Religion, Explicit Religion and Purpose in Life: An Empirical Enquiry among 13- to 15-year-old Adolescents." *Mental Health, Religion & Culture* 9 (2013) 909–21.
Frazer, James George. *Totemism and Exogamy: A Treatise on Certain Early Forms of Superstition and Society*. Vol. I–IV. New York: Cosimo, 2010.
Frei, Hans W. *The Eclipse of Biblical Narrative: A Study in Eighteenth and Nineteenth Century Hermeneutics*. New Haven: Yale University Press, 1974.

———. *The Identity of Jesus Christ*. Eugene, OR: Wipf & Stock, 1997.
Fries, Heinrich. *Fundamental Theology*. Washington, DC: Catholic University of America, 1996.
Funda, Otakar A. "Je teologie vědou?" *Acta Filosofické fakulty Západočeské University v Plzni* 1 (2011) 105–35.
Gallagher, Michael P. *What Are They Saying About Unbelief?* New York; Mahwah, NJ: Paulist, 1995.
Gallus, Petr. "Orientující teologie." In *Teologie jako věda: Dvě perspektivy*, edited by Petr Gallus and Petr Macek, 11–145. Brno: CDK, 2007.
Gauchet, Marcel. *The Disenchantment of the World: A Political History of Religion*. Princeton, NJ: Princeton University Press, 1999.
Geiser, Hans-Peter. *The Community of the Weak: Social Postmodernism in Theological Reflections on Power and Powerlessness in North America*. Eugene, OR: Wipf & Stock, 2013.
Ghiloni, Aaron J. "On Writing Interdisciplinary Theology." *Practical Theology* 1 (2013) 9–33.
———. "Review of *Theology Made in Dignity: On the Precarious Role of Theology in Religious Education*." *International Journal of Practical Theology* 2 (2017) 326–28.
Giddens, Anthony. *Sociologie*. Prague: Argo, 2000.
Green, Laurie. *Let's Do Theology: Resources for Contextual Theology*. New York: Mowbray, 2009.
Grenz, Stanley J., et al. *Pocket Dictionary of Theological Terms*. Downers Grove, IL: InterVarsity, 1999.
Guarino, Thomas G. "Why Avery Dulles Matters." *First Things*, May 1, 2009. https://www.firstthings.com/article/2009/05/why-avery-dulles-matters.
Hábl, Jan. "Problem of Epistemological Foundationalism." *Paideia: Philosophical e-Journal of Charles University* 4 (2011) 1–14. https://ojs.cuni.cz/paideia/article/view/1778/1356.
Haight, Roger. *Dynamics of Theology*. New York: Orbis, 2001.
Halík, Tomáš. *Chci, abys byl: Křesťanství po náboženství*. Prague: Nakladatelství Lidové Noviny, 2012.
———. *Night of the Confessor: Christian Faith in an Age of Uncertainty*. New York: Image, 2012.
———. *Patience with God: The Story of Zacchaeus Continuing in Us*. New York: Doubleday, 2009.
———. *Vzýván i nevzýván: Evropské přednášky k filosofii a sociologii dějin křesťanství*. Prague: Nakladatelství Lidové Noviny, 2004.
Hall, Douglas J. *The End of Christendom and the Future of Christianity*. Eugene, OR: Wipf & Stock, 2002.
Hamplová, Dana. "Religiozita dospělých v České republice na počátku 21. století." In *Náboženství v menšině: Religiozita a spiritualita v současné české společnosti*, edited by Dušan Lužný and Zdeněk Nešpor, 20–30, Prague: Malvern, 2008.
Hauerwas, Stanley. *After Christendom*. Nashville: Abingdon, 1999.
Havel, Václav. *O lidskou identitu*. Prague: Rozmluvy, 1990.
———. "Power of the Powerless." 1978. https://www.nonviolent-conflict.org/wp-content/uploads/1979/01/the-power-of-the-powerless.pdf.
Hellwig, Monika K. "Foundations for Theology: A Historical Sketch." In *Faithful Witness: Foundations of Theology for Today's Church*, edited by Leo J. O'Donovan and Howland T. Sanks, 1–13, New York: Crossroad, 1989.

Hoebel, Thomas. *Laity and Participation: A Theology of Being the Church.* Bern: Peter Lang, 2006.
Holland, Dorothy, et al. *Identity and Agency in Cultural Worlds.* Cambridge, MA: Harvard University Press, 1998.
Hughes, Kathleen. *Saying Amen: A Mystagogy of Sacrament.* Chicago: Liturgy Training (Archdiocese of Chicago), 1999.
Huxley, Aldous L. *Brave New World & Brave New World Revisited.* New York: Harper Colophon, 1965.
Imbelli, Robert Peter. *Rekindling the Christic Imagination: Theological Meditations for the New Evangelization.* Collegeville, MN: Liturgical, 2014.
Jenkins, Philip. *The Next Christendom: The Coming of Global Christianity.* 3rd ed. New York: Oxford University Press, 2011.
Jensen, Jeppe Sinding. "Narrative." In *The Oxford Handbook of the Study of Religion*, edited by Michael Stausberg and Steven Engler, 290–303. Oxford: Oxford University Press, 2016.
Joest, Wilfried. *Fundamentální teologie: Problémy základů a metody theologie.* Prague: Oikúmené, 2007.
Jones, Tony. *Postmodern Youth Ministry: Exploring Cultural Shift, Creating Holistic Connections, Cultivating Authentic Community.* Grand Rapids: Zondervan, 2001.
Jüptner, Jan. *Civilní náboženství: Nový pohled na to, na čem skutečně záleží.* Prague: Karolinum, 2013.
Kaplánek, Michal. *Pastorace mládeže.* Prague: Salesiánská provincie, 1999.
Kasper, Walter. *Theologie—součást naší doby.* Prague: Fokus, Česká Křesťanská Akademie, 1994.
Kirmse, Anne-Marie, and Michael M. Canaris, eds. *The Legacy of Avery Cardinal Dulles, S.J.: His Words and His Witness.* New York: Fordham University Press, 2011.
Knauer, Peter. "Potentia oboedientialis en bovennatuurlijk existentiaal en hun verhouding tot het verlangen naar de godsaanschouwing." In *Op het ritme van de oneindigheid: Opstellen over het natuurlijke godsverlangen*, edited by Luc Braeckmans et al., 79–90, Leuven: Acco, 2000.
Korsmeyer, Jerry D. *God-Creature-Revelation: A Neoclassical Framework for Fundamental Theology.* Lanham, MD: University Press of America, 1995.
Kropač, Ulrich. *Religionspädagogik und Offenbarung: Anfänge einer wissenschaftlichen Religionspädagogik im Spannungsfeld von pädagogischer Innovation und offenbarungstheologischer Position.* Münster: Lit Verlag, 2006.
Küng, Hans. *On Being a Christian.* New York: Doubleday, 1984.
Lacoste, Jean-Yves. *From Theology to Theological Thinking.* Charlottesville, VA: University of Virginia Press, 2014.
Lang, Albert. *Wesen und Wahrheit der Religion: Einführung in die Religionsphilosophie.* München: Max Hueber, 1957.
Lorde, Audre. *Sister Outsider.* Berkeley, CA: Crossing, 2007.
Lucie-Smith, Alexander. *Narrative Theology and Moral Theology: The Infinite Horizon.* New York: Routledge, 2016.
Lyotard, Jean-Francois. *The Postmodern Condition: A Report on Knowledge.* Minneapolis: University of Minnesota Press, 1993.
Macek, Petr. "Teologie mezi vědami." In *Teologie jako věda: Dvě perspektivy*, edited by Petr Gallus and Petr Macek, 147–216, Brno: CDK, 2007.
Machula, Tomáš. "Teologie jako věda?" In *Teologická věda a vědecká teologie*, edited by Petr Gallus and Petr Macek, 35–50. Brno: CDK, 2006.

Marcel, Gabriel. *Homo Viator: Introduction to the Metaphysics of Hope*. South Bend, IN: St. Augustine's, 2010.
Martínek, Michal. *Ztracená generace? O duchovním dialogu mezi českou mládeží a katolickou církví*. Svitavy: Trinitas, 2006.
McCarty, Robert J., and Laurie Delgatto, eds. *The Vision of Catholic Youth Ministry: Fundamentals, Theory, and Practice*. Winona, MN: Saint Mary's, 2005.
McClendon, James W., Jr. *Biography as Theology: How Life Stories Can Remake Today's Theology*. Eugene, OR: Wipf & Stock, 2002.
McGowan, Michael W. *The Bridge: Revelation and Its Implications*. Eugene, OR: Pickwick, 2015.
McGrath, Alister E. *Christian Theology: An Introduction*. Malden, MA: Wiley-Blackwell, 2011.
Metz, Johannes-Baptist, ed. *The Development of Fundamental Theology*. New York; Mahwah, NJ: Paulist, 1969.
———. *Faith in History and Society: Toward a Practical Fundamental Theology*. New York: Crossroad, 2007.
———. *Theology of the World*. New York: Herder, 1971.
Milbank, John. "Foreword." In *Imaginative Apologetics: Theology, Philosophy and Catholic Tradition*, edited by Andrew Davison, xii–xxiv, Grand Rapids: Baker Academic, 2012.
Moltmann, Jürgen. *God for a Secular Society: The Public Relevance of Theology*. London: SCM, 1999.
Muchová, Ludmila. *Budete mými svědky: Dialogické rozvíjení křesťanské identity ve světonázorově pluralitní společnosti—pedagogická výzva*. Brno: Kartuziánské Nakladatelství a Vydavatelství, 2011.
Mueller, Jill J., ed. *Theological Foundations: Concepts and Methods for Understanding Christian Faith*. Winona, MN: Anselm Academic, 2011.
Murray, Stuart. *Church After Christendom*. Milton Keynes: Authentic Media, 2005.
———. *Post-Christendom: Church and Mission in a Strange New World*. Milton Keynes, UK: Authentic, 2004.
Neville, Robert C. *The Truth of Broken Symbol*. Albany, NY: SUNY, 1996.
Newlands, George. *The Transformative Imagination: Rethinking Intercultural Theology*. Burlington, VT: Ashgate, 2004.
Newman, John Henry. *Fifteen Sermons Preached Before the University of Oxford Between A.D. 1826 and 1843*. London: Longmans, Green and Co., 1909.
Ng, David. "A Path of Concentric Circles: Toward an Autobiographical Theology of Community." In *Journeys at the Margin: Toward an Autobiographical Theology in American-Asian Perspective*, edited by Peter C. Phan and Jung Young Lee, 81–102. Collegeville, MN: Liturgical, 1999.
Niebuhr, Helmut Richard. *The Meaning of Revelation*. New York: Macmillan, 1941.
Noble, Ivana. *Theological Interpretation of Culture in Post-Communist Context: Central and Eastern European Search for Roots*. Burlington, VT: Ashgate, 2010.
———. *Tracking God: An Ecumenical Fundamental Theology*. Eugene, OR: Wipf & Stock, 2010.
Norheim, Bård Eirik Hallesby. *Practicing Baptism: Christian Practices and Presence of Christ*. Eugene, OR: Wipf & Stock, 2014.
Noval, Christian. "Youth and Creation: A Biblical Theology of Growth & Development." *Journal of Youth and Theology* 1 (2013) 35–45.

O'Collins, Gerald. *Fundamental Theology*. Eugene, OR: Wipf & Stock, 2001.
———. *Rethinking Fundamental Theology: Toward a New Fundamental Theology*. New York: Oxford University Press, 2011.
———. *Revelation: Towards a Christian Interpretation of God's Self-Revelation in Jesus Christ*. New York: Oxford University Press, 2016.
O'Meara, Thomas F. *A Theology of Ministry*. New York; Mahwah, NJ: Paulist, 1999.
Ormerod, Neil, and Christiaan Jacobs-Vandegeer. *Foundational Theology: A New Approach to Catholic Fundamental Theology*. Minneapolis: Fortress, 2015.
Pederson, Ann. *God, Creation, and All That Jazz: A Process of Composition and Improvisation*. St. Louis: Chalice, 2001.
Plantinga, Richard J., et al. *An Introduction to Christian Theology*. Cambridge: Cambridge University Press, 2014.
Polanyi, Michael. *Personal Knowledge*. Chicago: University of Chicago Press, 1959.
Pospíšil, Ctirad Václav. *Hermeneutika mystéria: Struktury myšlení v dogmatické teologii*. Prague; Kostelní Vydří: Krystal OP; Karmelitánské Nakladatelství, 2005.
Putna, Martin C. *Spiritualita Václava Havla*. Prague: Knihovna Václava Havla, 2009.
Rahner, Karl. *Theological Investigations*. Vol. 4. Baltimore: Helicon, 1966.
———. *Základy křesťanské víry*. Svitavy: Trinitas, 2002.
Regan, David. *Experience the Mystery: Pastoral Possibilities for Christian Mystery*. London: Geoffrey Chapman, 1994.
Regner, Jan. "Víra a fundamentální teologie. Rozhovor s Karlem Skalickým." Radio Vaticana, Nov. 17, 2001. http://www.radiovaticana.cz/clanek.php4?id=653.
Roach, Jonathan C., and Gricel Dominguez. *Expressing Theology: A Guide to Write Theology That Readers Want to Read*. Eugene, OR: Cascade, 2015.
Robertson, Roland. *Globalization: Social Theory and Global Culture*. London: Sage, 1992.
Roebben, Bert. "International Development in Youth Ministry Research: A Comparative Review." *Religious Education* 2 (2012) 192–206.
———. *Seeking Sense in the City: European Perspectives on Religious Education*. Berlin: LIT, 2013.
———. "Shaping a Playground for Transcendence: Postmodern Youth Ministry as a Radical Challenge." *Religious Education* 3 (1997) 332–47.
———. *Theology Made in Dignity: On the Precarious Role of Theology in Religious Education*. Leuven: Peeters, 2016.
———. "Youth, Culture and Theology in Plural: Presenting the Work of the International Association for the Study of Youth Ministry." In *Global Youth Ministry: Reaching Adolescents Around the World*, edited by Terry Linhart and David Livermore, 247–52, Grand Rapids: Zondervan, 2011.
Root, Andrew. "Practical Theology: What Is It and How Does It Work?" *Journal of Youth Ministry* 2 (2009) 55–72.
Root, Andrew, and Kenda C. Dean. *The Theological Turn in Youth Ministry*. Downers Grove, IL: IVP, 2011.
Říha, Karel. *Filosofie konání: K 100. výročí Blondelovy "L'Action"*. Olomouc: Matice Cyrilometodějská, 1993.
———. "Fundamentální teologie v existenciálním horizontu myšlení." *Studie* 122–23 (1989) 133–52.
———. *Hledání středu*. Svitavy: Trinitas, 2010.
Sak, Petr. *Proměny české mládeže: Česká mládež v pohledu sciologických výzkumů*. Prague: Petrklíč, 2000.

Samohýl, Jan. *Židovské inspirace křesťanství*. Kostelní Vydří: Karmelitánské Nakladatelství, 2017.

Sanks, T. Howland. "Homo Theologicus: Toward a Reflexive Theology (With the Help of Pierre Bourdieu)." *Theological Studies* 3 (2007) 515–30.

Schambeck, Mirjam. "Mystagogisches Lernen." In *Religionsdidaktik. Ein Leitfaden für Studium, Ausbildung und Beruf* (3rd ed), edited by Georg Hilger et al., 400–15, München: Kösel, 2013.

Scheinerman, Amy. "Sukkot: The Harvest Festival", Mar. 7, 2017. http://scheinerman.net/judaism/Holidays/index.html.

Schelkens, Karim. *Catholic Theology of Revelation on the Eve of Vatican II: A Redaction History of the Schema De fontibus revelationis (1960–1962)*. Leiden; Boston: Brill, 2010.

Schillebeeckx, Edward. *Church: The Human Story of God*. New York: Crossroad, 1993.

Schlag, Thomas. "Systematic Topics." In *Basics of Religious Education*, edited by Gottfried Adam et al., 371–84, Göttingen: V&R Unipress, 2014.

Schlag, Thomas, and Friedrich Schweitzer. *Brauchen Jugendliche Theologie? Jugendtheologie als Herausforderung und didaktische Perspektive*. Neukirchen-Vluyn: Neukirchener Theologie, 2011.

———. *Jugendtheologie: Grundlagen-Beispiele-kritische Diskussion*. Neukirchen-Vluyn: Neukirchener Theologie, 2012.

Schreier, Monica, and Karel Skalický, eds. *Česko-římský teolog Vladimír Boublík: Symposium k jeho nedožitým 70. Narozeninám, 25.-26. listopadu 1998*. České Budějovice: Teologická Fakulta Jihočeské Univerzity v Českých Budějovicích, 1999.

Schüssler Fiorenza, Francis, and John P. Galvin, eds. *Systematic Theology: Roman Catholic Perspectives*. [2nd edition]. Minneapolis: Fortress, 2011.

Schweitzer, Friedrich. "Adolescents as Theologians: A New Approach in Christian Education and Youth Ministry." *Religious Education* 109:2 (2014) 184–200.

———. "Children as Theologians: God-talk with Children, Developmental Psychology, and Interreligious Education." In *Education, Religion, and Society: Essays in Honour of John M. Hull*, edited by Dennis Bates et al., 179–90, New York: Routledge, 2006.

———. "Was ist und wozu Kindertheologie?" In *Jahrbuch für Kindertheologie 2: Im Himmelreich is keiner sauer*, edited by Anton A. Bucher et al., 9–18, Sttutgart: Calwer, 2003.

Sedmak, Clemens. *Doing Local Theology: A Guide for Artisans of a New Humanity*. New York: Orbis, 2002.

Shea, John. *Stories of God: An Unauthorized Biography*. Chicago: Thomas More, 1978.

Shecterle, Ross A. *The Theology of Revelation of Avery Dulles 1980–1994: Symbolic Mediation*. Lewiston, NY: Edwin Mellen, 1996.

Shenk, Wilbert R. "Contextual Theology: The Last Frontier." In *The Changing Face of Christianity: Africa, the West, and the World*, edited by Lamin Sanneh and Joel A. Carpenter, 191–212, New York: Oxford University Press, 2005.

Skalický, Karel. "Geneze koncilního dokumentu o zjevení." *Teologické texty* 1 (2003) 22–23.

———. "Kdo je křesťan? K teologii křesťanské existence." *Teologické texty* 2 (2014). https://www.teologicketexty.cz/casopis/2014-12/Kdo-je-krestan-K-teologii-krestanske-existence.html.

———. *Po stopách neznámého Boha*. 4th ed. Svitavy: Trinitas, 2011.

---. *Radost a naděje*. 2nd ed. Kostelní Vydří: Karmelitánské Nakladatelství, 2000.
---. *Radost a naděje*. 1st ed. Roma: Křesťanská Akademie, 1968.
---. "Saggio Introduttivo: Vladimír Boublík e la sua teologia." In *Alla ricerca di Gesù di Nazareth: e altri scritti*, 11–85. Città del Vaticano: Lateran Univeristy, 2016.
---. "Současná křesťanská teologie, aneb pokus představit bohovědu přírodovědcům." *Teologické studie* 2 (2002) 33–42.
---. "Třetího dne vstal z mrtvých podle Písem." In *Věřím ve vzkříšení těla a život věčný*, 17–43. České Budějovice: Tomáš Halama, 2007.
---. *V zápase s posvátnem: Náboženství v religionistickém bádání*. Brno: CDK, 2005.
---. *Za nadějí a smysl*. Prague: Zvon, 1996.
Skalický, Carlo. *Teologia fondamentale*. 4th ed. Roma: Istituto Superiore di Scienze Religiose a Distanza dell'Ateneo Romano della Santa Croce, 1992.
Snow, David A. et al., "Identity." In *Encyclopedia of Social Theory: Volume II*, edited by George Ritzer, 390–93. London: Sage, 2005.
Song, Choan-Seng. "Five Stages Toward Christian Theology in the Multicultural World." In *Journeys at the Margin: Toward an Autobiographical Theology in American-Asian Perspective*, edited by Peter C. Phan and Jung Young Lee, 1–22. Collegeville, MN: Liturgical, 1999.
---. *In the Beginning Were Stories, Not Texts: Story Theology*. Eugene, OR: Wipf & Stock, 2011.
Stone, Howard W., and James O. Duke. *How to Think Theologically*. 3rd ed. Minneapolis: Fortress, 2013.
Stroup, George W. *The Promise of Narrative Theology: Recovering the Gospel in the Church*. 2nd ed. Eugene, OR: Wipf & Stock, 1997.
Sundermeier, Theo. *Den Fremden verstehen: Eine praktische Hermeneutik*. Göttingen: Vandenhoeck & Ruprecht, 1996.
Špidlík, Tomáš. "Skalického fundamentální teologie." *Studie* 78 (1981) 608.
Štěch, František. "Fundamental Theology, Dynamics of Christian Life and Identity: New Impulses for Fundamental Theology." *ET-Studies*. 1 (2014) 77–95.
---. "Fundamentální teologie a křesťanská identita." In *Církev a společnost: Karlovi Skalickému k 80. Narozeninám*, edited by František Štěch and Roman Míčka, 23–38. České Budějovice: Teologická fakulta Jihočeské univerzity v Českých Budějovicích, 2014.
---. "Here I Am: A Prolegomena to Theology of the Landscape." *Communio Viatorum* 2 (2017) 148–59.
---. "Integrální apologetika včera a dnes." In *Dialektika mysli a činu*, edited by František Štěch and Július Pavelčík, 59–76. Svitavy: Trinitas, 2014.
---. "John Henry Newman o víře a rozumu." *Communio* 2-3 (2011) 111–18.
---. "Love as the Core of Theology." In *In Love with the Bible and its Ordinary Readers: Hans de Wit and the Intercultural Bible Reading Project*, edited by Hans Snoek, 179–89. Mishawaka, IN: Dulley, Institute of Mennonite Studies, 2015.
---. "Od věrohodnosti křesťanského zjevení k teologii očekávání: Boublíkova fundamentální christologie a její inspirace pro současnou fundamentální teologii." In *Teologie v utkání s pluralitou náboženství: Přínos Vladimíra Boublíka v přístupech a hodnoceních jeho žáků*, edited by Kateřina Brichcínová et. al., 85–98. Kostelní Vydří: Karmelitánské Nakladatelství, 2009.
---. "Písmo a Tradice." In *Vydajte dôvod vašej nádeje: Vybrané témy z fundamentálnej teológie*, edited by Pavol Hrabovecký and Martin Maďar, 115–66. Brno: CDK, 2023.

———. "Teologie ve veřejném prostoru." In *Vykročit z uzavřenosti: Festschrift k 70. narozeninám Tomáše Halíka*, edited by Martin Kočí, 64–73. Prague: NLN, 2018.

———. *Tu se jim otevřely oči: Zjevení, víra a církev v teologii kardinála Avery Dullese SJ*. Olomouc: Refugium, 2011.

———. "Who Are Youth in Theological Perspective?" *Journal of Youth and Theology* 15:2 (2016) 124–45.

———., and Ludmila Muchová. "Sustainable Youth Ministry—Between Human and Divine." *Journal of Youth and Theology*, 1–2 (2012) 59–72.

Štofaník, Štefan. "Popularization and Autobiography: Towards an Accessible Theology." *Acta Universitatis Carolinae Theologica* 4:1 (2014) 67–83.

Teilhard de Chardin, Pierre. *The Divine Milieu: An Essay on the Interior Life*. New York: Harper & Row, 1960.

———. *Science and Christ*. New York: Harper & Row, 1965.

Thils, Gustave. *Théologie des réalités terrestres. I. Préludes*. Paris; Bruges: Desclée de Brouwer, 1947.

———. *Théologie des réalités terrestres. II. Théologie de l'histoire*. Paris; Bruges: Desclée de Brouwer, 1949.

Tillich, Paul. *Systematic Theology*. Vol. I. Chicago: University of Chicago Press, 1951.

United Nations. "Definition of Youth." https://www.un.org/esa/socdev/documents/youth/fact-sheets/youth-definition.pdf.

United States Conference of Catholic Bishops. "Renewing the Vision." Jun. 1997. https://www.usccb.org/topics/youth-and-young-adult-ministries/renewing-vision.

Vahland, Joachim. *Max Webers entzauberte Welt*. Würzburg: Königshausen & Neumann, 2001.

van Dijk-Groeneboer, Monique C. H. "Youth Ministry: About Youth?" *Journal of Youth and Theology* 2 (2015) 25–44.

van Huyssteen, Wenzel J. *The Shaping of Rationality: Toward Interdisciplinarity in Theology and Science*. Grand Rapids: Eerdmans, 1999.

Vanhoozer, Kevin J., et al. *Everyday Theology: How to Read Cultural Texts and Interpret Trends*. Grand Rapids: Baker Academic, 2007.

Veling, Terry A. *Practical Theology: On Earth as It Is in Heaven*. Maryknoll, NY: Orbis, 2005.

Vido, Roman, et al. "Czech Republic: The Promised Land for Atheists?" In *Annual Review of the Sociology of Religion: Sociology of Atheism*, edited by Roberto Cipriani and Franco Garelli, 201–31, Leiden: Brill, 2016.

Volf, Miroslav. *Exclusion and Embrace: Theological Explorations on Identity, Otherness, and Reconciliation*. Nashville: Abingdon, 1996.

———. "A Vision of Embrace: Theological Perspectives on Cultural Identity and Conflict." *Ecumenical Review* 2 (1995) 195–205.

Walton, Heather. *Writing Methods in Theological Reflection*. London: SCM, 2014.

Ward, Peter. *Participation and Mediation: A Practical Theology for the Liquid Church*. London: SCM, 2008.

Whapham, Theodore J. "Foreword." In *Expressing Theology: A Guide to Write Theology That Readers Want to Read* by Jonathan C. Roach and Gricel Dominguez, 8–9, Eugene, OR: Cascade, 2015.

Wilkins, Michael. *Matthew: From Biblical Text to Contemporary Life*. Grand Rapids: Zondervan, 2004.

Zimmermann, Mirjam. "What Is Children's Theology? Children's Theology as Theological Competence: Development, Differentiation, Methods." *HTS Theological Studies* 3 (2015) 1–6.

Zvěřina, Josef. *Pět cest k radosti*. Prague: Zvon, 1995.

———. *Teologie agapé I*. Prague: Scriptum, 1992.

Žůrek, Jiří. *Prolegomena k četbě Vladimíra Boublíka a analýza stěžejních témat jeho myšlenkového odkazu*. Prague: Krystal OP, 2008.

Name Index

Abelard, Peter, 56
Anderson, Ray S., 144
Anselm (Saint), 21, 43, 48, 55, 84
Aquinas, Thomas (Saint), 53, 55, 56, 83–84
Aristotle, 55, 93
Astley, Jeff, 30, 169, 170
Augustine (Saint), 21, 54, 55, 95

Bailey, David, 138
Bailey, Edward I., 198
Barth, Karl, 169
Bauman, Zygmunt, 17
Beck, Ulrich, 16
Becker, Matthew L., 55, 63, 116, 128, 147, 152
Becker, Ron, 152
Bellarmine, Robert, 208
Bennett, Byard, 207
Beran, Josef, 80
Berger, Peter L., 83
Bergmann, Sigurd, 111, 113
Berman, Rivka C., 46
Bernard (Saint), 92
Bevans, Stephen B., 17, 29
Blondel, Maurice, 58, 59, 60, 117, 220
Boff, Leonard, 147
Borgman, Dean, 41, 134, 140, 161, 164, 165, 181, 182
Boublík, Vladimír, 48, 66–78, 81, 85, 89, 91, 111, 114, 115, 194
Brofsky, David, 46

Browning, Don S., 145
Bucher, Anton A., 168, 180
Budden, Chris, 66
Burrell, David B., 23
Büttner, Gerhard, 168

Cahalan, Kathleen A., 216
Canaris, Michael M., 96
Carey, Patrick W., 92, 96, 98, 99, 100, 102
Chan, Simon, 192, 193, 196
Charry, Ellen, 147
Chesterton, G. K., 231
Coe, Shoki, 112
Comstock, Gary L., 35, 36
Cullmann, Oscar, 45

Davidsen, Markus A., 35
Dean, Kenda C., 16, 125–31, 136–44, 148, 149, 151–53, 158, 176, 204, 207, 213
de Kock, Jos, 139, 144, 145, 149, 151
Delgatto, Laurie, 152
de Lubac, Henri, 60, 106
Descartes, 85, 93, 192
Doehring, Carrie, 30
Dominguez, Gricel, 31, 32, 41, 88, 205, 218
Doolin, Paul, 94
Dreyer, Yolanda, 132
Driscoll, Jeremy, 51
Duke, James, 205, 206, 218, 219

Dulles, Avery, 13, 14, 52, 57, 60, 66–69, 83, 91–104, 107, 111, 113–17, 198, 199, 207, 209
Dulles, John Foster, 92
Duns Scotus, 56
Dupuis, Jacques, 184–87
Durkheim, Émile, 2, 83

Ebeling, Gerhard, 63
Egan, Harvey D., 211
Eisenhower, Dwight D., 92
Ellis, Wesley W., 156, 157, 187
Elshof, Toke A. J. M., 208, 211, 214
Erikson, Erik H., 156, 191
Eusebius (Saint), 8

Faix, Tobias, 159–61, 173, 175, 178, 179
Farley, Gerard, 169
Feldman, Daniel, 46
Fichte, Johann Gottlieb, 57, 192
Fischer, Kathleen R., 37
Francis, Leslie J., 169, 198
Frazer, James George, 9
Frei, Hans W., 34, 35
Freud, Sigmund, 83
Freudenberger-Lötz, Petra, 168
Fries, Heinrich, 51
Funda, Otakar A., 29

Gallagher, Michael P., 208, 211
Gallus, Petr, 28, 29
Galvin, John P., 23, 24
Gauchet, Marcel, 16
Geiser, Hans-Peter, 9, 15, 17, 30, 63–65, 114, 116, 118, 119, 122, 142, 143, 225, 227, 228, 230
Ghiloni, Aaron J., 8, 9, 167
Giddens, Anthony, 190
Gilson, Étienne, 94
Green, Laurie, 205, 206
Grenz, Stanley J., 21
Guardini, Romano, 207
Guarino, Thomas G., 98, 99
Gutiérrez, Gustavo, 147

Hábl, Jan, 53
Haight, Roger, 117
Halík, Tomáš, 8, 15, 16, 42, 195, 210

Hall, Douglas J., 16
Hamplová, Dana, 198
Hauerwas, Stanley, 35, 113
Havel, Václav, 22, 201, 202, 203
Heidegger, Martin, 70, 145, 221
Hellwig, Monika K., 14, 54, 56, 58, 60
Hoebel, Thomas, 30
Holland, Dorothy, 190, 191
Hughes, Kathleen, 209
Hull, John M., 168
Hume, David, 93
Hus, Jan, 56
Huxley, Aldous L., 14

Imbelli, Robert Peter, 158

Jacobs-Vandegeer, Christiaan, 63, 116
Jenkins, Philip, 16, 114
Jenks, Chris, 156
Jensen, Jeppe Sinding, 35
Joest, Wilfried, 52, 63
Jones, Tony, 128
Jung, Carl Gustav, 83
Jüptner, Jan, 23
Justin Martyr (Saint), 54

Kant, Imanuel, 93
Kaplánek, Michal, 152
Kasper, Walter, 196
Kempis, Thomas à, 79
Kierkegaard, Søren, 44
Kirmse, Anne-Marie, 96
Knauer, Peter, 105
Komonchak, Joseph, 99–100
Korsmeyer, Jerry D., 224
Kraft, Friedhelm, 168
Kropač, Ulrich, 5
Küng, Hans, 147, 225

Lacoste, Jean-Yves, 40
Lang, Albert, 83, 84
Lang, Andrew, 83
Levinas, Emanuel, 8
Lindbeck, George, 35, 147
Loder, James, 164
Loisy, Alfred, 58
Lonergan, Bernard, 63, 147
Lorde, Audre, 7

NAME INDEX

Lucie-Smith, Alexander, 36
Luke (Saint), 8
Lyotard, Jean-François, 16

Macek, Petr, 28
Machula, Tomáš, 28
Marcel, Gabriel, 166, 167, 217
Maréchal, Joseph, 60
Marion, Jean-Luc, 44
Maritain, Jacques, 94
Martínek, Michal, 152
Masaryk, Tomáš Garrigue, 82
McCarty, Robert J., 152
McClendon, James W., 35, 37
McGowan, Michael W., 101
McGrath, Alister E., 23, 24, 34, 35, 142
Melito of Sardis, 79, 87
Metz, Johannes-Baptist, 10, 112
Milbank, John, 62
Moltmann, Jürgen, 113, 147, 157
Muchová, Ludmila, 76, 179, 190, 195, 197
Mueller, Jill J., 222, 223
Murray, Stuart, 113

Neusch, Marcel, 227–28
Neville, Robert C., 100
Newlands, George, 184
Newman, John Henry, 53, 58
Ng, David, 11
Niebuhr, Helmut Richard, 34
Nietzsche, Friedrich, 194
Noble, Ivana, 1, 23, 30, 31, 44, 48, 49, 55, 116, 122, 220, 221
Norheim, Bård, 139, 144, 145, 149, 151, 158
Noval, Christian, 161–64, 172, 173, 177

Ockham, William, 56
O'Collins, Gerald, 9, 44, 49, 50, 52, 57, 61–63, 96, 102, 109, 110, 119, 120
O'Meara, Thomas F., 214–16
Origen, 54
Ormerod, Neil, 62, 116

Pannenberg, Wolfhart, 63, 147
Paul (Saint), 40, 87, 88, 141

Pedersen, Ann, 4, 64, 65, 122, 227
Peter (Saint), 5, 80, 185, 186
Pettazzoni, Raffaelle, 83
Piolanti, Antonio, 74
Plantinga, Richard J., 23, 24
Plato, 58, 93, 94, 152
Polanyi, Michael, 101
Pope John Paul II, 60, 81, 104
Pospíšil, Ctirad V., 27, 29
Putna, Martin C., 202
Pythagoras, 84

Rabba, Midrash Vayikrah, 46
Rahner, Karl, 20, 21, 60, 101, 105, 147, 200, 207, 211–13, 225
Regan, David, 207–10, 212, 213, 216, 229, 230, 231
Regner, Jan, 89
Ricoeur, Paul, 35
Říha, Karel, 9, 59, 84–90, 121, 203, 204
Roach, Jonathan C., 31, 32, 41, 88, 205, 218, 219
Robertson, Roland, 22
Roebben, Bert, 13, 125–37, 143, 153, 159, 161, 162, 165–67, 170, 171, 173–76, 178, 183, 191, 193, 213–15, 225, 228
Root, Andrew, 128, 131, 137–39, 141, 148, 151–53, 158, 176, 204, 207
Rupp, Hartmut, 168

Sak, Petr, 152
Samohýl, Jan, 45
Sanks, T. Howland, 99
Sartre, Jean-Paul, 194
Schambeck, Mirjam, 214, 215
Scheinerman, Amy, 46
Schelkens, Karim, 75
Schillebeeckx, Edward, 15, 37, 107, 187
Schlag, Thomas, 159, 161, 168, 172–79
Schleiermacher, Friedrich, 34, 57
Schmidt, Wilhelm, 83
Schönborn, Christoph, 100
Schopenhauer, Arthur, 192
Schreier, Monica, 74, 81
Schüssler Fiorenza, Francis, 23, 24
Schwarz, Elisabeth, 168
Schweitzer, Friedrich, 159–61, 167–81

Sedmak, Clemens, 20, 22, 39, 119, 204, 228
Shea, John, 37, 186
Shecterle, Ross A., 103
Shenk, Wilbert R., 112, 114
Skalický, Karel, 9, 14, 24–25, 27, 30, 40, 45, 65–69, 74, 78–92, 111, 114–15, 199–200
Snow, David A., 190
Socrates, 58
Song, Choan-Seng, 15, 34, 39, 40
Špidlík, Tomáš, 88
Spinoza, Baruch de, 84, 93
Štěch, František, 13, 14, 25, 27, 31, 32, 46, 57, 59–60, 68–69, 76, 78, 82, 90, 99, 103, 114, 165, 179, 190, 195, 197
Štofaník, Štefan, 11, 14, 31, 41, 88
Stone, Howard W., 205, 206, 218, 219
Stroup, George W., 35, 36
Sundermeier, Theo, 12

Taubes, Jacob, 10
Teilhard de Chardin, Pierre, 26, 40, 158, 187, 222
Tertullian, 54, 208
Thils, Gustave, 112
Tillich, Paul, 109, 147

Tracy, David, 35, 147
Třebín, Vladimír, 79, 80
Trésmontant, Claude, 83
Trump, Donald, 229
Tylor, Edward B., 83
Tyrell, George, 58

Vahland, Joachim, 2
van Dijk-Groeneboer, Monique C. H., 151, 152
Vanhoozer, Kevin J., 6, 30
van Huyssteen, Wenzel J., 8
Varro, Marcus Terentius, 23
Veling, Terry, 112, 145–47, 150
Vido, Roman, 1
Volf, Miroslav, 165

Walton, Heather, 39
Ward, Pete, 21, 32, 38–41, 48, 132, 140, 152
Whapham, Theodore J., 29
Wiesel, Elie, 37
Wilkins, Michael, 155
Wycliffe, John, 56

Zimmermann, Mirjam, 168, 180
Žůrek, Jiří, 71, 72, 76
Zvěřina, Josef, 27, 45, 46, 193

www.ingramcontent.com/pod-product-compliance
Lightning Source LLC
Chambersburg PA
CBHW050843230426
43667CB00012B/2130